Rural Credit and Self-help Groups

Rural Credit and Self-help Groups

Micro-finance Needs and Concepts in India

K. G. Karmakar

Sage Publications
New Delhi • Thousand Oaks • London

First published in 1999 by

Sage Publications India Pvt Ltd
M–32 Market, Greater Kailash–I
New Delhi-110 048

Sage Publications Inc.
2455 Teller Road
Thousand Oaks, California 91320

Sage Publications Ltd
6 Bonhill Street
London EC2A 4PU

Third Printing 2002

Published by Tejeshwar Singh for Sage Publications India Pvt Ltd., laser typeset by InoSoft Systems, Delhi and printed at Chaman Enterprises, Delhi.

Library of Congress Cataloging-in-Publication Data
Karmakar, K.G., 1952–
    Rural Credit and self-help groups: micro-finance needs and concepts in India/K.G. Karmakar.
        p. cm. (c)
    Includes bibliographical references and index.
    1. Agricultural credit—India. 2. Rural credit—India. 3. Rural development—India. 4. Self-help groups—India. 5. Microfinance—India. I. Title.
HG2051.I4K36   332.7'1'0954—dc21   1999   99-22518

ISBN: 0–7619–9345–2 (US Hb) 81–7036–810–3 (India Hb)

Sage Production Team: Nomita Jain, Parul Nayyar, R.A.M. Brown and Santosh Rawat

To my parents, teachers, fellow bankers and the rural people of India who have provided the inspiration for this book

Contents

PART I

Rural Credit: Problems and Prospects

PART II

Analysis of Micro-finance Needs

PART III

Role of Self-help Groups

PART IV

Strategies for Sustainable Rural Credit Delivery

List of Tables

List of Abbreviations

AAP	Annual Action Plan
ACRC	Agricultural Credit Review Committee
ADB	Asian Development Bank
AFC	Agriculture Finance Corporation
AGDP	Agricultural Gross Domestic Production
ANOVA	Analysis of Variance
APRACA	Asia-Pacific Regional Agricultural Credit Association
ARC	Agricultural Refinance Corporation
ARCS	A Registrar of Co-operative Societies
ARDC	Agricultural Refinance Development Corporation
ARDR	Agriculture and Rural Debt Relief scheme
ARF	Assets Reconstruction Fund
ARR	Agricultural Rate of Return
BAAC	Bank for Agriculture and Agricultural Cooperatives
BCP	Block Credit Plan
BLBC	Block Level Bankers Committee
BSRBs	Banking Service Recruitment Boards
CBs	Commercial Banks
CCBs	Central Cooperative Banks
CDF	Cooperative Development Foundation
CIDA	Canadian International Development Association
CPI	Consumer Price Index
CRR	Cash Reserve Ratio
DCB	Demand Collection Balance
DCCBs	District Central Co-operative Banks
DCP	District Credit Plan
DDC	District Consultative Committee

DDM	District Development Manager
DF	Degrees of Freedom
DFIs	Development Financial Institutions
DICGC	Deposit Insurance and Credit Guarantee Corporation
DLRM	District-level Review Committee
DRCS	Dy, Registrar of Co-operative Societies
DRDA	District Rural Development Agency
DWCRA	Development of Women and Children in Rural Areas
FAO	Food and Agriculture Organisation
GB	Grameen Bank (Bangladesh)
GDP	Gross Domestic Product
GM	Gross Margin
GNP	Gross National Product
GOI	Government of India
GS	Gram Sabha
IBA	Indian Banks' Association (Mumbai)
IFAD	International Fund for Agricultural Development
IMF	International Monetary Fund
IRDP	Integrated Rural Development Programme
ITDA	Integrated Tribal Development Agency
LAMPS	Large-sized Adivasi Multi-purpose Societies
LT	Long-term loans
LBO	Lead Bank Officer
MDA	Multiple Discriminant Analysis
MFP	Minor Forest Produce
MNC	Multi-National Corporation
MoU	Memorandum of Understanding
MT	Medium-term loans
MYRADA	Mysore Resettlement Development Agency
NABARD	National Bank for Agriculture and Rural Development
NACREF.	National Agricultural Credit Relief Fund
NAFSCOB	National Federation of State Co-operative Banks
NCARDBF	National Confederation of Agriculture and Rural Development
NGO	Non-Government Organisations
NIBM	National Institute of Bank Management (Pune)
NIS	Non-Institutional Sources
NM	Net Margin
NPAs	Non-Performing Assets
NAC (LTO)	National Agricultural Credit (Long-term Operations) fund
OSCB	Orissa State Co-operative Bank
PACSs	Primary Agricultural Credit Societies
PC	Personal Computer
PCARDBs	Primary Cooperative Agricultural and Rural Development Banks

PLDBs	Primary Land Development Banks
PLP	Potential-Linked Credit Plan
PO	Project Officer
RBI	Reserve Bank of India
RCMS	Regional Co-operative Marketing Societies
ROFE	Return on Funds Employed
ROSK	Return on Skills Employed
RRBs	Regional Rural Banks
SAP	Surplus Agricultural Produce
SARCS	Sub-Registrar of Co-operative Societies
SBIRD	State Bank Institute of Rural Development (Hyderabad)
SCARDBs	State Cooperative Agricultural and Rural Development Banks
SCBs	State Cooperative Banks
SC/ST	Scheduled Castes/Scheduled Tribes
SD	Standard Deviation
SDOs	Sub Divisional Officers
SFC	State Financial Corporation
SHGs	Self-help Groups
SIDBI	Small Industries Development Bank of India
SLDBs	State Land Development Banks
SLR	Statutory Liquidity Ratio
SSI	Small-scale Industry
ST	Short-term loans
ST(SAO)	Short-term (Seasonal Agricultural Operations)
TC	Transaction Costs
THRTI	Tribal and Harijan Research Training Institute (Bhubaneswar)
TNC	Transnational Corporation
TPE	Total Public Expenditure
TPEA	Total Public Expenditure on Agriculture
TV	Television
ULR	Ultimate Lending Rate
UNICEF	United Nations International Children's Emergency Fund
USAID	United States Agency for International Development
VLMS	Village-level Mahila Sabha
VVVs	Vikas Volunteer Vahinis
VLWs	Village-level Workers
WB	World Bank
WSM	Womens Saving Movement

Foreword

The performance of the Indian economy continues to be linked to beneficial monsoons, given the importance of the agricultural sector in the economy. Provision of adequate and timely institutional credit to the rural sector is one of the basic requirements of the rural credit delivery system. Sustainable agriculture and sustainable rural credit systems are imperatives for sustainable growth in the rural sector. Gaps in rural infrastructure and in the rural credit delivery system are among the many constraints which have hampered the growth of the rural economy.

The multi-agency approach to rural credit is an integral component of our credit system. Various factors have led to the poor performance of the rural credit system such as poor resource base, low business and outreach levels, poor loan recovery performance, poor income margins due to increasing management costs and inadequate lending margins. Rural credit agencies are constrained by inadequate managerial and operational skills, and weak human resources due to poor training. Rural credit growth has been further hampered by the high loan default rate (exceeding 50 per cent) and the rising level of non-performing assets. Unless banks gear up their recovery mechanisms, the rural credit agencies will remain weak.

Critics have maintained that the banking system is over administered and under-regulated. With the implementation of prudential norms and strengthened bank supervisory systems following improved on-site inspection systems, off-site surveillance techniques, supplementary supervision mechanisms and signing of DAPs/MoUs setting out the minimum performance parameters, there is bound to be all-round improvement. With increasing operational freedom for rural credit agencies from the RBI/NABARD, allowing banks to fix their own interest rates and more lending autonomy, banks are expected to accelerate the pace of internal reforms so as to emerge as strong and viable institutions capable of standing on their own feet.

The high cost and halting flow of formal institutional credit has led to innovative/alternative credit systems such as Self-help Groups (SHGs) set up with the help of NGOs and banks. These SHGs have emerged as viable credit mechanisms and have succeeded in reducing transaction costs for banks and borrowers alike, apart from posting very high loan recovery rates. The large number of women SHGs has also enabled women to have easy access to credit in recent years. These initiatives need to be replicated so as to involve the rural poor in rejuvenating the rural economy and ensure that they do not continue to be marginalised.

Dr. K.G. Karmakar has made an in-depth study of the existing rural credit delivery system and has made many valuable suggestions for strengthening and restructuring the system, based on Asian financial role models. The thoughts and experiences of Dr. Karmakar are lucidly exposed in this publication—the second in his series. This book will be of assistance to rural bankers, NGO volunteers, credit specialists and social scientists, who are involved with the rural credit delivery system; to reflect on issues related to rural credit.

P.V.A. Rama Rao
Ex-Managing Director
NABARD
Mumbai

Author's Note

The views/opinions expressed in the book are those of the author as an individual and not those of the organisation he serves or is associated with.

Preface

Why have I inflicted one more book about rural credit on an unsuspecting audience? An explanation is needed! Having worked as an officer in various banks for over 22 years, I have come to respect our rural people who comprise the heartland of India. It is they who have constantly defied all odds to feed us all, assimilating new technologies and systems over the years.

From time immemorial, it is the urban dweller who has had access to the seats of power and utilised the wealth of rural India to build cities and towns and monuments. This deprivation continues even today with the powerful and the mighty continuing to rule in favour of the urban elite, ignoring the real problems of India's poverty. Today, rural credit is good for ritual speeches, some peripheral reports and studied neglect. The sad truth is that rural India is being served by an unhealthy credit delivery system and that institutional credit meets only about 12 per cent of the annual credit requirements of the farm sector. The rural non-farm sector also suffers from neglect and lip-service.

As if by rote or ritual, every few months, speeches can be heard stating that the rural credit delivery system needs to be revamped. But as there is no one who wishes to commit political suicide, very little is done. Over 35 per cent of the people below the poverty line (constitute about 50 per cent of the population) are untouched by the various credit schemes and government programmes! India can never attain its rightful place in the world's economy, unless we ensure that the genuine credit requirements of the rural economy are met. But with a poor resource base and lack of political will in diverting crucial financial resources for creation of an adequate economic infrastructure, rural India continues to suffer from official apathy and perennial lack of funds. We tend to ignore the fact that the largest private sector investment is in the agricultural sector!

To break the grinding cycle of rural poverty, we need to ensure that a chance is given to micro-entrepreneurs and potential micro-entrepreneurs; or else, in a market-driven economy, the rural poor will not have any chance to secure their rightful place. This book seeks to examine the state of the rural credit system and study the micro-finance needs of the rural poor. It offers the solution of Self-help Groups (SHGs) to enable the rural poor to aim for economic empowerment and a right to live with dignity! These SHGs offer the easiest and most economical method of enabling the rural poor to contribute their mite to the rural economy. The rural poor do not deserve to be marginalised forever. Hence this book!

Dr. K.G. Karmakar

Acknowledgements

This book would not have been possible without the help of my Ph.D. guide Dr. (Ms.) V.V. Manerikar, Director, JBIMS, University of Mumbai, who brought about order from chaos. I must also thank Dr. P.D. Ojha, Ex-Dy. Governor, RBI, and Dr. M.V. Gadgil, Ex-Managing Director, NABARD, for their helpful suggestions and encouragement. To the University of Strathclyde, faculty and computer staff and Ms. Alka Chadha, Officer, Punjab & Sind Bank, I acknowledge my gratitude for having prepared the entire computer data analysis from raw field data. I am grateful to Shri. J.C. Maharana, AGM, NABARD, Bhubaneswar, for having done the entire proof-reading of the thesis and for his perseverance. I am grateful to the rural borrowers/bankers in Dharwad, Karnataka, and the NGOs/SHGs in Orissa who helped me with all data collection and gave me a rare insight into rural credit aspects. I am extremely grateful to the entire NABARD Parivar for the unstinted affection, cooperation, assistance and for their generosity which has been a tremendous source of inspiration. And to my loving wife Dr. Rita Karmakar and children who have stood by me and egged me on, I remain forever indebted.

I also wish to record my appreciation for the editor and staff of Sage Publications who made several constructive suggestions for improving this book and making it a really useful book for all rural bankers and NGOs. For the various short-comings and inadequacies, I alone am responsible. However, any feedback would be welcome, for improving the book and enhancing its utility value as a source-book for micro and rural credit institutions.

PART I

Rural Credit: Problems and Prospects

1

Introduction

Since the 1950s, development strategies have aimed at enhancing agricultural productivity and profitability for farmers. In developing countries, helping the rural poor and meeting their basic needs have been additional goals. The low economic growth of these countries was perceived to be due to the lack of capital resources, especially in the rural areas. A vicious cycle of low capital, low productivity, low incomes, low savings and consequently, a weak capital base was perceived to be operating, perpetuating a permanent poverty syndrome. Cheap rural credit policies were designed to provide rural areas with access to adequate capital.

In India, a multi-agency approach for providing working capital and assets acquisition to rural borrowers has been in operation since 1969. The multi-agency approach to the rural credit delivery system arose due to challenges posed by the system at various points of time. The *taccavi* loans issued by the government in 1793 gave way to short-term cooperative credit institutions in 1904 and after 1929, cooperative land mortgage banks were started to help farmers redeem land mortgaged to private money-lenders. The partial nationalisation of the Imperial Bank of India and the formation of a large number of new branches after 1955, coupled with the continuing failure of cooperative credit institutions, led to the nationalisation of 14 largest commercial banks (comprising 90 per cent of the banking assets) in 1969. This led to a significant expansion of the number of rural branches for the purpose of monetising the rural economy. However, with increasing emphasis on 'priority' sector loans targeted at the poor and the weaker sections of society, Regional Rural Banks were formed from 1975 onwards. Though formal credit institutions have made a dent in providing finance for rural households (from 5 per cent in 1951 to 62 per cent in 1981), non-institutional sources of credit still play a significant role.

The reasons for providing cheap credit to rural borrowers (with small farmers, marginal farmers and landless agricultural borrowers forming over 66 per cent of total borrowers) have been summarised by J.L. Walinsky as:

> Farmers in the developing countries are generally hampered by high interest costs for short-term crop loans, usually from small-scale private money-lenders, and by the almost complete lack of sources from which they can borrow the longer term loans they need to purchase animals and equipment, upgrade their stock, reclaim acreage, execute soil conservation measures and finance similar capital needs. High cost loans from money-lenders constitute a major charge against their current income and depress their living standards. The unavailability of longer-term credit prevents them from improving and expanding their output. Both limitations can be overcome by a well-designed agricultural credit programme at the core of which would be an agricultural bank.

It was thought that credit provided by informal lenders (registered/unofficial money-lenders, commission agents, traders, landlords, etc.) was exploitative and expensive for small farmers and their hold needed to be counteracted by extending low-interest institutional credit.

The rural credit delivery system in India has been built on this classical approach. Today, however, the entire system is on the verge of a major shake-down due to the poor impact of these credit policies on rural development efforts. The problems of the rural credit delivery system have been documented by the Agricultural Credit Review Committee, 1989. The major problems appear to be that of repayment and recovery of loans at the borrower level and the consequent weakening of the entire institutional credit system.

Repayment ethics and recycling of credit are crucial to the smooth functioning of any credit delivery system. The incidence of overdues in the agricultural credit system has been increasing over the years. This, coupled with other weaknesses, has been steadily eroding the financial soundness of the system and at end June 1990, agricultural credit overdues at the borrower's level amounted to Rs 7,557 crore, constituting 26.42 per cent of the outstanding loans and 52.66 per cent of the demand. The causes on the internal front were defective loan policies and procedures, inadequate supervision and monitoring and unprofessional management.

On the external front, the problems were occurrence of natural calamities like floods and droughts, absence of backward and forward linkages, defective legal framework and lack of support from the government machinery in recoveries. In addition, there has been active interference in the system (especially cooperatives) through bans on coercive action for recoveries and announcement of interest subsidies, debt reliefs and write-off of bank dues (ARDR scheme 1990).

Thus, instead of mobilising resources for rural development, the programme for rural credit has actually been consuming scarce monetary resources and has not worked out to the advantage of the rural borrowers, the banks and the government. Instead, new problems have been created These include:

- Inadequate procedures for loan appraisal.
- Insufficient effective demand in some areas.
- Non-viability of rural credit institutions.
- Maintenance of a cheap/administered credit system.
- Debt write-offs leading to fall in bank recoveries.
- Bureaucratisation of rural credit and non-availability of skills in rural branches.
- Inadequate loan monitoring systems leading to poor recoveries.
- High transaction costs for banks and for borrowers.

There are several misconceptions about rural credit. It is viewed as an input rather than a claim on resources and services. Fungibility of finance is often ignored by those who target credit for specific uses. Also, politicians favour cheap credit as an easy means for helping the rural poor. Further, bank nationalisation and the creation of new credit institutions are seen as a step for cheap credit. It is felt that a government-owned bank can defy laws of 'financial gravity' and yet remain profitable/viable. In many developing countries, such weakened rural financial institutions are common. Low interest rates are also prescribed to offset price distortions, to transfer income to the rural poor and to induce farmers to adopt new technologies. With inflation rampant in most low-income countries, interest rates charged on financial instruments are negative in real terms. Borrowers repay lending less in purchasing power than they borrow and savers are returned less in purchasing power than they deposit. Recycling funds is thus difficult and hence, reliance on the government/Central Bank for funds is inevitable and also susceptible to political control. Also, low interest rates make it difficult for lenders to cover their operating costs. This forces banks to depend on external funds at concessional rates, rationing of cheap loans among potential borrowers and to restrict lending.

A weak bank provides unsatisfactory financial services and its employees become demoralised. Accusations of fraud, mismanagement and incompetence proliferate and for these, individuals not faulty policies, are blamed. The solution is generally to tighten the administration, appoint new leadership, combine weak organisations with better managed ones or create yet another institution. The undermining of financial institutions as a deliberate policy can be accepted if the objectives of equity and efficient resource allocation are met. But cheap credit does not make an unprofitable activity, profitable. Also, low interest rates force banks to concentrate loans in the hands of relatively few people and ensures that credit subsidy is not equitably distributed. (Adams et al. 1984 : pp. 2–3)

Cheap credit cannot offset the misallocation caused by prices and yield distortions. Low production prices, low and unstable yields and the lack of new technologies make farming a low return activity in most countries. This, in turn, reduces savings capacity and efficient financial intermediation to realise economies of scale. Much more needs to be done to study the reasons for the failure of the rural credit delivery system and to ensure that an efficient, effective system provides loans to those who have the economic opportunities that exceed their resource capacity. A rural credit delivery system cannot be used to make income distribution more equitable. Cheap credit also cannot compensate farmers for low product prices and yields. The reasons for the failure of the Indian rural credit delivery system need to be analysed so as to test whether the present system is able to meet the requirements of the central/state governments, rural financial institutions, and, rural borrowers.

Central/State Government Requirements

The primary requirement of the government is to increase production, enhance rural productivity and provide gainful employment to the increasing rural masses.

The problems on the demand side are:

* Declining profitability and sustainability of agriculture.
* Continuing stagnation in rural employment
* Marginalisation of land holdings.
* Need for self-employment for the rural masses especially in off-farm and non-farm sectors.

- Rising aspirations of rural disadvantaged people expecting instant solutions to age-old deprivations.
- Increasing regional imbalances.
- Poor ecological management leading to wastage of land/water resources.
- Degradation of resources and inefficient use of rural skills/resources.

The problems on the supply side are:

- Reduction of state subsidies due to deficits.
- Financing constraints.
- Reduced financial returns.
- Increasing budget deficit.
- Reduced ability to subsidise (IRDP, fertilizer subsidies, etc.).
- Growth/Distribution-oriented policies.
- Increasing cost of lending.
- Insufficient infrastructure.
- A bloated bureaucracy and inefficient bank officials,
- Insufficient resources for growth-led development leading to huge external/internal debt.
- Wastage of scarce financial resources due to leakages.

The rural credit delivery system has to meet the borrowers' requirements. The rural credit deposit ratio, the credit flow to priority sectors and weaker sections of society, balanced sectoral credit flow, rural assets creation and lessening of the credit gap are the crucial factors determining the efficiency of the system.

Requirements of the Rural Credit Delivery System

The rural credit delivery system requires a huge volume of low-cost deposits that has to be lent at subsidised rates yet show profits and meet development targets. The rural credit delivery system is beset with a number of problems that are affecting its viability. The increasing cost of lending and declining profitability of the banking system as a whole results in negative margins for most rural credit institutions. This is compounded by manpower constraints leading to poor monitoring of rural advances; poor motivation of urban-oriented staff posted in rural areas and lack of amenities/facilities; weakening of customer relationship between rural borrowers and bank staff; poor house-keeping and increasing number of frauds perpetuated by bank staff; very high transaction costs;

high cost of loan recovery; poor working conditions and a heavy work load due to non-computerisation of transactions; lack of adequate supervision and control; and, poor industrial relations climate leading to poor staff productivity. In the face of these problems, the following major factors need to be studied:

- Interest rates, operational costs and profit margins.
- Sectoral flow of credit to remove regional disparities and ensure credit flow.
- Reduction of credit gaps.
- Viability of rural credit agencies.
- Profitability of rural credit agencies.
- Repayment, overdues and loan recovery.
- Reduction of loan transaction costs, especially for subsidised low-interest loans.

Requirements of Rural Borrowers

Rural borrowers require a credit delivery system that ensures:

- Adequacy of loan amounts.
- Loans sanctioned in time and without long-drawn procedures.
- Low transaction costs and low incidental costs due to delays.
- Low interest costs.
- Adequate repayment period, with some gestation period.
- Savings and thrift opportunities.
- Proper and courteous services without additional 'rent' costs.

The rural borrower has been depending upon institutional sources for production/investment credit requirements. But, for consumption credit needs (social functions, births/deaths, medical needs, etc.), she/he is forced to go to non-institutional sources (registered/unregistered money-lenders, traders, commission agents, etc.).

For the rural poor, there is a very thin boundary line between consumption and production credit needs. Rural borrowers are keen on timely and adequate loans with low transaction costs.

Factors Affecting Rural Credit

The rural credit system has been evolving over a period of about 90 years. Various policy initiatives, constraints, thrust areas and the factors/linkages that have helped in shaping the system, need to be studied. The major factors influencing the existing rural credit delivery system have been set out in Table 1.1. Broadly, these can be grouped as:

- Social factors
- Economic factors
- Technological factors
- Political factors

The Rural Credit Delivery System

The organisational framework of the rural credit system has evolved into a very complex multi-agency system (see Table 1.2) and an equally complex credit system for non-institutional sources which, however, charges high interest rates due to risk evaluation, limited funds for consumption purposes and a limited area of operations. They still account for 38 per cent of rural credit while 62 per cent is purveyed by institutional sources. Expansion of the rural credit system is severely restricted due to scarce financial resources, profitability considerations and the consolidation of the banking system. While rural credit agencies provide term loans/working capital loans, non-institutional sources provide working capital loans and consumption loans; the latter hence, provide complementary services. Credit monitoring functions and coordination with government agencies are done through various committees set up at the block/district/state – levels and supervised by the lead bank officer and DDM at the district level. Rural credit agencies, the controls exercised by GOI/RBI and the refinance arrangements from SIDBI/NABARD are part of the system.

The rural borrower requires both credit and non-credit inputs (apart from infrastructure, entrepreneurial skills and marketing inputs). The non-credit inputs are provided by government/private and voluntary agencies. Credit inputs are provided by the multi-agency credit system with its attendant problems of screening, incentives and enforcement. The system, as it has evolved, is complex and involves a high degree of development banking elements, in addition to normal banking business. To maintain this credit flow into desired sectors, the Lead Bank Scheme and Service Area Approach, have been adopted.

In consonance with the official policies of the Government of India, credit-based development activities are being encouraged with the twin objectives of equity and growth. Rural development is linked with

Table 1.1
Rural Credit System—Factors/Linkages

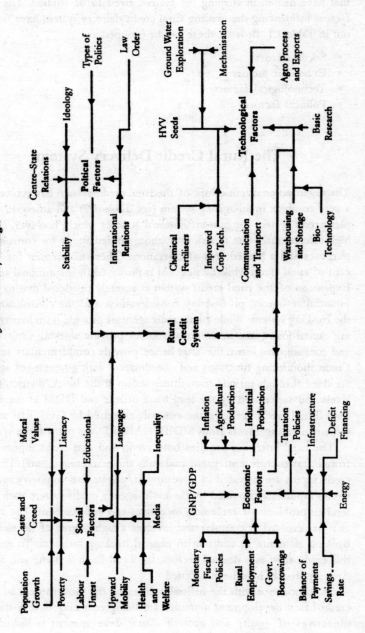

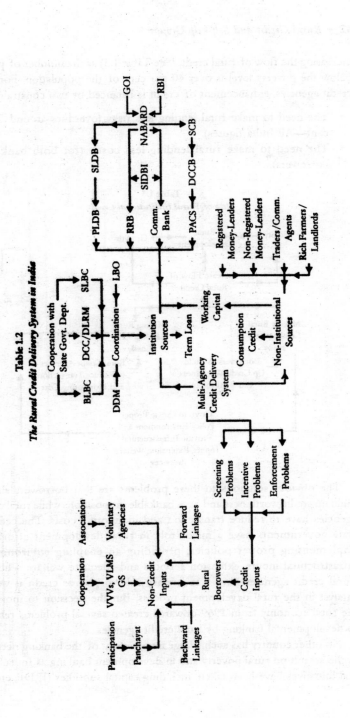

Table 1.2
The Rural Credit Delivery System in India

increasing the flow of rural credit (See Table 1.3) as the number of people below the poverty level is over 40 per cent of the population. For rural credit agencies, enhancement of credit is balanced by two constraints:

- The need to make rural lending less risky (overdues around 56 per cent—All India figures).
- The need to make rural lending less costly (for both banks and borrowers).

Table 1.3
Flow of Rural Institutional Credit

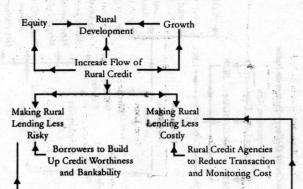

The obvious solutions to these problems are that borrowers should build up credit-worthiness and have bankable propositions while rural credit agencies have to reduce transaction and monitoring costs. The central/ state governments have a major role in rural development efforts by implementing proper policies, providing an enabling environment, infrastructural inputs, extension services and adequate welfare schemes. Rural credit agencies have a secondary role to play as credit is only a catalyst in the rural development process. But the decision to monetise the rural economy from 1969 onwards created several problems relating to developmental banking by rural credit agencies.

No other country has such a large involvement of the banking network in the assault on rural poverty and in development banking as India. Several initiatives have been taken, including capital subsidies (IRDP, etc.), a vast rural banking network, creation of a multi-agency system and interest subsidies (DRI, etc.) However, these pioneering efforts have not been implemented properly and the fact that so many institutional/policy changes are being initiated shows that there is little stability in policy making and a tendency towards quick results. Without waiting for these changes/initiatives to stabilise and be properly assimilated or institutionalised, new initiatives are explored. This injects a half-hearted approach to rural development without the stamina to push through the initiatives. These half-hearted efforts reveal the lack of credible rural development planning and quality in the implementation of efforts that should supplement rural development policies.

The issue/problem areas confronting rural credit agencies have been set out in Table 1.4. But, the major issues confronting rural credit agencies are:

- Reduction in profitability.
- Reduced viability.
- Administered interest and lending costs leading to reduced margins.
- Poor monitoring and poor loan recovery.
- Efficiency of mandatory/directed lending and assessment of credit gaps.

Table 1.4
Rural Credit—Areas/Issues

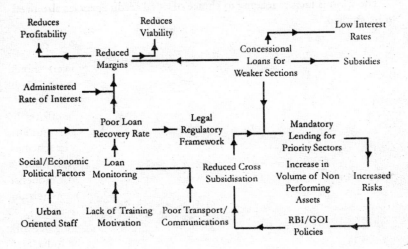

These five major factors will be studied in depth to assess their impact on rural credit agencies and the government. The other factors are difficult to quantify and have not been studied mainly because they are secondary factors.

The profitability factors deserve in-depth analysis as fears about the basic profitability of rural credit agencies have been frequently expressed and an attempt has been made to isolate the factors (see Table 1.5). The reasons for better profitability amongst the rural credit agencies need to be studied.

Rural Credit—Borrowers' View Point

In most efforts to study the rural credit system, the borrowers' view point is frequently left out or is treated as inconsequential. It is important to assess the impact of the present system and the transaction costs of an 'administered' rural credit system vis-à-vis its clients. The rural borrower is interested in:

- Adequate loan amount.
- Timely disbursals.
- Low interest rates.
- Efficient and courteous customer services.

The various factors relating to choice of rural credit agencies also need to be studied.

Table 1.5

Profitability Factors—Rural Credit Agencies

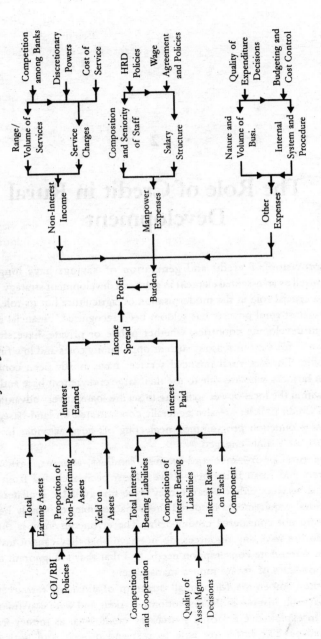

2

The Role of Credit in Rural Development

The provision of credit and generation of savings have long been recognised as an essential element in any rural development strategy. Credit plays a crucial role in the modernisation of agriculture but its role in the fight against rural poverty has seldom been recognised. Financial institutions in developing countries, whether public or private, have shunned rural areas for various reasons such as opportunity costs and low financial credibility. Further, rural financial services have mostly been controlled by rich farmers, who are able to use their large endowment base and influence within the local power structure to secure loans at very advantageous terms. Credit policies are also generally concentrated on land-based agricultural production programmes, neglecting off-farm activities in which the poor are mainly engaged.

The rural poor—men and women, landless, artisans, agricultural labourers and small fishermen—have almost been excluded from these financial services either because they were not available (collateral and procedural requirements rendered them inaccessible) or simply because they were not considered creditworthy. The erroneous view is that the poor do not have any resources, do not save, that they cannot invest in view of immediate consumption needs, and that they are ignorant of the basic principles of sound money management.

In the competition for a small quantum of financial resources, the poor naturally lost out in the institutional markets and were constrained to resort to exploitative informal sources of credit such as money-lenders and traders. The latter are able to respond quickly and with great flexibility to pressing demands, and exploit the poor and further compound their poverty.

Many national rural development programmes in the form of integrated efforts or cooperatives have endeavoured to increase the availability of financial services, reduce collateral or other requirements, and adapt procedures to rural clients. Credit cooperatives are widespread in South Asian countries. But because of the principle of open membership, most cooperatives have come under the control of well-to-do powerful farmers and have failed to make any contribution in the alleviation of poverty. The benefits of cooperative institutions have frequently been diverted to serve the interests of a select few.

Government policies of many developing countries are built around the premise that by increasing the flow of agricultural credit, rural regeneration is possible. But it is wrong to equate credit flow with capital creation in rural areas. Credit cannot be created merely by increasing money supply; nor can capital be used for developmental purposes if farmers divert savings for consumption purposes. By combining additional labour with more capital, both production and productivity can be enhanced, i.e., more produce and more income. Credit for rural development depends upon two vital factors—rural savings and provision of liquidity to farmers without sufficient funds to invest in improved technological advances. There must be sufficient investible funds to exploit opportunities created due to technological breakthroughs. Credit enables extension of control as distinct from ownership of resources; but, it should be extended for investment in 'clearly spelt out' opportunities or it will surely end up as additional consumption. This is not to state that new technologies necessarily need additional credit or that new rural technologies are not adopted without credit. Thus, credit is neither essential nor sufficient for initiating rural development. Rural credit agencies can, however, encourage the efficient reallocation of tangible wealth as also new investment through intermediation between savers and entrepreneurial investors, and also increase the rate of accumulation of capital by providing increased incentives to save, invest and work. The characteristics of rural credit are:

- Provides a command over resources but is not a need.
- Is not income but could lead to income, if properly utilised.
- Is tangible and hence, it is difficult to evaluate the impact of credit programmes.
- Tends to flow to borrower-preference activities.
- Absence of mutual confidence between borrowers and lenders leads to increased transaction costs.
- Cheap cost of funds increase the demand for credit.

In South Asian and other developing countries, rural credit is generally earmarked for the agricultural sector as it supports 70 to 80 per cent of the work force and the development of small farms is crucial for rural development.

The main reason for low average incomes in the so-called overpopulated areas is the abundance of unskilled or semi-skilled labour relative to the available land, capital and other inputs, especially land, improved by application of capital. Improvement of the majority depends ultimately on increasing the volume of capital and skills, thus changing the ratio between the various classes of resources. The reforms now being implemented merely alter the institutional framework without influencing the availability of resources and, therefore, do not get to the root of the problem. Credit-related rural development strategies have shifted focus to the rural disadvantaged due to the following factors:

- Failure of past growth-oriented strategies (trickle-down effect) leading to increase in poverty and inequality.
- Need for productive employment for rural labour, especially in off-farm and non-farm activities.
- Availability of appropriate technologies leading to higher yields per hectare.
- Higher productivity of small farmers per hectare vis-à-vis large farmers, thus enhancing rural purchasing power so that increased agricultural profit can be used to buy goods and services, provide more jobs, etc.

The safest path to rural economic prosperity is through the continuous improvement of agricultural productivity without harming the environment.

Rural Poverty and Small Farmers

According to USAID norms, small farmers are grouped into four categories:

- Commercially viable—have access to commercial credit
- Potentially viable—i.e., technology, inputs and market available
- Potentially viable with subsidy (special incentives, etc.)
- Non-viable—very poorly endowed

Thus we can conclude that a small farmer can be defined as one whose resources are too small to qualify for existing bank credit. He may or may not have the appropriate growth potential as a farmer but he has to be assisted to be viable. The International Fund for Agricultural Development (IFAD) uses the following criteria to identify the rural poor.

1. regional criteria	• assuming that all households in the region are poor
2. asset criteria	• prescribing a cut-off level of assets and income depending on the incidence of poverty.
3. activity criteria	• by selecting activities attractive only to the rural disadvantaged
4. a combination of the above	

In India, the levels of poverty are defined on the basis of average annual family income (a family consisting of five persons):

Poverty Groups	*Annual Income Groups 1992 (Revised) (in Rs)*
Destitute	0–4000
Very very poor	4001–6000
Very poor	6001–8500
Poor	8501–11000

In the past, rural credit agencies preferred to lend to the richer sections of the rural people for the following reasons:

- Loan administration costs are proportionately less.
- Collateral terms can be complied with.
- Safety for lenders in view of collateral.
- Enhanced food production is possible in order to meet national objectives.
- Completing loan targets is easier with a smaller number of borrowers.
- The rural poor are viewed as unreliable clients with unstable incomes and irregular savings.

Small and poor farmers, on their part, also kept away from rural credit agencies due to:

- Cultural gap between the rich and rural poor, especially in borrowings.
- Information relating to credit schemes, terms, obligation, etc,. were not known.

- Restricted banking hours leading to lower accessibility.
- Institutional procedures not appropriate to clients' needs.
- Cash flow of small producers is not conducive to flexibility in loan repayment.
- Consumption credit needs are not met.

Various reviews of rural credit programmes by USAID (1972) and the World Bank (1974–75) revealed that the design and implementation of rural credit programmes were very complex and that traditional models were irrelevant. Rural credit is but one of the many inputs necessary for rural regeneration and if it is to be effective, it has to be supported by improved technology, infrastructure, inputs, extension services and markets, i.e., the economic opportunities associated with rural credit. The viability of rural credit agencies could be eroded by interest rates, high administrative costs associated with small loans and shoddy banking practices inappropriate to the needs of small farmers. It must be remembered that the factors that have retarded agricultural development (economic, social, political, etc.) also hinder the development of credit institutions which serve the rural poor. The reviews concluded:

- There is no preferred model for rural credit delivery and credit agencies reaching the maximum number of clients with minimum costs were successful.
- The factors responsible for a successful rural credit delivery system were decentralised operation, appropriate grouping of farmers, use of intermediaries with an existing rural network, tapping rural savings and providing access to private/institutional financial sources.
- Private money-lenders could be utilised as on-lending agencies by institutional lenders to reach large numbers with minimum cost.
- All rural credit agencies should work collectively, retaining their particular attributes while coordinating with government agencies and others dealing with marketing, extension and input supply to link up with the credit supply.
- Rural credit agencies should be viable and programmed goals should be pursued.
- Adequate number of trained and rural-oriented staff should be available.
- A self-evaluating mechanism to monitor progress and assess quality of goal achievement should be incorporated.

Existing Systems

The rural credit delivery system has centred around some very erroneous assumptions:

- High interest rates are a critical factor in borrowing decisions as they contribute to the bulk of borrowing costs.
- Poor rural households have limited or no savings capabilities.
- Consumption credit being unproductive, it should not be granted by rural credit agencies.
- Adverse effects of pricing and exchange rate policies through subsidiary interest rates.

Consequently, it was observed that a rural credit delivery system based on consumption would face several problems:

- Non-viability due to high inflation, fixed interest rates, overdues and defaults.
- Serious organisational and management problems and tendency to concentrate on short-term loans rather than investment loans.
- Poor mobilisation of voluntary rural savings and heavy dependance on central banks or foreign aid.
- High transaction costs for small loans which cannot be covered through the interest income, thus eroding the profits of rural credit agencies.
- Benefits were collected only by big borrowers (income transfer due to negative real rates, non-repayment of loans, etc.).

Credit programmes in Indonesia and in Latin America have shown that 'cheap' credit has numerous defects. The adoption of new technology does not necessarily depend on the availability of credit. Low-interest rates generate excess demand, requiring credit rationing which, in turn, leads to corruption and political intervention to corner credit for bigger borrowers. This secures 'over-financing' for a privileged few. Low interest rates for credit ensure lower rates for saving deposits and dependence on external agencies and central banks for 'cheap funds'. Low interest rates (often dictated by political reasons) secure low margins and ensure that banks are unable to offer a variety of services needed by rural borrowers. As credit provides additional liquidity, it has an impact on all activities of the borrower, including those not financed by the bank. Thus, assessment of impact becomes difficult.

The latest credit strategies for rural farmers and rural disadvantaged are:

- Due to seasonal agricultural production, there is more liquidity in rural areas and rural people are responsive to interest rate changes and appropriate financial services. Mobilisation of voluntary financial deposits in rural areas is the first priority of rural credit agencies.
- Deposit mobilisation enlarges the resource base of lending agencies, reduces external dependence and may often help to reduce loan defaults.
- Supervised credit leads to lower interest rates on credit and deposits.
- Real interest rates reflecting the general scarcity of capital would revive market forces. This would increase operating margins, reduce transaction costs for small rural borrowers and ensure adequate credit flow to the rural poor as also avoid pre-emption of credit by 'vested interests'.
- Interest forms only a small part of the total cost of borrowing by small farmers while borrowers' transaction costs are very high. Credit from the informal sector has much lower transaction costs and may be cheaper than formal credit for short-term loans. If borrower transaction costs are reduced, borrowers may prefer a higher interest rate to formal lenders. In their relative effect on farmer behaviour, product prices rank first, yields second, input prices third and credit availability and interest rates a distant fourth.
- Higher interest rates would enable rural credit agencies to offer a range of financial services and enable more people to participate in financial intermediation. This helps rural credit agencies to become better integrated with the rural people.
- With the revived effect of market forces, targeting the loan and supervision of compliance would not be necessary, cutting lending costs. Borrowers will be more prudent in resorting to high-cost resources.
- The money-lender will continue to remain a valued source of credit in rural areas for a long time due to his immediate approachability, informality and flexibility. Rural credit agencies have a lot to learn from him.

For over 40 years, governments and aid agencies have been devoting considerable resources to supply cheap credit to rural borrowers through various institutional frameworks. This was possibly due to an inadequate understanding of rural financial systems. Prior to intervention in the rural credit markets, the village money-lender charged very high interest rates, perhaps due to his monopoly. Hence, cheap institutional credit was seen as an alternative. But 51 years after Independence, the money-lender coexists in the rural credit system (albeit with a reduced market share) and continues to charge high interest rates. Their default rates are very low compared to those of rural financial institutions. These institutions are not self-supporting in spite of massive doses of cheap government funds. There are still some puzzling issues that remain:

- The formal and informal sectors coexist despite the fact that formal interest rates are lower.
- Interest rates do not equilibrate credit supply and demand. There may be credit rationing and during bad harvests, credit may just not be available.
- Despite high interest rates and margins, the number of money-lenders is not increasing sharply in the rural credit market.
- In the informal sector, linkages between credit transactions and trans-actions in other markets are common.
- Rural credit agencies specialise in areas where collateral is available (e.g., land)

For appropriate policy interventions, it is necessary to understand the role of rural credit markets. An initial picture can be drawn from:

- Borrower behaviour, especially as regards default, is difficult to pre-dict and it is costly to determine the extent of the risk for each bor-rower. This is the 'screening problem'
- It is also costly to ensure that borrowers perform so as to ensure repayment. This is the 'incentives problem'.
- It is very difficult to force repayment of rural credit. This is the 'en-forcement problem'.

An understanding of the complex issues involved is necessary before a good rural credit delivery system can be designed. Increasing access to the rural poor has not helped and neither has subsidised credit led to reducing poverty levels. A prime example being the Integrated Rural Development Programme (IRDP) in India which succeeded in increasing the assets of large numbers of the rural poor, but failed to ensure sustainable financial returns to them. Public funds are better spent on infrastructure and ser-vices such as agricultural extension and marketing information. Informal financial sources, with flexible collateral terms and repayment schedules, are better placed for serving the rural people. But here, too, there are deficiencies such as reduced access to funds and competition, non-provi-sion of term finance and large loans. A variety of innovative credit programmes targeted at the rural poor—without subsidised interest rates and the group lending approach of the Grameen Bank and BRAC in Bangladesh—can be tried. Well-designed credit programmes can provide group access and still remain viable. Other important areas are improving access to appropriate technology and providing rural infrastructure responsive to the people's needs.

Finally, though credit is only one of the components of a rural credit delivery system designed to bring about rapid socio-economic changes along with rural development, it is nevertheless a very crucial component. A component is as important as the right dose of medicine for a patient. The illness is a sign of deficiency in the body which has to be remedied. For the patient's recovery, the right dose of medicine at the right time is vital. Too much medicine can be harmful while too little can delay recovery. And for this, the patient has to trust the doctor implicitly. A poor patient cannot afford costly medicines and if the medicine is not taken, he/she may die.

Similarly, credit has to be administered in the right doses, at the right costs (interest, etc.) and at the right time. If this is not done, there is a chance of the project failing. Also, the borrower has to trust the bankers' prescription with the banker too trusting the borrower for repayment. These confidence-building measures are a must for any rural credit delivery system to perform efficiently.

3

Evolution and Growth of the Rural Credit Delivery System

Rationale

The history of rural banking in India is the story of a newly independent, predominantly agricultural nation where vast numbers of resource-poor farmers, caught in a cycle of low productivity and low investment, had been ignored by bankers for decades. Observers in the West were ready to write off India as a 'basket case', incapable of feeding itself. Today, it has come a long way. The far-reaching developments in the last 30 years of Indian agriculture have their origin in a combined effort launched by the government, bankers and scientists. The government invested huge amounts of capital in irrigated agriculture, the banks built from scratch a rural credit delivery system reaching the far corners of the country, and the scientists brought the bio-technological revolution to the farmers' doorstep. It is interesting, therefore, to review India's rural banking from a historical perspective.

All productive activities, agricultural or industrial, intended for the market or self-consumption need some degree of credit for their sustenance and growth. The amount and duration of credit, as well as other terms and conditions, depends on the nature and time involved in production, on the types of financial institutions supplying credit and the availability of internal funds with the production units. Thus, effective demand for credit in productive activities is partly conditioned by the existence of credit institutions (i.e., supply side) and partly by the needs of the market and producing units (i.e., demand side). Lack of certain facilities such as irrigation, non-availability of timely and adequate inputs, hesitation on the part of some producing units (i.e., cultivators and artisans to break away from traditional methods of production) have been responsible for holding up the desired growth on the supply side. At the same time, recent changes in production practices and adoption of modern techniques by some of the progressive units have enlarged the scope of credit institutions, thereby increasing the demand side. Further, though there exists various financial institutions in rural areas, their functioning during the past few years has shown that institutional credit generally benefited creditworthy borrowers, leaving the majority of small and marginal farmers, artisans and landless labourers to depend on non-institutional sources.

In promoting a balanced, equitable and self-reliant pattern of development, the central monetary authority can never lose sight of the strategic role of agriculture and agro-based activities in the rural areas. Hence, the central monetary authority in most countries is involved in the process of institution-building in rural credit. This ensures that the system serves both the cause of accelerated growth in production and income, and greater equity in distribution of credit (and hence, assets and income). The central monetary authority also pays attention to rectifying the structural and organisational deficiencies or weaknesses of the rural credit delivery system.

Though *taccavi* loans for providing agricultural credit at low interest rates started in 1793, the Land Improvement Loans Act of 1883 was the first consolidated law aimed at providing agricultural loans. But the response to it was poor due to its stringent procedures. The regressive and exploitative land revenue system, compounded by low productivity and recurrent natural calamities, caused heavy indebtedness among the peasantry. This led to a large proportion of them losing their lands and turning into landless labourers.

It was against this background that ideas based on cooperation, stressing thrift and mutual help among the peasants, emerged, which led to the Cooperative Credit Societies Act. Under this Act, small cooperative societies were to be organised to meet the short-term credit needs of the farmers. Adoption of the Act in 1904 marked the beginning of efforts to build an institutional finance system for agriculture. The Committee on Cooperatives (Maclagan) in 1915 recognised the need for the provision of capital to agriculture and to relieve farmers from indebtedness if the nation wanted to achieve agricultural growth.

The Central Banking Enquiry Committee (1931), after a detailed investigation into the problems of agricultural credit, rural banking and agrarian indebtedness, suggested linking agricultural finance with central banking functions. It felt that as agriculture was an important activity in the national economy, a sound and stable monetary (credit) system could not be expected to operate unless the needs and requirements of this sector were brought within the purview of the central banking system. Sir Malcolm Darlings' Report in 1934 pointed out the need to examine whether the operations of commercial banks could be coordinated to the advantage of agriculturists; and, whether provincial or central cooperative banks could be made to secure a proper level of financial efficiency and soundness. It is clear that right from the beginning, the government made serious attempts to nurture the cooperative movement and until 1947, the general thinking was in favour of promoting primary credit cooperative societies in rural areas.

The depression of the 1930s led to a catastrophic fall in the prices of agricultural commodities. As a result, farmers became heavily indebted and their lands began to pass into the hands of money-lenders. Cooperative Land Mortgage Banks were then founded for issuing long-term loans for the redemption of such debts. In short, in the pre-Independence period, the major thrust of rural credit from cooperatives was more towards preventing the usurious exploitation of peasants by money-lenders rather than promoting capital formation in agriculture.

Commercial banks had no interest in the agricultural operations of the peasantry as their role was confined to financing trade and exports. The Royal Commission on Agriculture (1928) and the Central Banking Enquiry Committee had emphasised that cooperatives would have to be the mainstay of rural credit. This led to the establishment of the Agricultural Credit Department in the Reserve Bank of India in 1935 to promote and assist cooperative credit development.

The Rural Banking Enquiry Committee (Sir Purshottamdas Thakurdas) in 1949 found that the cooperative infrastructure was quite satisfactory and that commercial banks had not shown any appreciable interest in agricultural and rural credit and had not gone beyond taluka headquarters. The All India Rural Credit Survey (Gorwala) in 1954, however, pointed out that the development of the cooperative credit movement had been inadequate in coverage and recommended its strengthening by developing a three-tier cooperative structure. The Committee on Cooperative Credit (Mehta) in 1960 recommended the development of a strong and stable institutional framework for cooperative societies, suggesting they should follow sound business methods, distribute assets properly, maintain fluid resources, attract local deposits, develop proper lending norms, supervise the utilisation of credit, improve recovery, maintain a good audit report, etc.

The first real move to plan for rural credit came when the Reserve Bank of India set up the All India Rural Credit Survey Committee (1951–52). While assessing the role of cooperatives, the Committee found that agriculturist money-lenders together supplied about 70 per cent of the total borrowings of agriculturists, whereas government agencies and cooperatives supplied only 6.4 per cent and commercial banks only 0.9 per cent. The Committee, therefore, recommended an integrated reorganisation of the cooperative credit system, which envisaged state partnership through contribution to the share capital of the cooperative credit institutions; coordination between credit and other economic activities, especially marketing and processing; and, administration through adequately trained and efficient personnel responsive to the needs of the rural population.

The Committee emphasised the need for progressive cooperative organisation for marketing and processing along with financial, administrative and technical assistance from the state and the development of storage and warehousing through state-partnered organisations. The key role of coordinating the extensive efforts on the credit side was assigned to the Reserve Bank of India. Two funds were constituted in the RBI. One, National Agricultural Credit (LTO) fund meant to provide long-term funds for State partnership in cooperatives and subscription to the debentures of the Land Mortgage Banks. Two, the National Agricultural Credit (Stabilisation) fund to facilitate conversion of short-term crop loans issued by cooperatives during natural calamities into medium-term loans.

The National Credit Council Study Group on Orgnisational Framework for the Implementation of Social Objectives (Gadgil) in 1968 recommended that the main aim of future national credit policies should be to involve commercial banks in providing rural credit. But the All India Rural Credit Review Committee (Venkatappiah) in 1969 recognised that commercial banks being essentially urban in origin, conception and operations, do not have the organisational machinery or the expertise to deal with rural producers. But, at the same time the Committee hoped that progressive and far-sighted banks would boldly enter rural areas. With such divergent views from different committees, it appeared natural for the Banking Commission (Saraiya) in 1972 to comment that changing the organisational pattern of rural credit too often was undesirable.

It is however, interesting to note that at this stage, little attention was paid to planning to exploit the development potential or the promotion of technology. It would seem that resource development in agriculture was left mainly to government investments in medium and major irrigation projects, land developments, etc. During the 1950s and till the mid-60s, Indian agriculture qualitatively travelled on the traditional path, except for the extension of irrigated agriculture. Weather-induced instability, limited scope for area extension and low productivity posed serious problems. It was recognised at this juncture that a major factor hindering the modernisation and growth of the sector was the low rate of capital formation in agriculture—at around 4 per cent to 5 per cent of the Gross Domestic Product (GDP)—and the inadequacy of institutional finance for promoting long-term investment.

The Third Five-Year Plan, which began in 1961, emphasised the urgent need to step up agricultural production and to create an institution to provide funds by way of refinance to financing institutions. The Agricultural Refinance Corporation (ARC) thus came to be established in 1963. This marked the beginning of a systematic effort for agricultural development banking. The role of the private sector in the development of resources like ground water had become important and was catalysed by the ARC's refinancing and development role in areas like minor irrigation, plantation and horticulture.

The Agriculture Finance Sub-committee (Gadgil) in 1964 examined the question of finance, both short term and long term, and felt that cooperative financing agencies provided the best and lasting solution to the problems of rural credit. It also recommended linking credit with marketing, proper supervision, efficient end-use, greater efforts to mobilise deposits and greater participation of commercial banks in agricultural credit.

In the wake of the disastrous droughts of the mid-60s, the Reserve Bank of India set up the All India Rural Credit Review Committee in 1966 to reassess the developments since the All India Rural Credit Survey of 1951. The Committee pointed out the lapses in disbursal of credit in states with weak cooperatives, especially the eastern states. Low deposits, poor management, apathy in implementing the integrated scheme of rural credit and high overdues were observed in other parts of the country also. It recommended the setting up of the Small Farmers Development Agency in each of the selected districts to help potentially viable small farmers. One could see here the first stirrings or concern for the resource-poor farmer.

To examine the area approach to rural development, the RBI constituted a Committee chaired by F.K.F. Nariman and on its recommendation, the Lead Bank Scheme was introduced in 1969. The scheme involved commercial banks, cooperative institutions, government and semi-government agencies in the process of economic development. Lead Banks for each state/district were appointed to play a catalytic role, especially in rural development of backward areas. The Lead Banks were responsible for surveying credit needs, developing a branch network and extending adequate credit facilities in cooperation with other banks. This was a major step taken by the RBI in expanding the rural banking network and in providing adequate credit for priority sectors and weaker sections of the society, with monitoring of the credit flow being done at district/state fora.

The Committee further recommended the creation of a Rural Electrification Corporation to strengthen the infrastructure for minor irrigation development. The Committee also envisaged a more active and a bigger role for the ARC, subsequently renamed the Agricultural Refinance and Development Corporation (ARDC) in 1975, to emphasise its developmental and promotional role in rural banking.

The advent of new high-yielding seed, fertilisers and technology around the mid-60s marked the beginning of an era of technology-oriented agriculture. The development of minor irrigation, largely based on ground water exploitation, came to acquire much greater significance in the context of the high-yielding technology. The significance of credit as a prime mover was recognised and it began to serve the developmental role on a much wider scale than before. The spurt in demand for credit following the diffusion of the new technology exposed the inability of cooperatives to meet the challenge. It was becoming clear that the commercial banks had to be brought into rural banking. The nationalisation of the 14 scheduled commercial banks in 1969 made this transition easier and influenced the subsequent sizeable growth of development banking in agriculture.

The Working Group on Rural Banks (Narasimhan) in 1975 concluded that the main disabilities in cooperatives arose from their inability to mobilise deposit resources, their managerial weaknesses and dominance of vested interests. Other defects were lack of effective supervision, inadequate coverage of small and marginal production units and limited absorptive capacity of refinance from the higher tiers of the financial institutions because of high overdues of the societies. It noted that efforts over the years towards the rehabilitation of the cooperative credit structure did not appear to have yielded any appreciable results. Hence, the group concluded that there was an urgent need to try new experiments; especially in rural credit.

Here, the central question that needs to be answered is whether it is better or proper organisationally to reorient attitudes and to improve the working of already existing institutions to meet the needs of rural credit, or to create an entirely new institution. Further, the problem of vested interests cannot be isolated from the wider issue of such interests operating in the political, economic and social spheres. Instead of removing vested interests, basic problems may only be avoided by creating new institutions. Creation of new institutions can provide a short-term solution; the long-term remedy is to correct the fundamental problems of rural credit. Without solving those problems, new institutions will face the same or similar problems faced by the old institutions.

Potential Linked District Credit Plan (1987–88)

The National Bank for Agriculture and Rural Development (NABARD) has been preparing Potential Linked Credit Plans (PLPs) since 1987–88 for all rural districts in the country. The basic objective is to map the existing potential for development and evolve an appropriate mechanism through which these could be exploited over a specified time frame. These plans reflect an effort at projecting credit requirements in different sectors in a district, taking into account the long-term physical potential, availability of infrastructure, marketing support, credit absorption capacity and strengths and weaknesses of the credit institutions. These plans aim at reflecting in a more realistic way the micro-credit needs of the villages, the potentials and linkages established/to be established by development agencies. The PLP is aimed at being a total plan document, giving all the relevant information relating to economic activities in the district so as to assist different rural development institutions by providing a valid basis to search for investment alternatives.

The PLP has contributed to perceptible improvements in rural credit planning even under the present Service Area Approach and has pointed out existing inadequacies in the rural infrastructure.

Service Area Approach (1989)

The Service Area Approach was introduced by the RBI on 1 April 1989. Under it, a group of 20 to 25 villages were assigned to each bank branch (commercial bank/RRB) for meeting the credit needs of potential borrowers in the designated 'Service Area'. An annual credit plan for the service area was to be prepared by each branch on the basis of the village economic profiles prepared by them. These branch credit plans were aggregated to form the district credit plan. The district plans were in turn aggregated to form the state credit plan. The implementation of the plans at various levels is continuously monitored. With a view to improving credit flow and its monitoring, both quantitative and qualitative aspects, a computerised Service Area Monitoring and Information Systems (SAMIS) was introduced in 1991.

The Service Area Approach has greatly helped in the preparation of micro-credit plans on the basis of the potential available for exploitation, avoidance of incidence of double financing and creating a database, etc. Its implementation has also brought to the fore several drawbacks and constraints. Instances of service area violations and the inability to adequately meet credit needs have been on the increase, reflecting the incoherence between the service area plan and the performance budget of the branch.

The evolution and growth of the rural credit system needs to be analysed in terms of the changes introduced at various points of time and the compulsions for such changes.

Administrative Interventions in Rural Credit Since 1947

If one looks chronologically at the events which have had a far-reaching impact on the Indian rural credit system, the events prior to 1947 have been few. The few changes then were introduced as a result of a deliberate policy by the authorities and not because of any ground-level requirements as such. Prior to 1947, the changes introduced were:

- 1793—introduction of *taccavi* loans as a measure of administrative relief after recurring famines.
- 1904—introduction of a cooperative credit system based on the Raifessian Model for providing cheaper credit alternatives.
- 1928—introduction of land mortgage banks in the cooperative system to provide for long-term loans for redemption of debts to moneylenders.
- 1935—creation of the Agricultural Credit Department in the Reserve Bank of India, a revolutionary step undertaken for supervising agriculture credit operations.

These changes were introduced by the then administrative powers, with a vision for the future. Coupled with the creation of major irrigation systems, these had a lasting impact on agricultural production, productivity and rural employment. The Indian peasant on his own just did not have the means to make changes/improvements in a feudal zamindari system. Thus, changes had to be introduced from the 'top' and in a phased manner for improving the agricultural credit scenario.

After Independence, the benign and paternalistic attitude towards changes in agricultural credit policies continued but with more significant ideological inputs, which in retrospect did more harm to the rural credit delivery system. The latter, though inadequate, was shaping up well without any significant stresses. But changes introduced after 1947 have been responsible for the sad state of the rural credit delivery system, introducing in it a state of 'forced growth', leading to quick changes and policy 'turnarounds'. These changes were due to the reports of the:

- 1949—Rural Bankers' Enquiry Committee
- 1954—All India Rural Credit Survey
- 1955—Formation of State Bank of India
- 1960—Committee on Cooperative Credit
- 1963—Agriculture Refinance Corporation set up—changed to ARDC (1975) and then to NABARD (1982)
- 1968—National Credit Council Study Group on Organisational Framework for Implementation of Social Objectives.
- 1969—Rural Credit Review Committee
  —Nationalisation of 14 largest banks
- 1972—Banking Commission
- 1972–75—Setting up of REC, SFDA
- 1975—Working Group on Rural Banks
- 1989—Agricultural Credit Review Committee
- 1991—Report on the Financial System
- 1998—R.V. Gupta Committee on Rural Credit

These are some of the major committees which have tried to make the rural credit delivery system more effective. There were many other committees constituted by the government and the RBI which made many conflicting suggestions. Without considering the effect of the policy changes already introduced, further changes were recommended. These policy interventions introduced in a piecemeal, casual and half-hearted manner, further tampered with the system, creating more problems.

Instead of analysing why the pre-Independence policy-induced changes did not succeed, major structural changes were introduced in the rural credit delivery system after 1947 with the hope that such committee-induced changes may prove beneficial to the rural poor. It was as if 'social engineering' was done on a vast scale without any insight into the consequences and the result is clear. The rural credit delivery system is now on the verge of collapse with poor interest margins, very high overdues, untrained staff, poor monitoring and control by regional offices, and very poor working results. Commercial banks are seriously contemplating closure of rural branches, which have been loss making for very long periods. Cooperative banks have been depending solely upon cheap refinance while the Regional Rural Banks (RRBs) have run into huge losses that have wiped out their share capital and a portion of the deposits. The assault on the rural credit delivery system continues with politicians often encouraging non-repayment of bank dues, loan melas and loan write-offs. This has subjected the rural banking system to undue stresses and strains apart from high administrative costs and poor interest margins as per the ACRC (1989) and the Narasimham Committee findings. In short, the official intervention in the rural credit delivery system after 1947 and particularly after 1969 has been often harmful.

Institutional Mechanism for Credit Delivery

NABARD (and ARDC) opted for providing loans by way of refinancing credit institutions, cooperative banks and commercial banks, rather than undertaking direct financing through outlets of their own. This was because with 90 million farmers spread over half a million villages in 25 States and seven Union Territories, direct financing would have been a far more costly operation involving a parallel set of outlets. Refinancing the existing institutions and also over-seeing and coordinating their activities to ensure that development finance does flow into the rural sector in accordance with the national priorities made for greater efficiency.

Under the prevailing multi-agency approach, agricultural credit is provided in India at the base level by cooperatives, commercial banks and the RRBs (see Table 3.1). Cooperatives are divided into two types—the first providing short- and medium-term loans (state cooperative banks numbering 28, district central cooperative banks, 366 and primary agriculture cooperative societies over 88,000); and, the second providing long-term loans (19 Cooperative Land Development Banks operating through 1,412 primaries or branches). Hundred commercial banks with a network of more than 44,000 rural and semi-urban branches provide direct, as well as indirect, credit for agriculture. The indirect forms being the loans extended to state electricity boards for the energisation of irrigation pumpsets and the distribution of fertilisers. The 196 RRBs operating through about 14,000 branches in 369 districts provide agricultural credit with a focus on small and marginal farmers and landless persons. At the apex of the structure is NABARD, which is supported by the RBI.

Table 3.1
Institutional Arrangements—Agriculture and Rural Credit

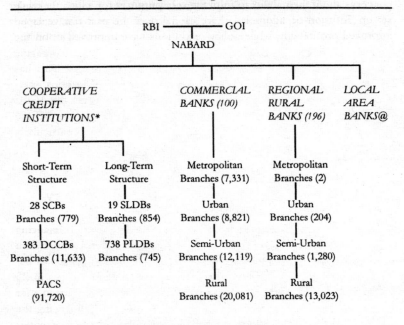

DEPOSITORS AND BORROWERS

Number of branches as on 31 March 1997.
@ 8 licensed but yet to commence operations.
* In AP, the short-term and long-term cooperative credit institutions have been integrated.

The emergence of the RRBs as an important arm of agricultural development needs special mention. Though the new strategy of high-yielding technology in agriculture was scale-neutral, it was not resource-neutral. Rural power structures dominated the cooperative system, which also suffered from structural weaknesses and poor management. The commercial banks lacked a rural development orientation. Between these two types, it was feared the weaker target groups would be bypassed. An institution was needed which combined the advantages of the cooperatives' familiarity with rural problems and the commercial banks' ability to mobilise deposits and function with a modern outlook and access to money markets. The RRBs were designed to meet this need and were set up in 1975. There has been a rapid expansion of their branch network, deposits and credit business. Exclusive lending to the weaker sections at low rates of interest has, however, adversely affected their financial viability, leading to concerns about their ability to fulfil the very purposes for which they were set up. Infusion of additional share capital over the past few years has improved profitability, while policy relaxations have improved viability.

4

Credit Recycling and the Problem of Overdues

Repayments ethics and recycling of credit are crucial to the smooth functioning of the institutional credit delivery system. The incidence of overdues in the agricultural credit system has been increasing over the years and, coupled with other weaknesses, has been steadily eroding its financial soundness.

Impact of Overdues

At the end of June 1990, the overdues of all agricultural credit agencies at the ultimate borrowers' level amounted to Rs 7,557 crore, constituting 26.42 per cent of the loans outstanding and 52.66 per cent of demand. As can be seen, overdues are an all-pervasive phenomenon and their extent varies only in degree between different categories of credit institutions and in different regions.

The poor recovery performance of credit institutions has been influenced both by internal and external factors. Factors internal to the banks include defective loan policies and procedures, inadequate supervision and unsatisfactory management. Factors external are occurrence of natural calamities like floods and droughts, absence of linkages, defective legal framework and above all, lack of support from the government machinery in recoveries. Not only is government support in recovery not forthcoming but there has also been active interference, particularly in cooperatives, through the ban on coercive action for recoveries, announcements of interest subsidy and loan write-offs. This has vitiated the climate for recovery. The All India Rural Credit Survey Committee, in fact, recommended for the setting up of a National Agricultural Credit (Relief and Guarantee Fund) to write-off loans which have become irrecoverable due to genuine hardships caused by natural calamities. However, appropriate schemes for such deserving cases were not evolved. The schemes announced by state governments envisaged across-the-board write-offs. In the process, those borrowers who had repaid their dues to banks in time did not get any relief, thus sending wrong signals.

The more recent Agricultural and Rural Debt Relief scheme (1990) has apart from writing off substantial amounts (of the order of Rs 4,672 crore in the case of cooperatives and RRBs covering 1.93 crore beneficiaries), so vitiated the climate for recovery that many borrowers defaulted in repaying their current dues, in anticipation that these would also be written off. In the process, credit flow has been choked and the eligibility of the units of the credit delivery system to have recourse to higher financing agencies has been severely curtailed. The delay by the Government of India/state governments to provide the relief amount to the banks has caused a serious resource crunch. The health of credit institutions has also been seriously jeopardised due to the inadequate margins available to them on rural lending. This has further aggravated the situation.

NABARD had to make several relaxations in its disciplines every year to encourage credit flow for agriculture and has been forced to extend concessions in this regard since the 1991 kharif season.

Deterioration in Recovery Levels

Various committees, including the Agriculture Credit Review Committee made several recommendations aimed at improving the recovery climate as a key step for ensuring the health of rural credit institutions. However, the ARDR scheme (1990) vitiated the recovery climate and fresh lending regressed to the lending levels of 1980. This deterioration has to be urgently corrected. As pointed out by the ACRC strong political will is required to check the politicisation of agricultural credit institutions. A general consensus is also needed among all political parties to ensure that agricultural credit is not used as an instrument for political purposes. It is advisable to send a clear message that no waivers would be announced and state governments should be requested to desist from announcing similar relief schemes in future. The Central and state governments should also evolve a concrete long-term policy for recovery of agriculture dues and take a firm and objective view in respect of wilful defaulters. The hypothesis that the ARDR scheme (1989) has affected recovery levels in the rural areas needs to be tested. The impact of ARDR scheme (1989) has been studied at the field-level and a medium-sized district selected for the purpose of sampling loan recovery data from all operating rural credit agencies. Dharwad district in Karnataka is a district which is neither very agriculturally developed nor under-developed, and the proportion of irrigated lands to total land cultivated there is around 25 per cent (as is the all India proportion). Dharwad's loan repayment performance before/after the imposition of ARDR scheme (1989) has been studied so as to have a fair idea of the impact on loan recovery.

Recovery Performance—Dharwad District

Recovery of Advances—1989–90

The position of demand, collection and overdues as on 30 June 1990 has been reviewed (See Table 4.1 and 4.2). As against total demand of Rs 188.25 crore in respect of priority sectors, total recovery was Rs 42.45 crore and overdues Rs 145.80 crore.

Table 4.1
Institution-wise Demand and Recovery—Dharwad District

(Rs crore)

Agency	Total Demand	Total Collection	Total Overdues	% of Collection to Demand
1. Commercial Banks	87.59	30.98	56.61	35.38
2. Regional Rural Banks	42.30	5.98	36.32	14.13
3. Cooperatives	58.36	5.48	52.87	9.38
	188.25	42.45	145.80	22.54

It was observed that the percentage of collection to demand was lowest for cooperatives at 9.38 per cent, followed by Malaprabha Grameena Bank at 14.13 per cent and 35.38 per cent in respect of commercial banks. All banks/institutions have shown a declining trend in recovery.

Table 4.2
Sector-wise Demand and Collection—Dharwad District

(Rs. crore)

Agency	Total Demand	Total Collection	Total Overdues	% of Collection to Demand
1. Agriculture and Allied Activities	135.00	21.16	113.84	15.67
2. Small-Scale Industries	21.53	8.36	13.17	38.80
3. Tertiary Sector	31.72	12.93	18.79	40.77
	188.25	42.45	145.80	22.54

As regards sector-wise recovery position, against a collection of 39.87 per cent in respect of agriculture and allied activities during 1989–90, recovery during 1990–91 was only 15.67 per cent. However, in respect of small scale industries the percentage of collection improved from 32.66 per cent to 38.80 per cent. In the tertiary sector, against a collection of 48.27 per cent during 1989–90, recovery during 1990–91 declined to 40.77 per cent.

There were 2,30,649 overdue accounts with amount outstanding of Rs 145.80 crore at the end of June 1990 (See Table 4.3). The age-wise classification of these accounts is given below.

Table 4.3
Classification of Overdue Accounts

Age of Overdues	No. of A/cs	Amount (Rs crore)
1. Up to One Year	57,680	34.48
2. One to Three Years	93,030	70.26
3. Above Three Years	80,039	41.06
	230,649	145.80

Recovery of Advances—1990–91

The bank-wise and sector-wise recovery position as on 30 June 1991 in Dharwad district was:

The consolidated data of all the banks relating to demand, recovery and collection reveals that there is an improvement in the overall recovery position during the year 1990–91. However, the actual recovery position would have been far below the progress reported, but for the Agricultural Rural Debt Relief scheme, 1990 of the Government of India, which has come in a big way in reducing the overdues of the banks.

The consolidated data of the banks indicates that as against a total demand of Rs 237.44 crore, total recovery was Rs 113.91 crore (i.e., 47.97 per cent) leaving overdues of Rs 123.53 crore. There was an improvement of around 109.79 per cent in the recovery position during the year 1990–91 over the previous year 1989–90. The institution-wise demand, collection and overdues are given in Table 4.4.

Table 4.4
Agency-wise Demand, Collection and Overdues Position

(Rs crore)

Agency	Total Demand	Total Collection	Total Overdues	% of Collection to Demand
1. Commercial Banks	125.11	63.57	61.54	50.80
2. Regional Rural Banks	50.46	24.57	25.89	48.68
3. Cooperatives	61.87	25.77	36.10	41.65
Total	237.44	113.91	123.53	47.97

The sector-wise demand, collection and overdues are given in Table 4.5.

Table 4.5
Purpose-wise Demand, Collection and Overdues Position

(Rs crore)

Sector	Total Demand	Total Collection	Total Overdues	% of Collection to Demand
1. Agricultural and Allied Activities	167.35	77.50	89.85	46.31
2. Small-Scale Industries	40.88	25.09	15.79	61.36
3. Tertiary Sector	29.21	11.32	17.89	38.16
Total	237.44	113.91	123.53	47.97

The recovery position of commercial banks increased from 35.38 per cent in 1989–90 to 50.80 per cent in 1990–91. It may also be observed that there was a remarkable improvement in the recovery position of RRBs and cooperatives over the last year. As already stated, this was mainly due to the ARDR scheme (1990) and cash recoveries from borrowers had reduced. However, the actual recovery atmosphere is yet to be geared up, since 'overdues' in the banks are increasing at a faster rate every year. However, in respect of cooperative banks, it was slightly less at 41.65 per cent.

In the sector-wise recovery position, we can observe that the recovery position under SSI sector was very good at 61.36 per cent followed by agriculture and allied sector at 46.31 per cent and tertiary sector at 38.16 per cent.

There were around 190,098 overdue loan accounts with an amount of Rs 123.53 crore at the end of June 1991.The age-wise classification of these accounts is given in Table 4.6.

Table 4.6
Age-wise Classification of Overdue Accounts

Age of Overdues	No. of A/cs	Amount (Rs crore)
1. Up to One Year	36,392	21.33
2. One to Three Years	89,702	64.40
3. Above Three Years	64,004	37.80
	190,098	123.53

It may be mentioned that the overdue priority sector accounts as on 30 June 1992 for Dharwad have increased to Rs 211.62 crore while that for Karnataka as a whole increased to Rs 4,383.46 crore.

Conclusion

The ARDR scheme (1990) certainly reduced overdues; the number of overdue accounts fell by 36.7 per cent (up to one year), 3.6 per cent (up to 3 years) and 20 per cent (over 3 years) upon comparing the 1990–91 position with 1989–90. Also, the total amount of overdues reduced by 16 per cent. However, the gains have to be consolidated by better and more effective loan recovery steps. The ARDR scheme (1990) is perceived by the rural borrowers as having discriminated against those who repaid their loans on time, sometimes by recourse to other loans from friends/relatives and even money-lenders while the wilful defaulters have benefited. Even money-lenders have stated that after the ARDR scheme (1990) was implemented, those borrowers, who hitherto paid their debts regularly, had become restive and wanted similar facilities from them. Also, there is always the expectation that further loan waivers will be given, purely for political purposes when elections are due. Thus, debt write-offs have severely affected recovery of banks dues at the grassroots levels. All state governments should realise that debt write-offs only serve to help the wilful defaulters while penalising those farmers who repay their loans in spite of crop failures, by resorting to income generation from labour employment, remittances, etc. If at all there is a need to help farmers in distress, then the state governments should:

- Strengthen rural credit agencies so that the credit gap is lowered and the spread of institutional credit is widened.
- Consider interest rebates for those repaying loans promptly.

Repayment Ethics

In a country where a large proportion of people are very conservative and orthodox in their thinking, taking loans from money-lenders/banks is considered to be a grave risk. If a person dies without repaying his debts, his sons and heirs feel it their duty do so or the father's soul will not rest in peace. Also, the fear of non-repayment of debts due to exorbitant interest rates, could lead to alienation of property rights.

However since 1969, bank nationalisation led to the popularisation of policies and programmes based on cheap credit availability. Cheap credit was coveted by the better-organised people, who also had the political clout, and so loan melas and loan write-offs became the order of the day in the 1980s. But in the 1990s, due to economic and banking reforms, there is a move to consolidate the banking sector and indiscriminate expansion has been stopped. The profitability of banks is being closely watched and prudential norms and NPA management have become key operational issues today.

Loan recovery has become very important as will be seen from Table 4.7.

The agency-wise/state-wise recovery figures on an institution-wise basis for 1995–96 (see Annexure 4.1) reveal that certain states like Bihar, Assam and other north-eastern states and Orissa have a chronic overdues problem due to weak monitoring systems and poor repayment ethics. Conversely, the variations in recovery between various credit agencies in a state, can be ascribed to good management and leadership as also proper monitoring of end-use. It is time that all those interested in the continued good health of rural credit agencies realise that bank deposits are not government funds and have to be returned. No bank can afford to operate on poor margins and earn losses, eroding not only their share capital and reserves but also the deposits and, sometimes, the borrowings too!

Table 4.7
Agency-wise Recovery Position

Agency	Percentage of Recovery to Demand				
	1991–92	1992–93	1993–94	1994–95	1995–96
SCBs	83	88	89	90	90
DCCBs	56	65	67	70	69
PACSs	57	49	56	59	53
LDBs	50	52	57	62	61
RRBs	40	41	46	51	55
Commercial Banks	54	54	55	57	59

Prudential Norms

The Committee of Financial Systems, 1991 (Narasimham Committee) had recommended that a bank's balance sheet should reflect its actual financial position and hence, a proper system for recognition of income, classification of assets, provisioning for bad debts on prudential basis was necessary. Income recognition should be objective rather than subjective, on the actual recovery of both principal and interest dues based on uniform worldwide norms (Basle Committee for Bank Supervision Norms). These prudential norms have been applied in a phased manner to all credit agencies, details of which are given in Table 4.8.

Table 4.8
Particulars of Application of Prudential Norms to Banks

Agency	Year of Application	Income Recognition	Assets Classification	Provisioning Norms	Capital Adequacy
Commercial	1992-93	A	A	A	A
RRBs	1995-96	A	A	A	NA
SCBs/DCCBs	1996-97	A	A	A	NA
PACSs	NA	NA	NA	NA	NA
SCARDBs/ PACRDBs	1997-98	A	A	A	NA
IDBI/IFCI/ IDBI/EXIM	1994-95	A	A	A	A
NB/SIDBI	1995-96	A	A	A	A

A—Applicable   NA—Not Applicable

While the Capital Adequacy Ratio (minimum 8 per cent) is to be attained by commercial banks and financial institutions, this norm has not been applied to RRBs and cooperative banks. However, the NPA percentage should not normally exceed 5 per cent, as per banking norms worldwide. The application of these prudential norms is expected to make bank balance sheets more transparent and more conscious of NPA management so as to reduce exposure to bad loans. Better recovery of bank dues is possible with coordinated efforts to reduce NPAs and effect loan recovery.

Overdues Management

Overdues arise due to non-payment of loan instalments on due dates. Wilful default is mainly due to the inadequate and ineffective organisational efforts of banks to receive dues. Clearly, overdues can result from external or internal factors. These need to be studied in some detail.

EXTERNAL FACTORS

There are factors over which the banks have no operational or administrative control, such as:

- Natural calamities like floods, drought and earthquakes.
- Political and government interference.
- Cropping pattern changes not adopted by farmers.
- Costs of inputs and prices of farm produce without price support.

INTERNAL FACTORS

There are factors related to organisational deficiencies and administrative ineffectiveness, such as:

- Defective loaning policies and procedures (loans for unproductive purposes, due date determination).
- Ineffective supervision machinery over loan utilisation.
- Lack of efforts for recovery and inadequate system for recovery.

There are certain other causes leading to loan overdues, such as:

- Under-financing or over-financing.
- Infructuous investments.

- Alienation of lands by borrowers by way of sale, gift, mortgage.
- Failure of projects like lift irrigation units, processing units.
- Sale of assets like tractors, power tillers.
- Demise of borrower and disputes among heirs of deceased.
- Lack of proper marketing facilities.
- Delay in getting power connection to well points.
- Non-availability/inadequacy of production credit.
- Shorter loan period and higher loan instalments.
- Uneconomic land holdings.
- Increased cost of living due to inflation or unforeseen social expenses.
- Power/fuel shortages.
- Absence of credit/market linkages for borrowers/defaulters.

Suggestions for Recovery Improvement

There are certain practical suggestions for improving loan recovery in rural credit agencies, such as:

- Reorienting loan policies and procedures to suit the borrowers.
- Ensuring effective monitoring and supervision of loans.
- Setting up loan recovery cells.
- Coercive, legal action to be taken up and followed.
- Coordination with government officials especially revenue officials, for recovery of bank dues.
- Rescheduling and postponing overdues.
- Sale of mortgaged property.
- Stringent recovery action against selected wilful defaulters.
- Seek involvement of youth clubs, NGOs and non-officials.
- Linking of credit with marketing.
- Sanction of cash credits in multi-cropped areas.
- Increasing commercialisation of agriculture.
- Chief ministers to launch public awareness campaigns for loan repayment.

The 'soft state' that India has degenerated to in the absence of a swift legal system, absence of follow up measures, and the proliferation of vested interests in rural areas make it difficult to ensure prompt repayment of bank dues. Unless swift steps are taken to bring down the high level of NPAs (totalling over Rs 42,000 crore for commercial banks alone) and enhancing loan recovery rate from 55 per cent to over 80 per cent, the future of rural credit is bleak.

It is estimated that the total NPAs of commercial banks in the loans for agriculture and priority sectors amount to Rs 10,000 crore—compelling the study of reasons for poor loan recovery especially in the rural areas. Many research studies have been made in different parts of the country. According to them, failure in repayment stems from:

- Defective loan deliveries, including sanctioning delays and inadequate loan amounts.
- Natural disaster leading to crop failures.
- Wilful defaults due to political intervention.
- Impact of a few politico-social decisions like debt waivers.

Unless these factors are taken care of, poor loan recovery in the agricultural sector will continue. However, a good banker can maintain a good working relationship with his clientele and overcome these problems to a large extent.

Annexure 4.1

Agency-wise/State-wise Recovery Performance—1995–96

State	Average % of Recovery to Demand				
	SCBs	DCCBs	RRBs	SCARDBs	PCARDBs
Haryana	99	83	64	95	86
Himachal Pradesh	34	39	66	85	89
Jammu & Kashmir	79	23	36	54	—
Punjab	99	89	65	100	89
Rajasthan	85	78	50	80	68
Chandigarh	55	—	—	—	—
New Delhi	53	—	—	—	—
Arunachal Pradesh	28	—	50	—	—
Assam	13	—	17	02	26
Manipur	10	—	23	14	—
Meghalaya	39	—	23	—	—
Mizoram	16	—	52	—	—
Nagaland	46	—	09	—	—
Tripura	24	—	07	86	—
Bihar	16	18	29	33	—
Orissa	77	53	58	09	34
West Bengal	81	69	34	60	60
Andaman & Nicobar	39	—	—	—	—
Madhya Pradesh	97	58	48	39	52
Uttar Pradesh	85	59	51	79	—
Goa	82	—	—	—	—
Gujarat	99	67	68	66	—
Maharashtra	86	66	67	54	—
Andhra Pradesh	83	70	58	—	—
Karnataka	82	70	68	37	39
Kerala	92	81	84	82	75
Tamil Nadu	100	78	79	49	85
Pondicherry	61	—	—	49	—
All India	90	69	55	61	61

Note: Recovery of Commercial Banks for 1995–96—59 per cent (All India).

5

Agricultural Credit Review Committee (ACRC), 1989

The Agricultural Credit Review Committee (ACRC) was engaged by the Reserve Bank of India to

> evaluate the major problems and issues currently affecting the Indian agricultural credit system, as outlined in the five review studies, and to make recommendations for a programme to strengthen the sector.

The five review studies were carried out by five separate consultancy firms and covered agricultural credit in general; the role of effectiveness of lending institutions; the role and functions of the apex level in agricultural credit; lending costs and margins; and, organisation and management study of NABARD.

The ACRC report is structured into seven parts—developments in agricultural sector and projections of agricultural credit; agricultural credit system, a review and measures for improvement; overdues in the agricultural credit system; strengthening the agricultural credit system; credit linked poverty alleviation programmes; role of apex level; and, summary of recommendations.

The report concluded that the Indian rural credit system, with its various inefficiencies—poor management, inadequate resources including inadequate deposit mobilisation, large-scale non-repayment, and inadequate rural people participation—would not be able to support emerging credit demands for the economic growth planned, including poverty reduction targets. Thus, the attainment of India's growth objective, particularly its poverty reduction targets, requires a revitalisation of the whole rural credit system. It observed that the banks were more concerned with credit disbursements and less so with recovery and promotional efforts. Also, that the banks were more concerned with the improvement of their own viability rather than that of the community they serve.

In reviewing demand and resources, the studies concluded that there may not be any appreciable constraint of resources in the commercial banking system assuming a 2.5 per cent annual increase in credit requirements. However, at 5 per cent which seems likely, there would be a constraint of resources for agricultural credit requirements. Cooperatives would continue to depend on refinance from NABARD. In both cases, effective steps for recovery of dues would be necessary to obtain the resources estimated. It was observed that by 1990, commercial banks including RRBs would finance 50 per cent short-term and 35 per cent medium and long-term requirements. It was also estimated that for commercial banks—deposits now growing at 16 per cent p.a. would average 12 per cent in the year 2000; advances to agriculture now mandated at 16 per cent of total net bank credit would average 18 per cent in the year 2000; and, credit deposit ratio now at 62 per cent would further decline to 52 per cent. For cooperatives—deposits now growing at 14 per cent would average at 15 per cent, and after allowing for liquidity and cash reserves of 35 per cent of deposits and 10 per cent to non-agriculture areas, 65 per cent would be advanced for agriculture. In 1986, overdues related to demand were 43 per cent for commercial banks, 45 per cent for RRBs, and 41 per cent for cooperatives including Land Development Banks (LDBs). In fact, 84 per cent of RRBs and 66 per cent of LDBs were either ineligible or subject to restricted eligibility for NABARD refinancing.

In reviewing the role and performance of commercial banks, it was observed that one of the specific objectives of bank nationalisation was to increase the flow of credit to weaker sections. Commercial banks are now mandated to achieve certain targets under priority sector lending: 40 per cent of total credit to be channelled to priority sectors including agriculture and small business; 17 per cent directed to finance of agriculture and related activities; and, 10 per cent of credit for weaker economic sections. Credit under various poverty alleviation programmes of which the IRDP is the largest, has substantially increased—commercial banks now finance nearly 70 per cent of the total programme (RRBs 23 per cent and cooperatives 8 per cent). As a result, branch coverage for rural areas has expanded, with rural branches coming to 56 per cent and semi-urban branches 26 per cent of total branches in 1986. These banks were required to maintain credit deposit ratios of at least 60 per cent for their rural branches so as to eliminate regional imbalances. This emphasis has naturally resulted in an increased number of small advances with the attendant higher transaction costs per loan. However, overall cost has been restrained through the tendency for understaffing at both the clerical and supervisory levels. While total overdues have averaged 43 per cent of demand, overdues related to IRDP lending were 54 per cent in 1987. Improvements were noted where special emphasis has been introduced in sub-loan appraisal and collection efforts at a higher transaction cost.

While commercial banks have been able to earn overall net profits, they have suffered losses in their rural business, because of declining margins (increased cost of deposits and the reduced percentage of concessional funds), the increase in transaction costs arising from the large number of rural branches, and reduced resources caused by the high level of non-performing loans arising from overdues. The average interest of 1.5 per cent earned on rural lending compares to 14 per cent on non-rural lending. In addition, overall profitability suffers from the high level of cash and liquidity reserves maintained with the RBI at low interest rates. With the view to strengthening the banks, the ACRC suggested the increase of 'own funds' (equity) at least to a level of 2 per cent of assets by 1990, 3 per cent by 1995 and about 4 per cent by the year 2000.

The review of commercial banks' performance shows that the steep increase in institutional credit has not resulted in a corresponding increase in agricultural production and productivity. To improve the quality of rural lending, the Service Area Approach was introduced in April 1989, whereby each branch would be allocated a designated area. Through branch credit plans, the banker at the grassroots level would determine the needs and potential of the likely clientele in a systematic way. This would form the basis of credit plans through to the district levels. While the ACRC has supported this approach with the modification of including the cooperatives and commercial banks in this scheme, it noted its concern that the allocated number of villages per branch were large and sometimes widely spread, and sub-borrowers would not be able to go outside their service area. Also, there arises the possible conflict between the government's role in development planning and that of the branches.

In summary, the assessment on commercial banks is that far too many targets, mandates, and detailed instructions on procedures have detracted from efficiency, making management difficult and professionalism the biggest casualty. Welfare orientation has substituted commercial judgement, including the autonomy of the manager, resulting in reduced motivation and accountability. The client–bank relationship has undergone a massive change due to mass loaning, and people have started to perceive credit as another public service disassociated with the capacity of profitable utilisation of the resources borrowed.

The RRBs were intended to combine the local feel and rural familiarity possessed by the cooperatives with the business organisation and modern outlook of the commercial banks. The aim being to reach the rural disadvantaged more extensively. These banks are owned by Government of India (50 per cent), state government (15 per cent) and a commercial 'sponsor bank' (35 per cent). They did reach the target group having expanded into far-flung rural and tribal areas. In 1987, they represented 40 per cent of all rural branches of the commercial banking system, but accounted for only 9 per cent of rural lending. While these banks suffer very much from the general problems of the commercial banking system non-viability was built into their very concept. RRBs lend at 10 per cent interest, pay 1/2 per cent higher interest for depositors. Almost all RRBs made losses from their lending operations and about 70 per cent have accumulated losses in excess of their share capital, thereby becoming legally bankrupt. Staff costs levels, which were initially expected to be low, are close to that of commercial banks and the management, including that at the board level, is considered unsatisfactory. In the ACRC's view, the logic and rationale which justified the setting up of RRBs no longer existed, as commercial banks have now expanded into rural areas much faster than was anticipated. Their recommendation is that RRBs be merged with the branches of their shareholders in accordance with their percentage ownership. To ensure increased lending to the weaker sections after the proposed merger, the ACRC recommended that the commercial banks be required to increase their lending to that section from 10 per cent to 15 per cent of net bank credit. It suggested that the commercial banks will be able to cross-subsidise such operations.

The cooperative credit system comprises both short-term and long-term structures. The short-term structure has as its base Primary Agricultural Credit Societies (PACSs), federated into District Central Cooperative Banks (DCCBs) which, in turn, are federated at the state level into State Cooperative Banks (SCBs). At the long-term level are the Land Development Banks (LDBs) which are unitary in some states and in some, they are federal. While the general consensus of past working groups has been that cooperative banks have not done well, the rather similar experience of the commercial banking system suggests that many of their problems relate

to the agricultural credit system in general. It has been said that cooperatives in India have experienced operational problems because they are
both, state sponsored and patronised, thereby negating democratic management. The basic principle of cooperative banking, namely reliance on
resources mobilised locally and lesser dependence on higher credit institutions, has historically been absent from the Indian system. The lower
tiers look up to the higher tiers and the government for refinance, and the
higher tiers ignore the interests of the lower tiers. This has resulted in ever
increasing state control over cooperatives, depriving them of their democratic and autonomous character. Also, an increased level of politicisation
has crept in with interference in recoveries by politicians promising to
write off loans and reduce interest charges.

Latest available data (1986) shows the PACSs having over 70 million
members with about 20 million borrowing from the cooperative system.
Deposits from members amounted to about 12 per cent of credit and
share capital and reserves were equal to another 25 per cent, leaving 63
per cent to be financed by borrowings. It should be pointed out that a
large percentage of PACSs' share capital is from the state government.
Overdues equalled about 42 per cent of demand and less than 60 per cent
of these PACSs were profitable, with their performances varying from
state to state. While credit is the primary role of PACSs, many are involved
in other activities such as input distribution. An issue raised was the lack
of a full-time staff (secretarial) in all PACSs and the inadequacy of
training.

The review highlighted many weaknesses in the operations of PACSs .

(a) About 50 per cent of all PACSs were not viable and it was recom-
    mended that an action programme be developed for each PACS to
    increase their deposit mobilisation, increase its loan business, and en-
    large profitable non-credit activities.
(b) NABARD should provide funds to state governments to allow them
    to invest additional share capital in PACSs to facilitate meeting their
    lending requirements, irrespective of current levels of overdues (many
    are now ineligible because of high overdues).
(c) Each PACSs should have a full time staff (secretarial) and that assist-
    ance should be given to pay their salaries and the reorganisation pro-
    cess for PACSs now in progress should continue to allow them to
    cover larger areas but this should be on a voluntary basis.
(d) Most PACSs are totally dependent on DCCBs' financing and are
    starved of credit where the DCCBs are weak. At the same time, they
    can not compete with the commercial banking system in deposit

mobilisation because of their inherent culture to be merely passers of funds, lack of secure and essential handling facilities, and the lack of deposit insurance enjoyed by the commercial banks. The report recommends that the SCBs/DCCBs finance a development fund with the assistance of the government for providing assistance to PACSs. Also, SCBs in coordination with their state governments should formulate suitable schemes for insuring deposits of PACSs in their states.

(e) To replace fixed short-term loans for 12-month periods or less, it is proposed that the cash-credit system already introduced in some areas be extended for all irrigated areas and where multiple cropping is practical. The cash-credit system would reduce transaction costs and provide more flexibility in determining repayment dates. Other recommendations addressed the problems of disbursements in kind, the fixing of recovery due dates and the adequacy of credit allowed.

(f) Proper office premises and godown space should be provided to PACSs to conduct their activities as multi-purpose societies (41 per cent now own godowns and 17 per cent have hired godowns).

(g) PACSs should be allowed to lend for non productive purposes from their own funds.

(h) Principal and interest on credit collected from PACSs' members should be the same as the DCCBs level, instead of being applied to interest first for the total recovery due from the PACSs to the DCCBs. This will avoid the principal repayment of some members being used to pay the interest of delinquent members at the higher tier.

The share capital of DCCBs is contributed by the PACSs, mainly on the basis of ratios linking share capital to borrowing. In 1986, 17 per cent of DCCBs' total resources were derived from own funds, 33 per cent from cooperative societies and 50 per cent from public and individuals. About 70 per cent of their lending was short term and overdues were 38 per cent of demand. Of 352 DCCBs, 173 were under rehabilitation and by far, the majority were in loss-making positions. DCCBs are at a disadvantage compared with commercial banks in deposit mobilisation, as not being 'scheduled banks', they cannot accept deposits from trusts, institutions, etc. Also, their basic weaknesses would not create the confidence essential for attracting deposits from such clientele. The major deficiencies observed in their operations included delays in sanction and disbursement of loans; provision of inadequate finance; insistence of disbursement in kind; improper repayment schedule; and, lack of monitoring and follow-up. The high level of overdues has affected their ability to obtain adequate refinance. A DCCB is put under rehabilitation when its accumulated losses and overdues above three years exceed 50 per cent of paid-up capital and reserves. Very few, if any, have emerged from rehabilitation successfully.

There are 28 SCBs, one for each state and union territory. In most states, membership is restricted to DCCBs, state-level cooperative institutions and some primary agricultural cooperatives (such as urban cooperative banks), and the state governments which on average own about 18 per cent. About 25 per cent of their deposits are low cost, being current and savings accounts, with the other 75 per cent being fixed and other deposits representing the statutory reserves of DCCBs and other cooperative institutions which are mandated to invest these with the SCBs. However, a handicap is that SCBs' branches are, except in certain circumstances, restricted to state capital cities. About one-third of their available resources are borrowed from NABARD for seasonal agricultural operations, for medium-term agricultural purposes and for conversion and rephasement of seasonal loans. NABARD provides only supplementary finance, usually to the extent of the deficit in DCCBs resources. As NABARD finance is at a concessional rate of interest, the higher cost of mobilising deposits mobilised acts as a disincentive to the SCBs for extra efforts at deposit mobilisation. Conversion/rephasement loans have increased during the three years from 1984 to 1986 due to successive natural calamities in several parts of the country. Overdues to demand averaged 11 per cent in 1986, that relating to agricultural lendings are usually absorbed at the DCCBs level and that for SCBs are mainly for non-agricultural lending to cooperative institutions.

The problems and weaknesses besetting the short-term cooperative structure in general were substantially those identified by earlier studies. These were said to be owing to certain structural weaknesses, failure to mobilise adequate deposits, mounting overdues and lack of trained staff. The need to establish a viable primary structure was lost sight of and a coordinated pattern of marketing and credit was not achieved. While the records showed that in 1986, SCBs and DCCBs relied less on refinancing as a percentage of working funds, only 23 per cent and 28 per cent respectively, that for PACSs was only 10 per cent. It was observed that no real progress was being made in the development of professional management, with blame attributed mainly to the control by state governments which allowed little or no say to the cooperatives themselves.

In summarising what was considered critical to the overall development of the short-term cooperative credit system, the ACRC report listed—

(a) development of the leadership role of the higher tiers; (b) greater deposit mobilisation; (c) development of project formulation and investment planning; (d) capability for better and diversified project lending; and, (e) rehabilitation of weak banks. There is a strong need to develop the cooperative credit system into a functionally integrated structure with a two-way system of obligations and rights. Each tier should be allocated its responsibilities for deposit mobilisation and demotivating policy constraints should be removed. SCBs should set up a technical cell to formulate sub-loan appraisals and monitoring, and utilise it to provide the necessary training throughout the system. Also, guidance on investment/portfolio management should be included. The programme for rehabilitating weak DCCBs should allow for the financing of non-defaulting members and assist non-wilful defaulters.

The long-term cooperative credit system operates through the Land Development Banks (LDBs), at the primary level (PLDBs) and the state level (SLDBs). LDBs have shown a declining trend in their share in agricultural lending, with increasing overdues (45 per cent of demand in 1986) resulting in restricted eligibility for lending. Memberships are restricted to land-owning farmers and the majority of their funding is by way of NABARD debentures supported by underlying mortgages. In 1986, 194 out of a total of 910 LDBs were under a rehabilitation programme. Problems other than overdues and restricted eligibility included inadequate operating margins compared to high operating costs and government intervention in management decisions. Staff development has been very poor with the majority of senior staff being government staff on deputation. To remedy the above problems, the ACRC report recommended that NABARD provide increased concessional funds for interim financing before the debenture issue and term loans instead of special development debentures; LDBs introduce a system for recruitment, development and training of staff; and that housing finance activity be taken up by LDBs on an agency basis. Increased margins were also recommended.

The question of integrating the short-term and long-term aspects of agricultural credit has always been a debatable issue. After reviewing the reports of earlier studies on the subject, in addition to its own observations, the ACRC recommended the establishment of the National Cooperative Bank of India (NCBI) as an apex body. Its main functions would be to act as a balancing centre for state-level cooperative institutions; accept deposits; make loans and advances; act as an apex cooperative bank providing leadership including development and promotion; and, evolve and administer an efficient national training system. It would be established by an Act of Parliament as a scheduled bank, fully owned by the cooperative system (75 per cent by cooperative banking system and 25 per cent by national-level cooperative organisations). NCBI would be a balancing centre for the surpluses of the SCBs, with up to 50 per cent of thier statutory liquid reserves deposited therein. It is expected that large national-level cooperatives such as fertiliser cooperatives would move some of their business from the commercial banks to this new bank. Apart from creating the normal reserves, it was recommended that NCBI should establish a development fund for training and research projects by appropriations from profits and contributions from cooperative federations, enterprises and state apexes.

The ACRC also studied the working of NABARD. NABARD provides refinance at concessional rates of interest—about 30 per cent being long-term refinancing to all participating banks and about 70 per cent being short-term confined to SCBs and RRBs. NABARD has no overdues as all repayments are deducted from new refinancing. The review of NABARD's refinancing activities found that investment guidelines were rigid; planning required strengthening; eligibility criteria did not improve loan recovery; and, more regional decentralisation was needed. It concluded that the refinance activity was not working effectively. However, it was also observed that corrective actions were in progress. While the ACRC felt that no major changes in NABARD's existing role and objectives were necessary, it made certain recommendations associated with its institutional development for better monitoring and inspection, with the view to integrate these functions more closely with refinancing. Some way had to be developed to ensure compliance by client banks. Also, training needs should be identified, strongly linked to training programmes and extended to support client banks.

In reviewing projections for refinancing, the ACRC believed that NABARD should play a more aggressive role in providing refinance support to agriculture and rural development programmes, concluding that resource needs have been much higher than NABARD can conceivably meet. The majority of its refinancing was at 6.5 per cent interest, and profitability was due to its large equity base. There is, therefore, no alternative, if NABARD's lending is to grow, but for additional equity contributions from the government or RBI. NABARD should also extend liberal assistance from their research and development fund on a priority basis to client banks for strengthening monitoring, evaluation and inspection.

Refinance facilities from NABARD for a schematic term loan depend on the level of overdues of each lending institution, known as the eligibility criteria. Because the commercial banking system and the SCBs/DCCBs have access to deposits, they are able to continue some lending even when their eligibility is restricted. However, their profitability is affected as the NABARD funds are concessional in nature and, therefore, cheaper than the deposits mobilised. The LDBs suffer more, as they are not allowed to take deposits and rely almost entirely on NABARD for financing through the sale of their debentures. In addition to the eligibility criteria is the impact of the statutory liquidity ratio and cash reserve ratio (commercial banks are required to place 38 per cent of their outside liabilities in eligible liquid assets and 11 per cent with the RBI as cash reserve). The Committee concluded that recovery performance due to regional diversity and the need for government assistance against wilful defaulters are not reflected in the application of the eligibility criteria. Also, recoveries have deteriorated over the years in banks with restrictions on fresh lending, and it was felt that in general the criteria had done more harm than good.

The Committee recommended the replacement of the eligibility system by a 'viability criteria', whereby solvency would be the basis for NABARD refinancing. The recommendations outlined the proposal for solvency and offered the following reasons in its support—the system will be easy to operate; will not finance non-solvent institutions; viability will provide more motivation to management; pressure for recoveries will not be reduced; and, the obligation of the government to contribute to compensate losses to maintain eligibility will deter their interference. Also, the viability criteria would be applied at a bank level and not at individual branches.

The Committee made several other recommendations for strengthening institutions, including the recommendation to replace the current rehabilitation programme of NABARD with an Institutional Strengthening Programme (ISP) which would identify problems and develop an action plan on an individual bank basis. NABARD would be concerned only with the apex agencies (SCBs/SLDBs), with the state governments and state agencies concerned with implementing action at the lower tiers.

As discussed above, overdues of credit to demand have become a major constraint to the expansion of credit and development of agriculture. The ACRC report stated that nearly 26 per cent of all resources deployed by the agencies in agriculture credit was locked up in overdues. Overdues cut off the borrower from additional institutional credit, reduce the ability of the credit agency to lend both to existing borrowers and to new borrowers. Though overdues range from 41 per cent to 45 per cent throughout the credit system, the report argues that bad debts should not be equated with overdues. A portion of overdues relates to late payments for different reasons, both the fault of the borrower and the lender. According to the age-old classification of overdues, the quantum declines with age, and the amount which eventually becomes chronic after five to seven years is only a small portion at any point in time. Estimates of provision of bad debts showed that overdues form 24 per cent of outstanding agricultural credit (not demand) and bad debts were 19 per cent thereof or 4.7 per cent of outstandings. While the ACRC continue to be concerned about the high level of overdues and did not suggest that overdues should be stated in relation to outstandings, but demand as it now is, they emphasised that overdues should not necessarily be viewed as bad debts. Also, it believed that the high level of overdues was somewhat affected by the lack of a definite policy to accurately determine and write off bad debts on a regular basis.

Contributory factors to overdues include agro-climatic factors, size of holdings, infrastructure available, types of crops, etc. Field surveys showed that for commercial banks, the bigger farmers accounted for a larger portion of overdues, and in the cooperative system, it was the small farmers and landless labourers. There was no significant relationship between staff strength and overdues in the commercial banking system, but moderate improvement with adequate staffing was noted in the PACSs. The mid-term review of the pilot programme (with high staff support) introduced for strengthening the credit delivery system suggested that lending and loan recovery may be helped through the formation of Self-help Groups (SHGs). Such groups would act as links between the credit agencies and the borrowers. Interviews with defaulters showed 54 per cent to be wilful defaulters without specific reasons for non-payments, 23 per cent attributed default to natural calamities and adverse weather conditions, 17 per cent to low-income generation, and 6 per cent to other causes. Wilful default was attributed mainly to politicisation—politicians promising postponement of loan recovery, granting of extension, to avoid/delay the enforcement process. This effectively puts institutional credit on par with government subsidies. The problem frequently begins at the time of granting or disbursement of the credit when loans are sanctioned at public functions in front of political dignitaries (loan melas). Such situations reduce the staff's ability to undertake proper loan appraisals, etc. Also, lending under poverty alleviation programmes is frequently under pressure to meet targets, with little attention paid to loan utilisation and ability to repay.

In sum, it was observed that overdues were all-pervasive and neutral to the type of credit agency. Perhaps the most important factor was the overall climate of credit recovery, and several recommendations were made to improve enforcement procedures, income generation particularly of small borrowers, and institutional development. The Committee also suggested the need for creating the necessary political will and observing a code of ethics so as to induce non-interference in the functioning of credit agencies.

In discussing natural calamities, the Committee observed that efforts to solve this problem was usually through the rescheduling of debts with the view to postponing recovery to a future date. Previous committees had agreed that in the case of successive calamities, the debt burden exceeding the borrowers' ability to repay would be written off, through relief and guarantee funds to be established at national and state levels. However, these provisions have been inoperative mainly because of the lack of such a fund at the national level. As a result, in most cases rescheduling of dues are being effected in a routine manner, without assessing the repayment capacity of the borrowers. RBI studies also showed that frequent rescheduling was carried out to circumvent repayment discipline. While crop insurance was considered one solution, areas which are chronically drought-prone required other approaches. Since 1985, there has been a comprehensive crop insurance scheme (CCIS) for certain specific crops, currently to the extent of the crop loan and applied at the option of individual state governments. Premiums are at 2 per cent for rice, wheat and millet and 1 per cent for oilseeds and pulses with the remaining premium subsidised by the central and state governments equally. Usually, the states only included adverse/unstable crop yield areas under the scheme. As a result, along with inadequate premiums, the scheme has acquired a welfare nature with significant losses. Apart from being unviable, the scheme has also failed in its basic objective of indemnifying the farmers' losses.

The Committee concluded that if the insurance scheme is to be viable, then the premiums should be fixed on an actuarial basis with the farmers paying 1 per cent to 2 per cent of the premia, the lending agency bearing 1/2 per cent and the balance borne by the government. In making other modifications to the scheme, the ACRC suggested that the indemnity amount should fully cover the principal and interest associated with the loss, enabling farmers to be eligible for fresh lending and also provide relief to the farmer beyond the amount of the indebtedness. The scheme should cover all cultivated areas and principal crops and also be eligible for non-borrowers on a voluntary basis. A separate corporation should be set up by the government for the implementation of this scheme.

The Deposit Insurance and Credit Guarantee Corporation (DICGC) is a merger of two schemes, one which provided guarantee for depositors and was financially very strong and the other which provided guarantee to credit institutions to cover risks in lending for priority sectors including small agricultural borrowers. The scheme now does not cover lending by the cooperative banking system. Because of the high level of claims influenced by the poor climate of credit recovery and the low premiums charged, claim payments far outweigh receipts and the scheme is no longer considered viable. The Committee has recommended that the following remedial actions be considered—rationalisation of the terms for invocation of the guarantee; increase in guarantee premiums/fees; and the government to subsidise the losses related to lending under the poverty alleviation and similar programmes.

In discussing development and credit planning, the Committee notes its broad agreement with the recently introduced Service Area Approach whereby every village will be allotted to one commercial bank. However, it recommended that the scheme be broadened to include the participation of cooperative banks and be designated as Development Area Scheme with both a commercial and a cooperative bank in each area. It is believed that this will reduce supervision and other transaction costs and allow more effective fund mobilisation and monitoring of lending. In such an approach, it is expected that banking will become more development oriented.

In reviewing the increased credit supply in the system, the Committee noted that expansion varied between different regions/states. This has been influenced by the imbalances in agricultural development itself. To assist in addressing this problem, the committee recommended the establishment of an Agricultural and Rural Infrastructure Development Corporation in each of these developing areas.

In the review of staff training and manpower development, the lack of adequate trained personnel, the low level of motivation, low level of sympathy for the disadvantaged class and bureaucratic approach was noted. In cooperatives in particular, recruitment based on patronage, caste and community considerations was found to be widespread. Several recommendations were made to improve these problems.

In the review of interest charges and margins, note was taken of the concessional interest rates for agriculture in general, and for weaker sections of rural communities in particular. The wider coverage to rural areas together with social obligations supported the position that interest rates cannot be left entirely to market forces and that a fair degree of control is necessary for orderly resource mobilisation as well as for the viability of the institutions. The analysis showed that PACSs were operating at a net loss of about 1 per cent after applying a risk factor for bad debts and an increase in margins of 1.5 per cent through the increase of short-term lending rates. The above increase in rates would also apply to the commercial banking system. It was felt that the DCCBs and the SCBs did not require any additional margins. However, the LDBs required an additional 2 per cent which could be financed by a 1 per cent reduction in the rates charged by the SLDBs to the PLDBs, and an increase of 1 per cent in lending rates which would only be applicable after the gestation period of the investment and not less than two years after the loan. The 1 per cent allowed by the SLDB would be financed by a reduction of 1 per cent in debenture interest rates charged by NABARD. The RRBs were estimated to require an additional 3 per cent margin, but as their merger into sponsor banks was recommended, no specific suggestions were made. In addition to the 1 per cent for short-term lending, no additional margins were considered necessary for commercial banks. The transaction costs associated with agricultural/rural lending are very high mainly because of the large volume of small loans. However, this is expected to decrease through the Service Area Approach.

It was observed that while the banking system maintained full accounting records, they did not generally follow a system of allowing for cost centres by type of lending, etc., and accounting was exclusively manual. Recommendations included provisions for the automatic ageing of loan accounts, the introduction of standard accounting policies which would also anticipate computerisation at a later date, a rationalisation of the many different returns with common data, and full accounting of bad and doubtful debt provisions irrespective of the profitability of the institution.

While reviewing the IRDP, the ACRC was concerned about the extent of involvement of institutional credit with fiscal subsidies in poverty alleviation programmes because of their impact on the credit system. Physical and financial targets had been exceeded and programme had probably grown too fast for its own good resulting in several deficiencies, including over-concern with targets which were determined on a uniform basis per block; wrong identification of 15 per cent to 20 per cent of beneficiaries; leakages through corruption and malpractices; absence of backward and forward linkages in project identification; inadequacies in the delivery and monitoring of credit; and, problem in the absorptive capacity of many beneficiaries. The programme has been reduced to meeting targets with constant pressure from government agencies. It was suggested that the

IRDP needs to be reoriented to provide services and inputs as part of a total package with credit. The recommendations included: The banks should not be mere windows for disbursement but be allowed to play a stronger part in the planning and monitoring of investments financed; the capital subsidy now allowed on the unit cost at investment should be retained for adjustment at the end of the repayment; and, the government should take part in building a bad debt reserve for this high-risk group.

The report is supported by over 300 recommendations, many of which are inter-related and deal with matters of reform detail. However, before the recommendations of the ACRC (1989)could be implemented, the financial crisis of the early 1990s brought in fullscale economic reforms. In 1991, the ACRC report was overtaken by the Narasimham Committee Report, and quietly shelved.

6

Narasimham Committee, 1991, and Gupta Committee, 1998

Narasimham Committee Report on the Financial System, 1991

The last two decades saw a phenomenal expansion in the geographical coverage and functional spread of our financial system, which significantly contributed to increase in our saving rate especially of the household sector. But, certain rigidities and weaknesses also developed in the system. To enable the financial system to play its role in ushering in a more efficient and competitive economy against this backdrop, the Government of India set up a high-level committee to examine all aspects relating to the structure, organisation, functions and procedures of the financial system under the chairmanship of M.Narasimham.

The Committee submitted its report on 30 November 1991. Salient features of the report are:

- Reputed banks may enhance capital through public issues.
- No bar on new private sector banks.
- Liberal policy towards foreign banks.
- Four-tier banking structure.
- Abolition of dual control.
- Depoliticisation of chief executives' appointments.
- Lower statutory liquidity ratio (SLR) to 25 per cent.
- Phasing out of concessional interest rates.

- New system for provision of debts.
- Special tribunals for recovery of dues.
- Scrapping of branch licensing.
- No further nationalisation of banks.
- RBI should be more liberal in allowing foreign banks to open branches.

The Committee's approach to the issue of financial sector reform was to ensure that the industry operates on the basis of operational flexibility and functional autonomy with a view to enhancing efficiency, productivity and profitability. A vibrant and competitive financial system was also necessary to sustain the ongoing structural reform in the economy. The Committee believed that ensuring the integrity and autonomy of operations of banks and Development Financial Institutions (DFIs) was by far the more relevant issue than the question of their ownership.

The Indian banking and financial system has made commendable progress in extending its geographical spread and functional reach. The spread of the banking system has been a major factor in promoting financial savings. The credit reach has also been extensive and the banking system now caters to several million borrowers especially in agriculture and small industry. The DFIs are a major institutional support for investment in the private sector. The last decade has witnessed considerable diversification of the money and capital markets. New financial services and instruments have appeared on the scene.

The Committee was of the view that the SLR instrument should be deployed in conformity with the original intention of regarding it as a prudential requirement and not as a major instrument for financing the public sector. In line with the government's decision to reduce the fiscal deficit to a level consistent with macro-economic stability, the Committee recommended that the SLR be brought down in a phased manner to 25 per cent over a period of about five years, starting with some reduction in the current year itself.

As regards the cash ratio, the RBI should have the flexibility to operate this instrument to serve its monetary policy objectives. The Committee believed that given the government's resolve to reduce the fiscal deficit, the use of cash reserve ratio (CRR) to control the secondary expansion of credit should also be less. The Committee accordingly proposed that the RBI consider progressively reducing the CRR from its present high level. With the deregulation of interest rates, there would be more scope for the use of open market operations by the RBI with correspondingly less emphasis on variations in the CRR.

With respect to direct credit programmes, the Committee was of the view that they have played a useful purpose in extending the reach of the banking system to cover hitherto neglected sectors. Despite considerable unproductive lending, there was evidence that bank credit has contributed to the growth of agriculture and small industry. This called for some re-examination of the present relevance of directed credit programmes at least in respect of those who are able to stand on their own feet, and to whom the directed credit programmes with its element of interest concessionality has become a source of economic rent.

The Committee recognised that in the last two decades, banking and credit policies have been deployed with a redistributive objective. How-ever, it believed that the pursuit of such objectives should use the instru-mentality of the fiscal rather than the credit system. Accordingly, the Committee proposed that directed credit programmes should be phased out.

It, however, recognised that as an interim measure, some special credit support through direction would be needed. The Committee, therefore, proposed that the priority sector be redefined to comprise the small and marginal farmers, the tiny sector of industry, small business and rural transport operators, village and cottage industries, rural artisans, and other weaker sections. The credit target for this redefined priority sector should henceforth be fixed at 10 per cent of aggregate credit which would be broadly in line with the credit flows to these sectors at present.

The Committee also proposed that a review may be undertaken at the end of three years to see if directed credit programmes need to be contin-ued. As regards medium and large farmers, and the larger among small industries, including large transport operators, etc., who would not now constitute part of the redefined priority sector, the Committee proposed that the RBI and other refinancing agencies institute a preferential refi-nance scheme under which incremental credit to these sectors would be eligible for preferential refinance subject to normal eligibility criteria.

The Committee felt that the present structure of administered interest rates was highly complex and rigid, in spite of recent moves towards de-regulation. It proposed that interest rates be further deregulated so as to reflect emerging market conditions. At the same time, the Committee be-lieved that a reasonable degree of macro-economic balance through a reduction in the fiscal deficit was necessary for the successful deregula-tion of interest rates. Premature moves to market-determined interest rates could, as experience abroad has shown, pose the danger of excessive bank lending at high nominal rates to borrowers of dubious credit-worthiness, eventually creating acute problems for both, the banks as well as the borrowers. Accordingly, the Committee recommended that for the present, interest rates on bank deposits may continue to be regulated, the ceilings on such rates being raised as the SLR was reduced progressively. Similarly, the interest rate on government borrowing may also be gradually brought in line with market-determined rates, which would be facilitated by the reduction in SLR. Meanwhile, concessional interest rates should be phased out.

The structure of interest rates should bear a broad relationship to the bank rate, which should be used as an anchor to signal the RBI's monetary policy stance. It would be desirable to provide for what may be called a prime rate, which would be the floor of the lending rates of banks and DFIs. The spreads between the bank rate, the bank deposit rates, the government borrowing rates and the prime rate may be determined by the RBI broadly in accordance with the criteria suggested by the Chakravarty Committee so as to ensure that the real rates of interest remain positive.

For the purpose of provisioning, the Committee recommended using the health code classification, which is already in vogue in banks and financial institutions. Assets should be classified into four categories namely, standard sub-standard, doubtful and loss assets. In regard to sub-standard assets, a general provision should be created to the extent of 10 per cent of the total outstandings under this category. In respect of doubtful debts, provision should be created to the extent of 100 per cent of the security shortfall. In respect of the secured portion of some doubtful debts, further provision should be created, ranging from 20 per cent to 50 per cent, depending on the period for which such assets remain in the doubtful category. Loss assets should either be fully written off or provision be created to the extent of 100 per cent. The Committee felt that a period of four years should be given to the banks and financial institutions to conform to these provisioning requirements.

The movement towards these norms should be done in a phased manner beginning with the current year. However, it was necessary for banks and financial institutions to ensure that in respect of doubtful debts, 100 per cent of the security shortfall is fully provided for in the shortest possible time.

The Committee believed that the balance sheets of banks and financial institutions should be made transparent and full disclosures made in the balance sheets as recommended by the International Accounts Standards Committee.

This should be done in a phased manner commencing with the current year. The RBI, however, may defer implementation of such parts of the standards as it considered appropriate during the transitional period until the norms regarding income recognition and provisioning were fully implemented.

Banks, at present, experience considerable difficulties in recoveries of loans and enforcement of security charged to them. The delays that characterise our legal system have resulted in the blocking of a significant portion of the funds of banks and DFIs in unproductive assets, the value of which deteriorate with time. The Committee, therefore, considered that there was urgent need to work out a suitable mechanism through which the dues to the credit institutions could be realised without delay. It strongly recommended that special tribunals on the pattern suggested by the Tiwari Committee be set up to speed up the process of recovery. The introduction of legislation for this purpose was long overdue and should be proceeded with immediately.

While the reform of accounting practices and the creation of special tribunals were essential, the Committee believed that an arrangement had to be worked out under which, at least a part of the bad and doubtful debts were taken off the balance sheet so that the banks could recycle the funds through this process into more productive assets. For this purpose, the committee proposed the establishment, if necessary, by special legislation, of an Assets Reconstruction Fund (ARF). This fund could take over from the banks and financial institutions a portion of the bad and doubtful debts at a discount, the level of discount being determined by independent auditors on the basis of clearly stipulated guidelines. The ARF should be provided with special powers for recovery, somewhat broader than those contained in Section 29–32 of the State Financial Corporations Act, 1951. The capital of the ARF should be subscribed by the public sector banks and financial institutions.

It is necessary to ensure that the bad and doubtful debts of banks and financial institutions are transferred to the ARF in a phased manner to ensure its smooth and effective functioning.

To begin with, all consortium accounts where more than one bank or institution is involved should be transferred to the ARF. The number of such accounts will not be large but the amounts involved are substantial enough to make a difference to the balance sheets of the banks. Gradually, depending on the progress achieved by the ARF, other bad and doubtful debts could be transferred over time. Meanwhile, banks and institutions should pursue recovery through the special tribunals. Based on the valuation given in respect of each asset by a panel of at least two independent auditors, the ARF would issue bonds to the concerned institutions carrying an interest rate equal to the government bond rate and repayable over a period of five years. These bonds will need to be guaranteed by the Government of India and should be treated as qualifying for SLR purposes. The advantage to banks of this arrangement would be that their bad and doubtful debts would be off their books—though at a price—but they would have in substitution of these advances, bonds up to the discounted value with a certainty of interest income, important from the point of view of income recognition. Further, by making these bond holdings eligible for SLR purposes, fresh resources could become available for normal lending purposes.

The Committee emphasised that this proposal should be regarded as an emergency measure and not as a continuing source of relief to the banks and DFIs. It should be made clear to the banks and financial institutions that once their books are cleaned up, they should take normal care and pay due commercial attention in loan appraisals and supervision and make adequate provisions for assets of doubtful realisable value.

Selling these assets to the ARF at a discount would obviously mean an obligation on the banks/DFIs to write off these losses which many of them are in no position to do now, given their weak capital position. The Committee proposed that to enable the banks to finance the write off, the Government of India would, where necessary, provide, as mentioned earlier, a subordinate loan counting for capital. As far as the government itself was concerned, the Committee believed that the rupee counterpart of any external assistance that would be available for financial sector reform could be used to provide this type of capital to the banks and DFIs.

The ARF would be expected to deal with those assets which are in the process of recovery. In respect of sick units which are under nursing or rehabilitation programmes, it was necessary to work out a similar arrangement to ensure smooth decision-making and implementation. The Committee recommended that in respect of all such consortium accounts, the concerned lead financial institution and/or lead commercial bank should take over the term loan and working capital dues from other participating institutions and banks. Such acquisitions should be at a discount, based on the realisable value of the assets assessed by a panel of at least two independent auditors as in the case of transfer of assets to ARF.

In regard to the structure of the banking system, the Committee is of the view that the system should evolve towards a broad pattern consisting of:

(a) Three or four large banks (including the State Bank of India) which could become international in character.
(b) Eight to ten national banks with a network of branches throughout the country engaged in 'universal' banking.
(c) Local banks whose operations would be generally confined to a specific region.
(d) Rural banks (including RRBs) whose operations would be confined to the rural areas and whose business would be predominantly engaged in financing of agriculture and allied activities.

The Committee was of the view that the move towards this revised system should be market-driven and based on profitability considerations and brought about through a process of mergers and acquisitions.

The Committee felt that the structure of rural credit would have to combine the local character of the RRBs and the resource, skills and organisational/managerial abilities of the commercial banks. With this end in view, the committee recommended that each public sector bank should set up one or more rural banking subsidiaries, depending on the size and administrative convenience of each sponsor bank, to take over all its rural branches and, where appropriate, swap its rural branches with those of other banks. Such rural banking subsidiaries should be treated on par with RRBs in regard to CRR/SLR requirements and refinance facilities from NABARD and sponsor banks. The 10 per cent target for directed credit, recommended as a transitional measure, should be calculated on the basis of the combined totals of the present banks and their subsidiaries.

The Committee proposed that while RRBs should be allowed to engage in all types of banking business, their focus should continue to be to lend to the target groups so as to maintain the present level of lending to these groups as the minimum. With a view to improving the viability of RRBs, the Committee proposed that the interest rate structure should be in line with those of the commercial banks. The Committee left the option to the RRBs and their sponsor banks as to whether the RRBs should retain their identity so that their focus on lending to the target groups is not diffused. Where both the RRBs and the sponsor banks wish to do so, they could be merged with the sponsor banks and in such cases, the sponsor banks should take them over as 100 per cent subsidiaries by buying out the shares from other agencies at a token price, and eventually merging them with the rural banking subsidiaries proposed by the Committee. For those RRBs that retain their identity and whose viability needed to be improved, the Committee proposed that instead of investing in government bonds as part of their SLR requirements, they could deposit the amounts stipulated under SLR with NABARD or some special federal type of agency that could be set up for this purpose. This would also be consistent with statutory requirements and NABARD or this agency could pay interest on such balances by investing or deploying these funds on their behalf, and thus help to augment the income of the RRBs.

The Committee proposed that the government should indicate that there would be no further nationalisation of banks. Such an assurance would remove the existing disincentive for the private banks to grow. The Committee also recommended that there should not be any difference in treatment towards public and private sector banks. There should be no bar to new banks being set up in the private sector provided they conform to the start-up capital and other requirements prescribed by the RBI and maintain prudential norms. This, in conjunction with the relevant statutory requirements governing their operations would provide adequate safeguards against misuse of bank resources to the detriment of the depositor's interests.

The Committee recommended that branch licensing be abolished and the opening of branches (other than rural branches for the present) be left to the commercial judgement of the individual banks.

The Committee also believed that, consistent with other aspects of government policy dealing with foreign investment, the policy with regard to allowing foreign banks to open offices in India either as branches or where the RBI considers it appropriate, as subsidiaries, should be more liberal, subject to the maintenance of minimum assigned capital and the statutory requirement of reciprocity. Joint ventures between foreign banks and Indian banks could also be permitted, particularly in regard to merchant and investment banking, leasing and other newer forms of financial services.

The Committee believed that the internal organisation of banks is best left to the judgement of the management of individual banks, depending upon the size of the bank, its branch spread and range of functions. However, for medium and large national banks, the Committee proposed a three-tier structure—head office, a zonal office and branches. In the case of very large banks, a four-tier organisation as is the case with the State Bank—head office, zonal office, regional office and branches—may be appropriate. Local banks may not need an intermediate tier between the branch and the central office.

The Committee endorsed the view of the Rangarajan Committee on computerisation that there was urgent need for a greater use of computerised systems than at present. Computerisation has to be recognised as an indispensable tool for improvement in customer service, the institution and operation of better control systems, greater efficiency in information technology and betterment of the work environment for employees. These are essential requirements for banks to function effectively and profitably in an increasingly complex and competitive environment.

Consistent with the Committee's view that the integrity and internal autonomy of banks and DFIs is far more important than the question of ownership, the Committee made some recommendations regarding recruitment of officers and staff, appointments of chief executives and constitution of the Boards of institutions.

It recommended that instead of having a common recruitment system for officers, individual banks should be free to make their own recruitment. This will provide scope for the banks to scout for talent and impart new skills to their personnel. Thus, there was no need to set up a Banking Service Commission for centralised recruitment of officers. At present, the recruitment of officers and clerical staff is being done through Banking Service Recruitment Boards (BSRBs). The Committee, however, recommended this on the assumption that the banks would set up objective, fair and impartial recruitment procedures and wherever appropriate, voluntarily come together to have a joint recruitment system. As regards clerical grades, the present system of recruitment through BSRBs could continue but the committee urged that the appointment of the chairman of the BSRBs should be totally left to the coordinating banks.

The Committee believed that managements and trade unions must recognise that the system could not hope to be competitive internally and be in step with the wide-ranging innovations taking place abroad, without a radical change in work technology and culture, and greater flexibility in personnel policies. The Committee was reassured to know that organised labour was as much convinced of the importance of enhancing the viability and profitability of the banking industry and providing efficient customer service. It was equally incumbent on management of banks to adopt forward looking personnel policies which would help to create a satisfying work environment.

The Committee was firmly of the opinion that the duality of control over the banking system between the Reserve Bank of India and the Banking Division of the Ministry of Finance should end. The RBI should be the primary agency for the regulation of the banking system. The supervisory function over banks and other financial institutions, the Committee believed, should be hived off to a separate authority—a quasi-autonomous body under the aegis of the RBI but separate from its other central banking functions. The Committee recognised that as long as the government had proprietary interest in banks and financial institutions, it would be appropriate for the Ministry of Finance to deal with other government departments and Parliament, and discharge its other statutory obligations but not to engage in direct regulatory functions.

Central to the issue of flexibility of operations and autonomy of internal functioning is the question of depoliticising the appointment of the chief executives, i.e., Chairman and Managing Director of the banks and ensuring security of tenure. The Committee believed that professionalism and integrity should be the prime considerations in determining such appointments, and while the formal appointments have to be made by the Government, they should be based on a convention of accepting the recommendations of a group of eminent persons who could be invited by the RBI Governor to make recommendations for such appointments. As regards the Boards of public sector banks and institutions, as long as the Government owned the banks, it would be necessary to have a government director to take care of 'proprietorial' concerns but the committee believed that there was no need for the RBI to have a representative on the board.

As regards DFIs, the main issue with regard to their operations is to ensure operational flexibility, a measure of competition and adequate internal autonomy in matters of loan sanctioning and internal administration. The Committee proposed that the system recommended for commercial banks in the matter of appointments of chief executives and boards should also apply to DFIs. The present system of consortium lending was perceived to be operating like a cartel. The Committee believed that consortium lending should be dispensed with and in its place, a system of syndication or participation in lending at the instance not only, as now, of the lenders but also of the borrowers, should be introduced. The Committee also believed that commercial banks should be encouraged to provide term finance to industry, while the DFIs should increasingly engage in providing core working capital. This would help enhance healthy competition between banks and DFIs.

The Committee proposed that the present system of cross holding of equity and cross representation on the board of the DFIs should be done away with. It welcomed the removal of the tax concession enjoyed by IDBI as an important step in ensuring equality of treatment between various DFIs. As a further measure of enhancing competition and ensuring a level playing field, the Committee proposed that the IDBI should retain only its apex and refinancing role, and that its direct lending function be transferred to a separate institution which could be incorporated as a company. The infected portion of the DFIs portfolio should be handed over to the ARF on the same terms and conditions as would apply to commercial banks.

In the case of state-level institutions, it was necessary to distance them from the state government and ensure that they function on business principles based on prudential norms and have a management set-up suited for this purpose. The Committee proposed that an action plan on these lines be worked out and implemented over the next three years.

The Committee's approach, thus, sought to consolidate the gains made in the Indian financial sector while improving the quality of the portfolio, providing greater operational flexibility and most importantly, greater autonomy in the internal operations of the banks and financial institutions so as to nurture a healthy, competitive and vibrant financial sector. This would, above all else, require depoliticisation of appointments, implying at the same time self-denial by the government and the perception that it had distanced itself from the internal decision-making of the banks and financial institutions. The proposed deregulation of the financial sector and the measures aimed at improving its health and competitive vitality would, in the Committee's view, be consistent with the steps being taken to open up the Indian economy. They would enable the Indian financial sector to forge closer links with global financial markets, and enhance India's ability to take competitive advantage of the increasing international opportunities for Indian trade, industry and finance.

Recommendations of the Gupta Committee, 1998

To give an impetus to the flow of rural credit from commercial banks, the RBI set up the Gupta Committee in December 1997. Its major recommendations released in April 1998,were:

- Commercial banks should be free to fix the interest rates for agricultural loans of all amounts, as is being done by cooperative banks and RRBs.
- Banks should prepare special agricultural credit plans to accelerate the flow and improve the quality of lending.
- 90 per cent of all loan applications should be decided at the branch level to ensure timely loans.
- State governments should constitute separate teams for improving

loan recovery, and through rurally oriented field publicity campaigns, inform borrowers to return loans and credit, for better relationships.

- Improved accounting systems for disaggregated recovery data as per loan products/time to enable managers to determine product viability.
- Substantial modification in Service Area Approach so as to provide borrowers a choice of banks and bankers, a wide area of operations.
- While timeliness and adequacy of credit are critical in increasing the credit flow to agriculture, the responsibility of a particular branch for the credit requirements for a particular village should, however, continue.
- State governments should abolish stamp duty on mortgage of agricultural land for obtaining loans from banks in view of high duty costs and procedural difficulties.
- Lending to the farm sector should be on the basis of confidence in the borrowers and the appraisal forms should shift from project-based considerations to a holistic assessment of the borrowers' income. The focus of credit appraisal should be on evaluation of income of the borrower and a comprehensive assessment of credit needs taking into account track record, credibility, capability and technical viability of the project.
- Appropriate incentive systems, including interest benefit or rebate to borrowers, for prompt repayment of dues. Farmers opting for savings module may get fixed rates on both deposits and advances linked to the loan product.
- Disbursing agricultural loans in cash and kind restricts borrowers choice and has given rise to false bills and receipts.
- Obtaining a 'no-due' certificate should be left to the discretion of the leading bankers.

7

Rural Credit Agencies Analysed

The Ninth Five-Year Plan (1997–98 to 2001–2002) has outlined an ambitious 7 per cent growth rate of GDP, with the growth rate of GDP in agriculture being 4.5 per cent. This is ambitious especially when the percentage share of agriculture in GDP has reduced from 48.66 per cent in 1950–51 to 24.35 per cent in 1996–97! With the share of the private sector increasing sharply in the gross capital fixed assets in agriculture over the Sixth and Seventh Five-Year Plans, the role of rural credit agencies hardly needs any emphasis, as revealed in Table 7.1.

Table 7.1
Flow of Short-term Agricultural Credit and its
Relation to Input Use and Output Use

(Rs Crore—1980–81 Prices)

Year	Value of Input	Gross Value of Output	SAO Credit	Flow of Proportion of Credit (%)	
				Input use	Output use
1960–61	2,592	29,297	782	30.18	2.67
1970–71	3,906	37,536	1,340	34.30	3.57
1980–81	7,122	46,278	2,043	28.69	4.42
1990–91	12,470	63,383	2,647	21.23	4.18
1992–93	13,026	64,506	4,339	33.31	6.73

Note: Inputs include seed, organic matter, chemical fertilisers, repairs and maintenance, irrigation charges, market charges, electricity, pesticides and diesel oil.

While input use proportion is fairly stable at around one-third of costs, the output use proportion is slowly increasing. More agro-processing is necessary if the Indian farmer is to get a better price for his products.

As far as production credit is concerned, the share of cooperative banks is falling while that of RRBs is stable and the share of commercial banks is increasing. For investment credit also, a similar trend prevails. The credit flow for the last five years from 1992–93 to 1996–97 and credit projections for 1997–98, are set out in Annexure 7.1. It is clear that the volume of credit flow has almost doubled during the last five years.

Credit Flow—Ninth Plan

The Ninth Five-Year Plan has ambitious plans (see Table 7.2) for credit flow to the agriculture sector.

Table 7.2

Projected Credit during Ninth Plan for Agricultural Sector

(Rs Crore)

Year	Production Credit	Investment Credit	Total	Growth Rate
1997–98	22,500	10,875	33,375	16.48
1998–99	25,650	12,995	38,645	15.79
1999–2000	29,250	15,530	44,780	15.88
2000–2001	33,500	18,608	52,108	16.36
2001–2002	38,500	22,342	60,842	16.76
Total	1,49,400	80,350	2,29,750	16.1

Some of the major recommendations are:

- Doubling of ground-level credit flow from Rs 46,276 crore to Rs 1,08,549 crore.
- Production credit to increase to Rs 21,398 crore from Rs 9,756 crore.
- Investment credit to increase to Rs 25,491 crore from Rs 10,367 crore.
- Share of commercial banks/RRBs to be 74 per cent in investment credit and 40 per cent in production credit.

- Share of cooperative banks to be 26 per cent in investment credit and 60 per cent in production credit.
- NABARD refinance to increase from Rs 9,000 crore to Rs 12,000 crore per year.
- National agricultural policy to be finalised.
- Reduction of regional, sectional and sectoral imbalances with appropriate credit packages.
- Commercialisation and diversification of agriculture for export promotion and employment generation.
- Evolving development packages and credit support for each agroecological regions.
- Increased investment in R&D by public and private bodies.
- More efficiency, autonomy and self-sustenance of rural credit agencies.
- Preparing sustainable development plans and dove-tailing these with credit plans.
- Monitoring rural credit flow through SAMIS.
- Improving crop insurance scheme and contributing to Risk Fund for risks.
- Providing Rs 6,600 crore for cooperatives and Rs 2,000 crore for RRBs for cleaning of balance sheets.
- Declaration of National Cooperative Policy and setting up of NACREF.
- More autonomy, professionalisation and viable operations of cooperatives.
- Improve professional management and training for cooperatives.

For rural credit agencies to attend to the tremendous responsibility of enhancing credit flow to agriculture, they have to be strong and healthy. The PCARDBs and RRBs continue to show losses while PACSs are only marginally profitable. The SCBs, SCARDBs and DCCBs earn healthy profits continuously (See Annexure 7.2). However, since the 1990s the combined losses of the RRBs are coming close to the combined profits of the cooperative credit banks. The working results of rural credit agencies for 1995–96 reveal that many are in the red and the trend is downwards. While there are many managerial and operational reasons for these crippling losses, a study of the interest rates, lending costs and margins would be helpful in understanding the reasons for the continued losses of most rural credit agencies.

Interest Rates, Lending Costs and Margins

A dynamic agricultural system should move towards higher levels of productivity. Growth requires higher levels of production as well as investment credit. Therefore, the major policy thrust in the sphere of agricultural credit in India has been progressive institutionalisation for supporting agricultural and rural development programmes through a multi-agency approach, in which formal financial institutions have witnessed a remarkable increase in the rural credit supply. The stock of production credit from all institutions have registered a growth rate of 15 per cent per annum while the stock of investment credit registered an annual growth rate of 20 per cent. The proportion of farm households availing of production credit and investment credit are estimated to be just 23 per cent and 2 per cent, respectively, of the total operational holdings in the country. Thus, there is a need to increase the rural credit outlay. The multi-agency approach has been adopted to ensure that such expansion is possible.

The viability of rural credit institutions are also to be considered. A credit institution is considered financially viable when the income generated by it can not only meet its financial and administrative expenses in order to disburse credit but should also enable the building up of a minimum reserve, which would enable writting off bad debts and help in institutional growth. Institutional viability provides the impetus to growth, and growth enhances viability. Despite the fears over institutional viability, agricultural loans of up to Rs 10,000 have been written off by central/state governments.

Costs in the Agricultural Credit System

There are two types of costs—direct and indirect.

Direct costs are those reflected in the income and expenditure account of the lender. All remaining costs associated with the credit business are referred to as indirect costs. The current study is confined to estimating direct costs in agricultural lending by different institutions or agencies at different levels engaged in formal credit operations. The objective of the study is to assess the cost of agricultural lending and thereby, to arrive at the sufficiency in the currently available margins realised by lending institutions in the country.

The various costs of lending depend on:

- The type of lending (short, medium or long-term) whether secured or unsecured, the purposes for which the loans are lent, whether many small loans are involved and what degree of technical and other supervison will be required.

- The risks involved in various types of lenders, the effectiveness or otherwise of collateral and the reserve requirements to protect the financial viability of institutions.
- The costs of raising funds internally and from other sources.
- The costs of overdues and bad debts in terms of reduced liquidity and costs of collection, taking into account the credit insurance scheme.
- Administration costs at all levels taking into account the importance of adequate supervision, particularly technical supervision at the field level.
- Present margins realised by various institutions and adequacy of incentives for effective lending.

The three major types of direct costs in the agricultural credit system are (i) cost of funds or financial costs, (ii) risk cost or cost of bad debts, and (iii) transaction costs.

FINANCIAL COSTS

The actual costs of raising financial resources are worked out and include dividend to shareholders, interest payment on borrowings, and interest payment for deposits.

A reasonable approximation in respect of dividend to shareholders shall have to be made to arrive at a particular cost of the same, as it normally does not fall under the purview of direct costs to the institution, unless otherwise declared. Hence, the actual financial cost implies interest payment essentially or borrowings made and deposits raised by the institution. The financial cost is generally computed as the interest payment due to borrowings and deposits expressed in percentages.

In the Indian context, the cost of maintaining liquidity too is considered one of the components of financial cost. This is due to the probable income foregone by the institution in adhering to liquidity requirements such as (i) CRR ranging from 3 per cent to 15 per cent and (ii) SLR ranging from 25 per cent to 38 per cent.

Till 1986, incomes due to CRR and SLR were less than normal interest income due to credit/deposits. However, recently an upward revision in the income from statutory maintenance of liquidity with a hike in priority sector lendings really warrants reservations as the same is computed as part of financial cost. Liquidity maintenance costs are to be computed wherever required.

TRANSACTION COSTS

These are essentially organisational costs for carrying out day-to-day institutional operations. They include the expenses towards staff salaries and allowances, rent on buildings, travel expenses, printing and stationery, postage and telegrams, audit and training etc. Transaction costs can be categorised as:

- Manpower costs
- Office rental costs
- Statutory requirements
- Others

Transaction costs may be segregated into the following activities:

- Agricultural credit
- Non-agricultural credit
- Non-credit activities such as trading, public distribution system and other banking operations

Appropriate apportionment of costs has been used to segregate the total transactional costs of an institution into the three listed activities. Loan transaction costs are asociated with operations such as loan appraisal, supervision of the end use, recovery (lawyer fees, court fees, etc.), rendering technical advice to the borrower, operations that influence the quality of lending, as well as a proportion of the cost of servicing deposits. The transaction costs due to credit operations are the actual costs incurred (after apportionment) on outstanding agricultural advances.

RISK COSTS

Debts which need to be written off and hence, the reserve for bad and doubtful debts to be created from the profits, fall under the purview of risk costs. Such costs could be the actual write-offs or reserve created for bad and doubtful debts arising from non-recoverable loans. The claims settled by DICGC is used as an approximation to the bad debts in CBs and RRBs. For cooperatives, depending upon the data available, appropriate techniques have been adopted to compute the risk costs.

MARGINS

Margins are the difference between costs and incomes. Income due to agricultural credit is computed as interest earned on outstanding agricultural advances expressed in percentages.

The difference between the financial cost and the agricultural income is the interest margin or the interest spread. This is referred to as gross margins to differentiate from the net margin, which is the difference between gross margin and transaction cost due to agricultural credit.

Margins have been worked out separately for agricultural credit agencies and for the various institutions as a whole. Further, wherever variations are large and conclusions based or averages, as a whole may not be meaningful, 20 institutions have been categorised into different strata depending upon size of operations. A thorough study of the margins available is necessary as the statutory interest rates, mandatory credit for the priority sectors and poor recoveries may have resulted in an unviable rural credit delivery system.

If there are negative margins, then the institutions would slowly lose their profitable/viable functioning and their functioning would follow a bureaucratic pattern. The ACRC has pointed out the increasing bureaucratisation of the banking system and its harmful effects on profitability.

LOSS OF FINANCIAL AUTONOMY AND ACCOUNTABILITY

There is a lack of clear demarcation between management and operations on the one hand, and political and strategic considerations on the other. This results in diffused and conflicting objectives, a loss of managerial autonomy needed for efficient commercial operations and a bureaucratic culture where officials are more administrators than bankers with commercial acumen. In such an environment, employment, investment and pricing decisions are more often made without due consideration for their financial consequences.

The confusion of operational and political responsibilities is often the starting point of a vicious circle for government-controlled credit agencies. Once a bank is driven into loss, staff morale suffers and performance then deteriorates even further. As financial problems accelerate, the government is forced to centralise decision-making even more and impose more controls.

The vicious 'Cycle of inefficient functioning' is set out below.

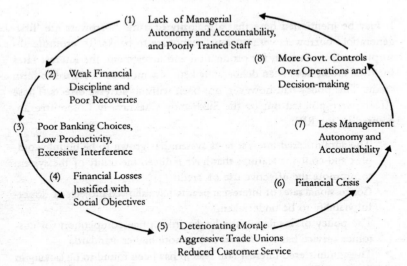

(1) Lack of Managerial Autonomy and Accountability, and Poorly Trained Staff

(2) Weak Financial Discipline and Poor Recoveries

(3) Poor Banking Choices, Low Productivity, Excessive Interference

(4) Financial Losses Justified with Social Objectives

(5) Deteriorating Morale Aggressive Trade Unions Reduced Customer Service

(6) Financial Crisis

(7) Less Management Autonomy and Accountability

(8) More Govt. Controls Over Operations and Decision-making

The entire 'Cycle of inefficient functioning' has already crept into the Indian banking system and as announced in the 1991–92 budget (July 1991), the Narasimham Committee was set up by the government to study the ailing financial system and suggest remedial measures. The Committee submitted its report on 30 November 1991 and many major recommendations have been accepted.

The obvious solutions as suggested by the ACRC and the Narasimham Committee are (in order of preference):

- Greater market orientation and interplay of market forces.
- Sound financial objectives.
- Clear social objectives.
- Elimination of subsidies (except for the very poor and needy).
- Appropriate capital and restructuring.
- Greater financial discipline and recovery norms.
- Establishment of performance measurement and incentives system for motivating staff.
- Trained staff with proper orientation, attitudes and good training facilities.
- Customer orientation and accountability.

Thus, to ensure that the 'Cycle of inefficient functioning' is not permitted to operate again, adequate margins are a must.

LENDING COSTS AND MARGINS

It may be mentioned here that a majority of rural borrowers are 'first-generation' borrowers without much exposure to banks. To promote absorption of credit both for production and investment, the interest rates for rural credit have been deliberately kept low more so in regard to term credit. This policy has, however, not been without adverse effects. These effects were pointed out by the Sukhamoy Chakravarty Committee appointed by the RBI:

- The administered interest rates system has grown to be unduly complex and contains features that have reduced the utility of the system to promote the effective use of credit.
- Concessional rates of interest appear to have allowed projects of doubtful viability to be undertaken.
- The policy of insulating the banks from price competition for customer service has not served to promote higher standards.
- The administered interest rate system has been found to be lacking in the flexibility necessary for augmenting the pool of financial savings by effecting suitable changes in the deposit rates from time to time, as low profitability has made banks wary of increasing the average cost of deposits.

Currently, the RBI has freed controls on the rates of interest for both lendings and borrowings as regards all rural credit except commercial bank branches for loans/deposits below Rs 2 lakh with effect from 24 October 1994. Annexures 7.3 and 7.4 show the de-regulated interest rates charged by SCBs/DCCBs/PACSs and the SLDBs, respectively. At the same time, the cost of raising resources by way of deposits has been going up. The increasing transaction/operating costs of banks arising mainly from the maintenance of a large number of small accounts, have resulted in their declining profitability. It is also significant to note that while the interest rates have been recently freed for loans involving larger outlays (above Rs 2 lakh), such a freedom for commercial banks is not available for the interest rates applicable on rural lending and the rates continue to be pegged at levels lower than the rest, even though some increases in the rates were affected depending on the size of loans in September 1990. The present interest rate structure and margins on lending are such that most banks are extending rural credit with an inadequate/negative margin. Rural credit agencies, in an effort to remain competitive, have yet to take recourse to the unregulated rates of interest for deposits and advances.

The concessionality in interest rates carries as a logical corollary, the need and scope for cross-subsidisation. While this is possible to some extent in the case of commercial banks where the non-agriculture portfolio is substantial, this is unfortunately not so with most cooperative banks and more particularly, the RRBs.

Another dimension to the operations of rural credit institutions, is the absence of operational flexibility due to mandatory lending under state-sponsored programmes. Mandatory lending inflicts a severe strain on credit discipline affecting loan recovery. The Narasimham Committee has recommended reduction of priority sector lending from 40 per cent to 10 per cent of total bank lending.

Role Played by NABARD

As part of its developmental efforts in institutional building, NABARD has been cross-subsidising rural credit institutions by providing refinance at concessional rates. After the reduction in interest rates in 1988, NABARD and the RBI reduced the interest rates on refinance support provided to the cooperative banks for production credit. They also assisted the banks in finding profitable avenues for surplus resources over and above their minimum involvement in production credit so as to compensate for their loss in earnings on production credit. The cross-subsidisation by the NABARD has, however, been more than offset by the escalating transaction costs as also the financial cost of raising resources. Besides, the increasing level of overdues has also affected the flow of refinance. The position of RRBs is even worse and as the ACRC report pointed out, non-viability was built into their structure inasmuch as 176 out of 196 RRBs incurred heavy losses during 1992–93. Further, out of 356 DCCBs, over 200 have become weak and, are under rehabilitation.

It is observed that cooperative banks are no longer enthusiastic about extending production credit because of the declining profitability and rising overdues. They have been pressing for reduction in involvement of their own resources, which is already low at 40 per cent in the case of DCCBs and 25 per cent in the case of SCBs. Similarly, LDBs are also experiencing serious erosion in their margins as transaction costs have gone up; rates of interest for mobilising resources for their ordinary lending programme (other than that refinanced by the NABARD) have also gone up in line with rates of open market borrowings. The commercial banks' involvement in rural credit is observed to be on a low key in recent years as an informal credit squeeze has been enforced upon rural branches due to poor recoveries and income-asset recognition norms of the RBI.

While some regulation of interest rate is essential, there is an urgent need to make the interest rates structure less complex and more flexible, and reduce the extent of concessionality in rural lending so as to provide adequate margin to the banks. The ACRC has recommended that there should be only two categories of rates, with a narrow band for concessional finance and no concessionality for other lending. It is pertinent to mention that the World Bank believes that the interest rate structure of rural lending leads to unviable funds as the present margins are very low. In view of the enhanced interest rates (from April 1992) the deficit margins have increased further, and all rural credit agencies have negative or very low margins. Hence, it is pertinent to recommend viable interest rates for credit disbursed by rural credit agencies.

The low rate of return on agricultural advances coupled with the high cost of funds and the retailing cost make the rural financial institutions unviable. It is estimated that an average lending rate of 15.5 per cent would be necessary to bridge the gap in respect of commercial banks. This will necessitate changes in the previous interest rates with a minimum slab of 15 per cent as against the prevailing 11.5 per cent. Long-term credit institutions in the cooperative structure would also be adequately covered by this average rate. The Government of India may have to consider making good the shortfall in the income of commercial banks if minimum economic rates as indicated are not acceptable for other reasons.

This average rate will not, however, be able to cover the cost of the short-term cooperative credit structures. Therefore, these will continue to remain weak primarily because of the high proportion of their low interest yielding assets and the higher cost of the existing three-tier structure resulting in a relatively higher retailing cost and the need for separate margins (viability) for each of the tiers. This situation leads to an average rate which is higher by 5–6 percentage points as compared to the economic rate (15.5 per cent) for the commercial banks.

The difference roughly corresponds to the establishment cost, which is the cost of retailing in respect of the PACSs—the retailing arm of the short-term cooperative credit structure. It does not seem feasible to provide for this extra cost by raising the interest rates beyond the level recommended for commercial banks. Therefore, the state government may have to make good the shortfall in the income of cooperative banks in the same manner as the Government of India may be expected to do in the case of commercial banks. As an alternative, cooperative institutions may be freed from the interest rate prescription. However, as the finances of the state government will not permit such a move and with the World Bank keen on restructuring the financial system and cutting loan subsidies, this move does not seem feasible. There is, thus, no alternative to closing down the cooperative credit structures in rural areas as they have been proved unviable. Only production cooperatives like milk/sugar have succeeded as also urban cooperative banks; most other cooperative credit agencies have failed and there is no need to support them any further.

The cooperative credit structure should not be merged into the rural credit subsidiaries envisaged by the Narasimham Committee report and instead, transformed into production cooperatives through the DCCBs/ PLDBs for short- or long-term loans, respectively, on the basis of credit requirements and backed up by a tripartite agreement with the society, if viability considerations are observed. Thus, each state will have a single subsidiary of one of the major commercial banks and a cooperative credit institution that will cater to all forms of rural credit and raise rural and other resources.

The ACRC had studied the margins available to rural credit agencies on the basis of data up to 1986. This data has been updated and margins recalculated for various credit institutions in Annexure 7.5. If we compare the interest rates being charged (in 1994) in Annexures 7.3 and 7.4 by cooperative banks with the economic rates of cooperative banks, calculated in Annexure 7.5, the lack of margin available for profitable lending operations is apparent. RRBs tend to follow the interest rate structure of their sponsor banks and while the economic rate works out to 15.10 per cent, they are found to charge 11 per cent as most of their loans are below Rs 25,000 due to the restricted nature of operations.

Thus, RRBs have had a negative margin since inception and though they can give 60 per cent of their total lending to non-target groups, due to business constraints and restricted business, they are unable to compete with either commercial banks or cooperative banks and hence, incur heavy losses.

The only way out is to restructure the rural credit agencies with minimum levels of business. RRBs could either be amalgamated at the state level or could be made subsidiaries of their sponsor banks. While the AP model has not been a success, there is a need to combine the short-term and long-term cooperative banks into a single entity that could challenge the commercial banks. Such consolidation is being carried out worldwide for better operational flexibility and successes. Rural credit agencies need to emulate such examples. No amount of funds for cleaning of balance sheets of rural credit agencies (estimated at Rs 6,600 crore) can ensure the future viability and profitability of these agencies in view of their structural weaknesses and operational inflexibilities.

Annexure 7.1

Percentage Share of Various Credit Agencies

(Rs Crore)

Particulars/ Agency	1992-93	Share %	1993-94	Share %	1994-95	Share %	1995-96	Share %	1996-97	Share %	1997-98	Share %
I. Production ST Credit												
Cooperative Banks	7170	71	7839	70	7250	91	8331	57	9750	55	11500	55
RRBs	489	5	732	6	688	9	849	6	1144	06	1200	6
Commercial Banks	2432	24	2700	24	@	–	5345	37	6797	39	8177	39
Sub Total (A)	10091	100	11271	100	7938@	100	14526	100	17691	100	20877	100
Growth Rate	(+43%)		(+12%)		–				(+22%)		(+18%)	
II. MT/LT Credit												
Cooperative Banks	2208	43	2278	43	2156	20	2148	29	2729	25	3275	24

Annexure 7.1 Contd.

Annexure 7.1 Contd.

Particulars/ Agency	1992–93	Share %	1993–94	Share %	1994–95	Share %	1995–96	Share %	1996–97	Share %	1997–98	Share %
RRBs	342	7	245	5	395	4	532	7	777	7	1010	8
Commercial Banks	2528	50	2700	52	8255@	76	4827	64	7456	68	9072	68
Sub Total (B)	5078	100	5223	100	10806@	100	7507	100	10962	100	13357	100
Growth Rate	(+23%)		(+3%)		(+14%)		(+18%)		(+46%)		(+22%)	
Grand Total (A + B)	15169		16494		18744	–	22032	–	28653		34274	
Growth Rate	(+35%)		(+9%)		(+14%)		(+18%)		(+30%)		(+20%)	

$ Revised Estimate (SAPs)

Projections under Service Area Plan (SAPs)

@ Separate break-up of Production Credit and MT/LT for CBs not available. Share of cooperatives in the GLC is declining but commercial banks share is increasing.

RRBs share is almost static.

Source: RBI/NABARD Annual Reports.

Annexure 7.2
Working Results of Rural Credit System

	1982–83	1985–86	1990–91	1994–95	1995–96 @
	Agency-wise Net Profit/Loss of the System				
SLDBs	14	15	78	78	53
PLDBs	(23)	(45)	(41)	(10)	(23)
LT COOP	(9)	(30)	37	68	30
SCBs	24	16	69	138	173
DCCBs	31	19	133	14	156
PACSs	(0.3)	0.56	1	(58)	N.A
ST COOP	55	36	203	94	329
RRBs	(3)	(27)	(73)	(394)	(426)

	Total Number	Number in Profits	Profit Amount	Number in Loss	Loss Amount
	Working Results for 1995–96				*(Rs crore)*
SCBs					
1994–95	28	25	141	3	3
1995–96	28	26	175	2	2
DCCBs					
1994–95	362	245	173	117	159
1995–96	363	276	266	87	110
PACSs					
1993–94	90783	41190	53	33069	104
1994–95@	90783	43102	68	34019	126
SLDBs					
1994–95	19	12	110	7	32
1995–96	19	12	71	7	18
RRBs					
1994–95	196	32	29	164	423
1995–96	196	44	42	152	468

Annexure 7.2 Contd.

Annexure 7.2 Contd.

( ) Figures in brackets indicate Loss   @ Provisional
Note: Working results of commercial banks have been omitted since working results for their rural branches are difficult to segregate from overall operations.
PACSs, PLDBs and RRBs are making losses, indicating low level of business to generate income.
Source: RBI Annual Report, 1998.

Annexure 7.3
Interest Rates Fixed by ST Credit Structure for SAO Advances after Deregulation of Interest Rates by RBI

Name of the State	Rate of Interest Charges (% P.A)		
	SCBs to DCCBs	DCCBs to PACSs	PACSs to Members
a. States where interest rates have been revised			
1. Assam		10–15*	12.5–16.5*
2. Himachal Pradesh		11.5(Uniform)	12.0–14.0
3. Punjab	5.5 to 6.5 +	Up to Rs 25000—11.5	14.5
		Above Rs 25,000—12.5	15.5
4. Andhra Pradesh	6.2 to 8.7 +	12.0 (Uniform)	15.25 to 16.75*
5. Gujarat	6.0 to 8.5 +	10.0 to 12.0 *	12.5 to 17.0*
6. Rajasthan	5.5 to 9 +	10 (Uniform)	14.0 (Uniform)
7. Madhya Pradesh	5.5 to 8 +	11.5/12.5	15.5 to 17.5*
8. Orissa	5.5 to 8 +	11.5 (Uniform)	15.5 and 18.5*
9. Karnataka	6.0 to 8.5	Up to Rs 25,000—10.5	13.5
		Rs 25,000–Rs 2 lakh—12	17
		Above Rs 2 lakh—free	free

Annexure 7.3 Contd.

Annexure 7.3 Contd.

No.	State			
10.	Maharashtra	7 to 8 +	10.0 to 12 *	13 to 18
11.	Bihar	6.5 to 9.0 +	10 to 11.5 *	12.5 to 14.0 *
12.	Pondicherry		10 to 13 *	13.0 to 16.0
13.	Mizoram		10.5	13.5 to 17.5 *
14.	West Bengal	5.5 to 8.0	10.0 (Uniform)	13.0 to 14.0 *
15.	Haryana	8.0 (Uniform)	12.0 (Uniform)	16.0 (Uniform)
16.	Kerala	8.5 (Uniform)	9.5 (Uniform)	12.0 to 15.0 *

b. States where interest rate revisions are yet to take place

No.	State			
1.	Tamil Nadu	0.5% above the		
2.	Uttar Pradesh	corresponding	9	12 to 15
3.	Jammu & Kashmir	refinance rate		
4.	North Eastern States (Other than Assam and Mizoram)	charged by NABARD		

+Depending upon extent of refinance
*According to loan size
Source: NAFSCOB publications.

Annexure 7.4

Interest Rates Fixed by SLDBs after Deregulation

Name of the State	ULR Prior to 18–10–94 SLDB			ULR after Deregulation SLDB			Deregulation (-)Extent(+) SLDB		
	Up to Rs 25,000	Rs 25,000 to Rs 2 lakh	Above Rs 2 lakh	Up to Rs 25,000	Rs 25,000 to Rs 2 lakh	Above Rs 2 lakh	Up to Rs 25,000	Rs 25,000 to Rs 2 lakh	Above Rs 2 lakh
1. Punjab	12	14	14/15	12	15	16	–	(+) 1.0	(+)2/1
2. Orissa	12	14	14/15	13	15	17.5	(+)1.0	(+) 1.0	(+)3.5/2.5
3. Gujarat	12	14	14/15	13	15	17.5	(+)1.0	(+) 1.0	(+)3.5/2.5
4. Haryana	12	14	14/15	13	15	17.5	(+)1.0	(+) 1.0	(+)3.5/2.5
5. Himachal Pradesh	12	14	14/15	13	14.5	16	(+)1.0	(+) 0.5	(+)2/1
6. Madhya Pradesh	12	14	14/15	13	15	17.5	(+)1.0	(+) 1.0	(+)3.5/2.5
7. Manipur	12	14	14/15	13	15	16	(+)1.0	(+) 1.0	(+)2/1
8. Meghalaya	12	14	14/15	13	14.5*	16.5*	–	(+) 0.5	(+)2.5/1.5
9. Pondicherry	12	14	14/15	13	15	16	(+)1.0	(+) 1.0	(+) 2/1
10. Tamil Nadu	12	14	14/15	13	15	14/15	(+)1.0	(+) 1.0	(+) 2/1
11. Tripura	12	14	14/15	13	15	16	(+)1.0	(+) 1.0	(+) 2/1

Annexure 7.4 Contd.

Annexure 7.4 Contd.

Name of the State	ULR Prior to 18-10-94 SLDB			ULR after Deregulation SLDB			Deregulation (−)/Extent(+) SLDB		
	Up to Rs 25,000	Rs 25,000 to Rs 2 lakh	Above Rs 2 lakh	Up to Rs 25,000	Rs 25,000 to Rs 2 lakh	Above Rs 2 lakh	Up to Rs 25,000	Rs 25,000 to Rs 2 lakh	Above Rs 2 lakh
12. West Bengal	12	14	14/15	12.5	15	17.5	(+)0.5	(+) 1.0	(+)3.5/2.5
13. Rajasthan	12	14	14/15	14	15	15/16	(+)2.0	(+)1.0	(+) 1
14. Kerala	12	14	14/15	12	15	15	–	(+)1.0	(+) 1
15. Assam	12	14	14/15	12	14	15	–	–	(+) 2/1
16. Andhra Pradesh	12	14	14/15	14	16	18	(+)2.0	(+)2.0	(+) 4/3
				C	C	C			
17. Arunachal Pradesh	12	14	14/15	12	14	15	–	–	–
18. Karnataka	12	14	14/15	13	15	16	(+)1.0	(+) 1.0	(+) 2/1
19. Jammu & Kashmir	12	14	14/15	14	15	16	(+)2.0	(+)1.0	(+) 2/1
20. Uttar Pradesh	12	14	14/15	13	14.5	17	(+)1.0	(+) 0.5	(+) 3/2

* Includes service charge @ 1.5%
C—Single Window
Source: CARDBP publications..

Annexure 7.5
Costs and Margins of Rural Financial Institutions

(in per cent)

	Financial	Transaction Cost	Gross Margin Required	Economic Rate
As per ACRC *				
CBs	7.48	6.00	7.00	14.48
RRBs	7.80	6.90	8.65	16.45
PLDBs	7.78	3.39	5.00	12.78
PACSs	9.90	5.40	6.00	15.30
As per April 1992 rate				
CBs	11.90	5.10 **	5.10	17.00
RRBs	9.10	11.80 **	11.80	20.90
LT Coop.	9.70	6.50 **	6.50	16.20
ST Coop.	8.90	12.50 **	12.50	21.40
As per March 1994 rate				
CBs	9.90	5.20 **	5.20	15.10
RRBs	7.90	11.80 **	11.80	19.70
LT Coop.	9.30	6.50 **	6.50	15.80
ST Coop.	7.90	12.50 **	12.50	20.40

Source: "National Seminar on Rural Credit—Background Paper" organised by RBI and NABARD, 1994.

Note:

*The costs and margins are based on the data for the years 1983–84, 1984–85 and 1985–86 in respect of cooperatives and the years 1984, 1985 and 1986 in respect of commercial banks and RRBs.

**Includes risk cost

8

Rural Credit at the Cross-roads

Non-institutional Sources

Money-lenders dominate the rural credit markets in developing countries and interest rates are usurious ranging from 2 per cent per month to even 30 per cent per month, depending upon the period of loan and the risks involved as also amounts and the collateral secured. Determined efforts have been made over the past 40 years (from 1951) to wean rural borrowers away from the money-lender (who could be a farmer, trader, commission agent, friend/relative or landlord) and build up an alternative rural credit delivery system based on cheap credit from institutional sources (subsidised). The money-lender, however, continues to thrive in modified forms.

In India, the proportion of rural credit owed to money-lenders was 80 per cent of all rural debt in 1951. This reduced to 24 per cent in 1981. During the same period, institutional debts rose from 7 per cent to 61 per cent. In spite of the rapid growth of rural credit from institutional sources in South Asian countries, particularly over the past 20 years, the percentage share of money-lenders and other informal sources of credit has not appreciably reduced. The intervention of the central and state governments in India over the past 40 years, has been substantial. Hence, India shows a low percentage share of the informal rural credit system to total credit outstanding possibly due to the large number of bank branches opened since 1969, the low rates for agricultural credit and the spread of the multi-agency system. From 1952 to 1982, the proportion of informal credit has come down from 86 per cent to 38 per cent but the money-lender has yet to disappear.

Rural credit markets of South Asia are still influenced heavily by money-lenders even though interest rates may exceed 75 per cent per month and in certain periods, may not even be available. The proportion of farmers served by agricultural financial institutions continues to be poor, except in Pakistan (80 per cent). A symposium on 'Imperfect Information and Rural Credit Markets' (World Bank Economic Review, 1991) concludes:

> creation of institutional alternatives has failed to drive traditional money-lenders out of the market and whatever competition it has provided, interest rates charged by traditional money-lenders remain high.

The informal sector still exists despite their high interest rates as compared to the subsidised rates provided by the formal sector. The interest rates offered by rural credit institutions are, in fact, subsidised heavily as any rate less than 15 per cent in India for rural credit, is likely to be unrealistic when compared to the agricultural rate of return (ARR). The components of the ARR are given in Table 8.1.

Table 8.1
Components of Agricultural Rate of Return

(in per cent)

Cost of Funds	–	7.9
Administration Costs	–	4.3
Liquidity Costs	–	1.5
Risk Costs	–	1.3
Max. Agricultural Rate of Return		15.0

Interest rates do not clear the market; there is credit rationing during bad harvests, with no lending being done. Credit markets are regulated with variable interest rates. There are a limited number of commercial money-lenders and high interest rates do not raise the number of lenders. In the informal sector, inter-linkages between credit transactions and transactions in other commodity markets are common. Formal lenders like banks tend to specialise in areas where farmers have firm land titles and other collateral. Informal lenders tend to give more credit for consumption and other needs. Rural areas with higher average incomes have lower interest rates (Burdwan in West Bengal is more prosperous and the interest rates range from 36–84 per cent, while Nadia in the same state is less prosperous so the interest rates range from 72–120 per cent).

There are new views on rural credit markets based on the following:

(a) Screening problem: Borrowers defer repayments in the likelihood that they will default and it is costly to determine each borrower's risk.
(b) Incentives problem: It is costly to ensure that borrowers take those actions which make repayments most likely.
(c) Enforcement problem: It is difficult to compel repayment. Rural financial agencies incur huge transaction costs to ensure that the above problems are 'minimised' or 'centralised' but the problem of overdues due to poor loan appraisal and monitoring systems continue to plague the institutional rural credit sector. Also, rural credit agencies either do not have the resources to finance all those requiring loans or have cumbersome procedures which drive a large number of the rural poor to money-lenders.

The market interface between the rural poor and the tentacles of the organised sector of the economy, is an unavoidable reality. One sees in the rural areas how the poor and unorganised are exploited. The interface is personified in the trader, middleman or money-lender, considered by those in the organised sector as a 'Devil' but by the rural poor as an 'Angel' because of his availability and willingness to advance credit. But it is an Angel who charges heavily for the services he provides, and the risks he takes. If this system continues for another 20 years or so, the rural poor will be sucked dry of whatever assets they may have and become bonded to the trader/money-lender. It is time that economists and planners have another look at how this negative interface with the organised sector and the rural poor can be avoided.

Informal Credit in Dharwad District

The total number of registered money-lenders/financial agencies as per records available with the ARCS, Dharwad, is given in Table 8.2.

Table 8.2
No. of Money-lenders/Other Agencies in Dharwad District

Category	As at end March 1990	As at end March 1991
Money-lenders (Regd.)	317	363
Pawn Brokers	143	174
Financial Companies	297	405
	757	942

However, all these cater exclusively to the urban sector and no loans are granted for agricultural operations. A few registered money-lenders do give loans for agricultural operations but only as 'bridge' loans to those farmers who are reliable and who have been sanctioned loans by commercial banks but are yet to receive the sanctioned amount. Bridge loans are given by the money-lender only after he confirms from the bank manager that the borrower has been sanctioned a loan by the bank, but its disbursal has been held up due to procedural delays. The bridge loans are given at an interest rate of 3 per cent per month for 100 days, deducted in advance. The borrower repays the bridge loan when the bank disburses the amount to him. However, in case of a default, the money-lender levies a penal interest at the rate of 1.5 per cent. The loan can, however, be renewed for another 100 days, if the borrower again pays the 3 per cent interest in advance.

The maximum amount of 'bridge' loan that can be disbursed by the money-lender is Rs 5,000 and that too only if two guarantors (who must be previous borrowers or businessmen or salary earners) provide securities on stamped papers of Rs 10 each. Advances to agriculturists against the security of gold ornaments are given up to Rs 10,000 on the same terms and conditions but if the risk factor is more, interest rates vary from 3 per cent to 5 per cent a month. However, annual interest rates usually range from 27 per cent to 40 per cent varying mainly due to the 'reliability' factor of the borrower, with respect to repayment and assessed risk.

Unofficial lenders also operate in the informal credit sector and their interest rates being unregulated, are higher at 3 per cent to 5 per cent a month. The major problem for official money-lenders is the Karnataka Rural Debt Ordinance passed in 1976 (during the Emergency) which wrote off the debt of all agriculturists from money-lenders without any compensation. Thus, money-lenders (unregistered) provide agricultural loans only against securities like gold and title deeds of houses after checking charge with the land revenue records/authorities and after getting the borrowers signatures on a blank paper, in case of non-repayment. Some lenders also provide crop loans against 'paddy' grown on irrigated (canal irrigation) lands for 4–6 months at the rate of 5 per cent. Further, interest payment in kind is also permitted at the rate of one bag of paddy for Rs 100. For other crops like chillies, cotton, tobacco, sunflower which are cash crops, there is no interest repayment in kind but all sale will be routed through the wholesale merchant/commission agent at the prevailing market prices. Many commission agents/wholesale traders also provide loans to their clients who have been dealing with them for over 15–20 years (or even 2–3 generations). The interest charged is 3 per cent per month till the crop is sold. The loan estimation is done by the farmer himself and the only security is the borrower's signature on blank paper.

Financial companies, operating since 1988, provide loans mainly for small business establishments (shop/service units) and not for agricultural rural borrowers. There is one guarantor (usually a salary earner) and interest is recovered in monthly equated instalments by means of 'advance'/undated cheques. There is also a facility for daily collection from the daily business turnover, if necessary. Loans are given on an annual basis. Pawn brokers charge 18 per cent interest per annum while financial companies charge 21 per cent to 24 per cent per annum.

Transaction Costs for Agricultural Loans from Informal Sources

For unregistered money-lenders like traders/commmission agents, there are almost no transaction costs involved, as borrowers invariably sell their crops/produce through them. Even if they attempt to sell to other agents, the lenders come to know about it through other farmers/informers as also other traders and hence, can take appropriate action. For registered money-lenders and financial companies depending upon the scale of operation, a clerk is hired for monitoring loans or for daily collection purposes. Their salaries range from Rs 500 per month for money-lenders to Rs 1,000 per month for financial companies. For a better understanding, the crucial transaction costs have been collated in a format:

	Transaction Costs for Money-lenders (regd.)	*Transaction Costs for Financial Companies*
1.	Maximum loan—Rs 1.00 lakh	Maximum loan—Rs 5.00 lakh
2.	No.of borrowers—20	No. of borrowers—10
3.	Professional tax—Rs 250 per annum	Professional tax—Rs.250 per annum.
4.	Registration fees— Rs 5,000 per year	Registration fees— Rs 5,000 per year
5.	Salaries of clerks— Rs 6,000 per year	Salaries of clerk— Rs 12,000 per year
6.	Other expenses Rs 500	Additional other expenses Rs 5,000 per year

Transaction cost per Rs 100 of loan	Transaction cost per Rs 100 of loan
$= \dfrac{11{,}750}{100{,}000} \times 100 = 11.75$	$= \dfrac{22{,}250}{500{,}000} \times 100 = 4.45$
Transaction cost per borrower per Rs 100 of loan	Transaction cost per borrower per Rs 100 of loan
$= \dfrac{11.75}{20} = .5875 = 0.59$	$= \dfrac{4.45}{10} = .445 = 0.45$

Thus, transaction costs per borrower are Rs 0.59 per Rs 100 of loan for registered money-lenders and Rs 0.45 for financial companies (who, however, do not lend for agricultural purposes).

Another important factor is that registered money-lenders disburse the loan amount net of interest cost. For a loan of Rs 5,000 for 100 days at the rate of 3 per cent interest per month, the actual amount given to the borrower is:

Amount of loan   = Rs 5,000
Period of loan   = 100 days
Rate of interest 10 per cent for 100 days

$$\text{Interest} = \frac{P \times R}{100} = \frac{5000 \times 10}{100} = \text{Rs } 500$$

Loan amount given = Rs 5,000–Rs 500 = Rs 4,500

Thus, the effective amount of loan is Rs 4,500 and in 100 days, Rs 5,000 has to be repaid by the borrower to the money-lender.

Transaction Cost for Informal Sources for the Borrower

The borrower's transaction costs are very low but could vary depending upon the source of informal credit. Transaction costs per Rs 100 of loan (say Rs 5,000) from varying sources are worked out as:

Transaction Costs for Rs 100 of Loan from the Registered Money-lender

1.	Cost of transportation (self + 2 guarantors)	Rs 25
2.	Incidental expenses for 3 persons	Rs 15
3.	Cost of stamp paper	Rs 15
4.	Cost of transportation for repayment	Rs 8
5.	Incidental expenses	Rs 5
	Total expenses	Rs 68

$$\text{Transaction cost} = \frac{\text{Rs } 68}{\text{Rs } 5,000} \times 100 = \text{Rs } 1.36$$

Transaction Costs for Borrowers per Rs 100 of Loan from Commission Agents/Traders

1.	Cost of transportation (self) for taking loan	Rs 8
2.	Cost of transportation to and fro (self for repayment)	Rs 8
3.	Incidental expenses	Rs 10
	Total expenses	Rs 26

$$\text{Transaction cost} = \frac{\text{Rs } 26}{\text{Rs } 5,000} \times 100 = \text{Rs } 0.52$$

Thus, the transaction costs for Rs 100 of loan for rural borrowers from a registered money-lender and commission agent/trader are Rs 1.36 and Rs 0.52, respectively, while the interest works out to 3 per cent a month; the maximum amount is Rs 5,000 and that too, for production loans and not for investment loans. However, 'bridge' loans are given when a bank loan has been sanctioned.

Informal Credit Markets

Informal credit markets form an important part of the financial system of developing countries, constituting as much as half of rural credit and in many countries, a significant part of urban credit. These markets play an important role in channelling credit to small and poor borrowers and assisting in generating employment, income and output. Moreover, informal credit markets contribute a major source of working capital for entrepreneurs. In general, these markets reduce discrepancies in the allocation of credit from institutional sources. Also, banks do not provide consumption credit which forms a significant proportion of the credit requirements of the rural poor.

The informal financial sector functions outside the purview of regulations imposed on institutional credit. Having no restrictions on capital subscription, liquidity, lending and deposit rates, informal lenders are able to avoid legal fees and reduce transaction costs relating to loan appraisal and documentation, to levels sharply below those for institutional credit sources. At the same time, the interest rate flexibility they enjoy enables them to cover any risk of default as well as the opportunity cost of their funds. Besides, credit from informal sources is seen as being more reliable due to its easy availability as also availability of credit for consumption purposes.

As risks are higher and the market small and fragmented, the cost of informal sector credit, is generally higher than that of formal sector credit even when the informal lender is not making monopoly profits. Also informal credit is more readily available to borrowers, whose credit needs tend to be neglected by the formal sector due to high risk factors, lack of collateral and high cost of administering small loans.

While informal lenders tend to rely on their own funds to a greater extent, some also accept deposits (e.g., temple trusts in Rajasthan). Informal lenders actually operate as individuals (e.g., relatives, rural moneylenders, agricultural traders and pawn brokers) or as groups of individuals organised for mutual interest, such as rotating savings and credit associations (ROSCAS)—also called 'chit funds'. However, in some countries, informal lenders are organised as 'indigenous bankers' and are partnership firms or even companies, such as informal finance investment, leasing and hire-purchasing companies. These lenders are usually exempt from central banking regulations and controls and take on the characteristics of the informal sector. The distinguishing feature of informal sources of finance is the informality and flexibility of lending operations that help make their transaction costs lower than in the formal sector.

Only very tentative estimates of the size of informal credit markets are available. As their size depends partly on the resources available and partly on the degree to which the financial sector is controlled, informal credit markets will continue to remain a significant feature in developing countries and may even grow. A useful distinction has been made between that part of the informal sector, which is to some extent autonomous and older than the institutional sector (indigenous bankers, chit funds, pawn brokers, etc.), and that part which has developed in response to tight controls and gaps in the formal credit delivery system (private finance companies). It is this second component that grows and contracts in reaction to regulations and liberal policies in the institutional credit sector.

In recent years, there has been a growing interest in informal credit markets for their role in the expansion of the rural credit system.

In parts of the informal sector without access to normal banking activities, the formal sector ought to provide more effective competition, perhaps, by adopting some of the former's practices. Measures for enhancing competition within the informal sector should also be part of this approach.

Another method could be to work through the informal sector in areas where competitive conditions do prevail but the cost of funds tends to keep interest rates high. The lower transaction costs of the informal sector can be used to 'retail' credit and this will lower borrowing rates as intermediation costs will be lower. This strategy will strengthen and expand the existing linkages between the formal and informal sectors. Access to institutional credit can be strengthened for several groups (agricultural inputs, dealers, traders and commission/transport agents), which can take advantage of the inter-linkage between credit and commodity transactions to reduce intermediation costs and risk premia only if monopoly market conditions are absent. But the greater availability of formal sector refinancing might itself induce better competition.

Some developing countries like Sri Lanka have experimented with schemes to use input and output dealers to 'on-lend' formally. There is a need for a pilot project to test this hypothesis further. Apart from the operational interest in informal credit markets, other issues like informal market savings mobilisation, allocative efficiency, equity and monetary policy need to be looked into. In many developing countries, there is a legislation having a bearing on the informal sector, including usury laws, restriction of the amount of loan or the purposes for which loans can be given, restrictions on deposit-taking, debt moratorium and registration requirements. Regulations may be framed keeping in mind that there are important trade-offs to be considered. There is conflict between restrictions on deposit-taking imposed in furtherance of selective credit controls and prudential concerns on the one hand, and the role of mobilisation of savings by informal credit markets, on the other.

Decisions regarding trade-offs need to be taken, if an 'optimal' regulatory environment towards the informal sector is to be instituted in keeping with the country's broad policy objectives.

Informal talks with both registered and non-registered money-lenders in Dharwad reveal that they are aware of the problems affecting the growth of institutional rural credit and the high administrative and transaction costs, and poor recovery rates. They are very efficient operationally and meet existing demands, but are restricted from wider coverage due to the lack of funds made available through a bank (with refinance from NABARD). In fact, a few money-lenders who usually charge interest between 3 per cent to 5 per cent per month (depending upon opportunity costs, operating margins and risk costs), have offered to act as agents for various rural credit agencies, if they are permitted to grant credit on flexible terms, with monthly commission of 1 per cent to meet operating costs.

Transaction costs (both for the borrower and the lender) for the non-institutional rural credit delivery system are very low mainly due to the lack of detailed documentation, immediate decision about loan sanction and disbursement and the lack of information costs. Involving them as agents for disbursal of crop loans or the working capital needs of small borrowers (village artisans, rural service industries and tiny rural industries) will reduce transaction costs and introduce better efficiency in the loan recovery mechanism.

Credit From Institutional Sources

The review of the existing rural credit delivery system has the following three major objectives:

- Efficacy of the existing system from the point of view of central/state governments.
- Impact of controls on the profitability and viability of rural financial institutions.
- Assessment of transaction costs of rural borrowers from institutional/non-institutional sources.

The conclusions arrived at on the basis of the analysis are:

- The existing rural credit delivery system has been created to meet government requirements and, especially after 1947, there has been lack of patience in making structural changes without correcting policy distortions and solving operational problems. These changes have met the government requirements in so far as targets set. Yet, development credit has flowed towards developed blocks/areas and not where resource potentials have been identified. Thus, the target orientation of priority sector credit has not achieved what it was expected to do. Credit gaps continue to exist. The entire system of 'guided' credit flow has achieved much but has fallen short in qualitative terms as rural development since 1947, commensurate with the efforts and money spent has not taken place. The qualitative aspect has been met only partially.

- The rigidly controlled and administered rural credit delivery system has had a harmful impact on institutional rural credit agencies due to low or negative interest margins, continued losses made by branches over many years or low profitability in some branches due to poor planning and operational problems. Branch profitability is even harder to achieve when politicians and staff vitiate the recovery climate, affecting field-level recoveries appreciably. The debt-relief schemes are perceived to have rewarded 'wilful' defaulters and punished those who repaid loans. The loan melas were also politically oriented and affected subsequent recovery. Indiscriminate expansion in the 1970s and 1980s further affected profitability and viability of the system. There is a need for flexible alternatives as further expansion of the rural institutional credit agencies is ruled out and consolidation needs to be done.

- An in-depth study of transaction costs reveals the various components of the total costs to the borrowers to be exorbitantly high. A careful analysis of transaction costs reveals that these vary directly with:

  (a) Number of days taken for disbursal of loans from the time of application.
  (b) Amount of loan.
  (c) Total number of visits to banks
  (d) Total number of visits to government agencies.
  (e) Total amount of bank and administrative charges.

Further, the average total loan costs of rural credit agencies is higher than that from non-institutional sources. Transaction costs are high for graduates but varies amongst others, with the next lowest being for illiterates. The transaction costs for Rs 100 of loan is the lowest for borrowers in the age group up to 40 years and below and highest for the 40–60 age group. Also, transaction costs are lowest for long-term loans and highest for short-term loans, possibly due to the short span of time of repayment. Transaction costs were the highest for commercial banks, followed by RRBs and the least for LDBs.

Rural credit institutions have high transaction costs due to:

• Inflexible lending terms not geared to the customers needs.
• Poor monitoring due to absence of marketing information.
• High default rate due to political intervention.
• High documentation/procedural costs for borrowers.
• Lack of market-orientation and improper targeting.

A detailed study of borrower's preferences for the five types of rural credit agencies over 12 different attributes, revealed that the main players in the system were non-institutional lenders, followed by commercial banks, with the LDBs, a poor third. The PACSs and RRBs have a marginal presence due to their limited financial services and inherent weaknesses. From the point of view of borrowers, the money-lenders are more efficient in assessing loan risks due to data availability as regards risk factors and hence, are able to dispense with costly documentation/procedures. Commercial banks have to gear themselves up in this area, for reducing their transaction costs.

The existing credit delivery system is, thus, unable to meet the needs and requirements of the central and state governments, the rural financial institutions and the rural borrowers. The system is neither cost-effective nor efficient and needs drastic overhauling. Here, it can safely be inferred that the existing rural credit delivery system is able to carry out its responsibilities and obligations only at the cost of viability and profitability, and needs to be replaced by a system that is more flexible, with cheaper transaction costs, timely disbursal of loans, with least documentation procedures and ensuring better recovery.

Rural Credit: Macro Issues

Rural development is a process and cannot be hastened. But a proper environment for it can be created. The rural credit delivery system is a 'facilitator' but rural credit by itself cannot bring about development; the rural poor have to be involved in their transformation, with credit and infrastructure being necessary inputs along with technology.

Cheap rural credit has been the bane of rural development efforts as it was felt that the poor have no resources, do not save and in view of their consumption requirements, cannot run their micro-enterprises and hence, are forced to fall back on exploitative money-lenders. Credit needs to be administered in the right doses and at the right time, while ensuring timely repayment.

Low interest rates generate excess demand for 'cheap' credit requiring rationing. This, in turn, leads to corruption and political intervention to corner credit for vested interests, resulting in over-financing a few and choking off finances for the really poor. Low interest rates ensure poor mobilisation of savings and dependence on external aid agencies and the RBI for cheap credit resources, which are inflationary in nature. Low interest rates also secure low margins and ensure non-availability of genuine financial resources to the rural poor. With credit providing additional liquidity, an assessment of its impact has become difficult.

The rural credit delivery system in India has evolved over a period of 90 years largely due to various demands made on the system. Since 1955, a large number of changes have been initiated without giving enough time for the system to stabilise. Loan waivers, loan melas, political intervention, wilful non-repayment of overdues have all adversely affected the credibility of the system.

The low rate of return on agricultural advances coupled with the high cost of funds and retailing costs makes rural credit institutions unviable. Even with the enhanced interest rates (22 April 1992), the economic interest rates for rural credit agencies work out to be 10.66 per cent for SCBs to 21.35 per cent for PACSs. It is recommended that there be a two-tier interest rate structure—15 per cent per annum as concessional interest for small and marginal farmers, agricultural labourers, village artisans and tiny industries while for all other rural borrowers, 18 per cent per annum interest should be charged. This will enable rural credit institutions to operate with positive margins. Rural credit agencies should work out their individual interest rates structure for better viability, as permitted under the latest RBI guidelines. 'Directed' credit or priority sector lending needs to be reduced sharply (to 10 per cent of the total advances in stages—Narasimham Committee Report) or abolished altogether.

Rural cooperative banks need to be merged and a single window concept, based on viability considerations, set up. Another solution is to have two types of banks—commercial banks (RRBs to be merged into them) and cooperative banks (merging the long-term and short-term cooperative structure as in Andhra Pradesh) and then have a two tier interest rate structure pegged at 18 per cent and 15 per cent (concessional). Or else, a mechanism of floating interest rates based on the credit agency's cost of raising resources, administration costs, risk and liquidity costs is evolved by the agencies without interference from the government or the RBI.

While other rural credit institutions have not increased their branches drastically, there has been a sharp reduction in the number of PACSs due to the amalgamation of unviable ones. The rate of increase in deposits of commercial banks has been very sharp mainly due to the full range of financial services being offered by them while that in other rural financial institutions has been minimal.

In advances, at end-1990, commercial banks had disbursed 52 per cent while the share of all other institutions came down sharply. The advances of cooperative banks registered a negative growth during 1989–90 and 1990–91. The CD ratio of the commercial banks was above the targeted 60 per cent while the RRBs had advanced 160 per cent for the priority sector. The achievement of the RRBs was double that stipulated at 40 per cent of total advances while commercial banks achieved 54 per cent. Over the last nine years, advances to weaker sections and to DRI sections were better than the targeted 1 per cent. Crop loans have almost doubled while term loans for agriculture increased by 2.5 times in percentage terms. Advances to the SSI have reduced by 20 per cent while advances to the tertiary sector have doubled. But the credit plan target achievements have reduced over the last nine years. The recovery position has been good for RRBs but has declined appreciably for CCBs and LDBs. Thus, there has been considerable progress in a large number of areas but the working results have been poor and recoveries have declined as have profits.

Credit Gaps

Credit flow has been uneven and in spite of existing potential, it has been directed to the richer talukas (or blocks) rather than poorer ones. Even after 22 years of credit planning, there has been no concerted move to direct credit to the underdeveloped areas to reduce the effect of disparities in natural endowments or earlier development. Potentials remain unexploited and there are huge credit gaps, both assets-wise and resources-wise. Bankers are seeking to reduce their volume of non-performing assets due to the resources crunch, poor recoveries due to the ARDR scheme, etc. Thus, credit targeting has succeeded but credit planning has failed.

The inherent viability of rural credit institutions is in doubt given the tightly controlled and regimented interest rate structure. The Z-score, which indicates corporate sickness or negative viability, has been prepared for various rural credit institutions (except commercial banks). Surprisingly, all rural credit institutions have been indicated as viable as their Z-scores are above the cut-off line. If used judiciously, the Z-score mechanism can give out warning signals to rural credit institutions.

Performance evaluation is a dynamic concept and on the 50 crucial ratios/factors studied for viability, the rank of rural credit agencies keeps fluctuating. Profitability is assured, if care is taken as regards management of non-interest costs, performance evaluation, etc. Self-monitoring and performance evaluation on a continuing basis will be effective for banks if adequate corrective action is taken in time. Commercial banks have the worst results as far as profitability-related factors are concerned. The CCBs and RRBs have the best working results due to low staff costs and better productivity. A better spread would be crucial for profitability. A higher deposit-growth ratio and a better managed spread are very important as is the quicker realisation of overdues and launching special recovery drives, better availment of refinance, yield on investments, etc., which are all crucial elements of profitability. Better staff productivity is a must, especially among demoralised officials in a rural area. Finally, a climate of cost-consciousness needs to be inculcated as also a profit-centre concept.

The ARDR scheme (1990) revealed that debt-write offs are not successful in reducing the substantially high rate of overdues. The risk factor of 60 per cent of outstanding loans is very high. The flow of credit to the rural areas has been reduced due to low recoveries and this is a matter of serious concern.

Conclusions

The low transaction costs of the rural non-institutional credit sector serve as an eye-opener for the formal rural credit agencies and offer valuable guidelines on reducing transaction costs for both the banks and also the borrowers. The main features are:

a) Flexibility

The size of the loan, the purpose for which it is granted, the timing and especially the quick decisions taken by the money-lender to lend (or not to) and the rate of interest are all important factors. Rural credit agencies have become bureaucratic and are rarely guided by business considerations. They prefer to follow 'instructions' rather than meet the borrowers' requirements. This is a very important factor for the continuance of the rural money-lender in spite of the latter's high interest rates.

b) Monitoring

The informal sector is able to monitor its loans at negligible costs due to the cheap information system it has developed, unlike that of a bank. The access to 'market' information and local gossip is a key factor for monitoring loan accounts. Rural credit agencies (except those in the cooperative sector) are handicapped by the lack of such reliable data. Also, the number of loans is kept at manageable limits by the money-lender so that monitoring is possible. Basically, the money-lender and the rural borrower exist in the same environment and understand each other thoroughly. Against this, rural credit agencies have little understanding of the environment in which they function and do not 'trust' the rural borrower.

c) Low Default Rate

As the loan interest rates of the money-lender are higher, there is a tendency to pay off the costlier loans first and thereby also maintain relations with the money-lender who can be relied upon in times of emergencies. With the rural credit agencies, due to 'rent costs' and changing rules, the borrower cannot be sure of getting another loan. Also, rural borrowers are misguided by politicians/vested interests about bank loans being in the nature of government grants which do not have to be returned.

These 'election promises' and the tendency to write off rural loans has made recovery very difficult. Also, the staff of rural credit agencies are perceived as 'outsiders' who have little or no local roots and hence, repayments to the informal sector receive first preference. There is also the effect of peer-pressure and 'coercive' action taken by money-lenders, which rural credit agencies are unable to resort to.

d) Transaction Costs

Loan transaction costs for money-lenders and for their borrowers are negligible due to the lack of extensive documentation/procedures. The large number of loans, which are a feature of the various central/state government programmes involving subsidised credit, increase transaction costs of the banks, which also have high loan recovery costs. The transaction costs of banks are also very high due to low staff productivity and lack of motivation among staff to work in rural branches. Transaction costs both of the rural credit agencies and the borrowers need to be lowered considerably.

e) Market Orientation

The market orientation of rural money-lenders is unique. Loans are 'packaged' by them for the rural borrower while the loan schemes of rural credit agencies are not targeted properly. The major constraint of money-lenders in expanding their business is the lack of funds; many money-lenders take loans from banks for 'on-lending' operations. Their repayment terms are also flexible and repayment in kind is also possible. With their numerous constraints, banks are in no position to offer better services to rural borrowers. However, their main advantage has been the low interest rates they charge. But, with the liberalisation of the Indian banking system (Narasimham Committee Report, 1991) interest rates are bound to go up. The only way out for Indian banks then will be to integrate the money-lender into the system as is being done in Sri Lanka.

The high transaction costs for rural credit agencies are due to the complexities imposed by rules and regulations and also the desire of bank officials to protect themselves in the event of loans turning 'bad and doubtful', especially in the case of targeted government programmes. The average total loan costs of rural credit agencies are more than the average total loan costs of the rural money-lender and hence, the reason for continuance of the money-lender in the rural financial market. Another important factor is the reliability of the money-lender in disbursing loans quickly as opposed to the dilatory tactics, corruption and non-flexible operations of rural credit agencies. The failure of cooperative credit agencies, due to bureaucratisation and politicisation, has added to the problems of rural credit agencies.

The only methods by which loan transaction costs can be reduced are by setting up Self-help Groups (SHGs) with the help of voluntary agencies (non-government); following the example of the Bangladesh Grameen Bank; or by integrating money-lenders into the institutional credit system as 'bank agents' as is being done in Sri Lanka and also with the help of Mobile Credit Officers (MCOs) as in Pakistan. There is a need to reduce the number of rural credit agencies—by merging RRBs into sponsor banks or into an all-India bank and merging the DCCBs and the PLDBs at the state/district level—so that the cooperative banking system offers one-window services to the rural borrowers. The introduction of the loan pass-book system since 1998 or the 'Krishi Vikas Card' enables the farmers to have easier access to credit without the hurdles associated with the bank loans. The rural borrower is not getting a fair deal at present and a rural market-orientation needs to be inculcated into the rural credit system. A thorough revamp of the system is overdue. It is a pity that the Narasimham Committee Report, 1991, did not delve deep into the problems of the rural financial sector and come up with comprehensive reforms. It is time to initiate reforms urgently before the rural financial system collapses.

PART II

Analysis of Micro-finance Needs

9

Credit Requirements of Tribal People

Exploitation of the Tribal Economy

Tribal people have all along been subjected to large-scale exploitation by non-tribals. Even though a series of measures have been initiated after Independence to ameliorate their economic condition, the degree of exploitation, instead of declining, is on the rise. The development of the tribal economy has been seriously hampered by the lack of infrastructural facilities, such as transport and communication, an organised/monetised market system, and an adequate organisational base. In addition to the exploitation by non-tribals, money-lenders and traders, intensive industrial/mining activities in tribal belts, inefficiency and callousness of state-owned agencies as also the high degree of land alienation and indebtedness have impoverished the tribals.

Absence of Tribal Land Rights

Tribal land rights, for example, in Orissa, are almost non-existent. The status of tribals with regard to land rights is clear from the fact that in government records, the tribal is an 'encroacher' on the land he has been occupying through the ages. Whether he lives deep in the forest or in inaccessible hilly regions, he has no legal right over the land.

The 1991 report of the Planning Commission on land holding systems in tribal areas, with a special reference to Orissa, highlighted the shocking state of affairs with regard to tribal land rights. The report notes that sometimes not even 1 per cent of the land occupied by the tribals is recorded in their favour. Moreover, it points to the fact that the laws do not recognise the communal holdings of the tribals. Thus, the land the tribals use to meet their basic needs of food, fodder and fuel are on record the preserves of the State Revenue and Forest Departments.

The report makes another significant revelation. The 'value' of land is perceived in terms of a market economy. So often, the land that is basic to the survival of the tribals, is designated as waste land in the records. Further, irregularities are reported to have been committed in settlement and survey operations, resulting in the transfer of large tracts of land, customarily held by tribals, to a new breed of non-tribal owners. Such abuses in settlement are a common phenomenon given the collusion between the settlement officials and non-tribals for mutual profit. Bribes, tampering of records, use of force and other methods have been used to deprive the tribal of his land. This, of course, is a gross violation of the law which explicitly declares that all land transfers from tribals to non-tribals are illegal and void without the permission of the proper authority.

A massive influx of coastal people to the uplands took place after the Bengal–Orissa famine of 1866–67. The famine took a toll of almost one-fourth of the population of the coastal districts of Orissa. This movement increased and continued till the mid-20s. The non-tribals called *Ghatidinha* (i.e., crossers of Ghats) settled under the auspices of the feudal rulers and British-appointed agents for collection of land revenue and other taxes.

Land Holding Pattern

The land holding pattern prevailing in tribal-dominated districts (undivided) of Orissa was studied on the basis of the Bench Mark Survey conducted by Tribal and Harijan Research Training Institute (THRTI), Bhubaneswar, in 1978–79. While landless and marginalised ST families constitute as low as about 30 per cent of the total tribal families in the district of Sundargarh, the same form as high as 72.8 per cent of the total tribal families in the district of Koraput. The position in other districts is 37 per cent in Phulbani, 39 per cent in Sambalpur, 44 per cent in Mayurbhanj and 64 per cent in Ganjam. The lesser percentage of landless and marginalised families found in the districts of Sundargarh, Phulbani, Keonjhar and Mayurbhanj due to the impact of opening of the areas to mining/industrial activity and the spread of Christianity. The latter checked the tribals from exploitation by traders and money-lenders, as awareness increased with their advent.

Limitations of Forest Rights of Tribals

The drive towards better forest management and development led the then British Government and later the central and state governments to enact stringent laws and policies, with regard to forests, thereby, gradually enhancing and monopolising their power over it. Far from recognising the relationship of the tribals to the forest, these laws squarely blamed the tribals for its degradation. Moreover instead of legalising the existing rights and privileges of the tribals and forest dwellers, the laws deprived them of these. The legal position remained fluid till the promulgation of the Indian Forest (Orissa Amendment) Act, 1954, and the Orissa Forest Act, 1972.

Exploitation and Land Alienation Caused by the Traders

A study made by the National Institute of Community Development, (now National Institute for Rural Development) Hyderabad, observed that in southern Orissa, non-tribal immigrants had become a dominant group, economically and politically. Land alienation and other forms of exploitation, such as debt bondage, money lending at exorbitant rates of interest are causing tribal unrest. However, the tribal communities in northern Orissa appear to be more careful and are asserting revivalism of their culture and nativism.

Closely observing the economic activity of the tribals, it is learnt that their basic requirements are salt, kerosene, oil, onions, molasses, dried fish, cattle, goats, poultry and some clothing. Except the livestock, they get the rest of the items mostly through barter. Salt or a handful of onions or dried fish, for example, is procured in exchange of some good quality vegetable seeds or forest produce/products and often, millets and other crops are exchanged for clothes. The traders take advantage of the simplicity and innocence of the tribal people and cheat them, using sub-standard weights and measures.

In the pre-Independence days, the merchants/traders used to come with their pack animals loaded with the daily requirements of the tribal people, such as salt, tobacco, onions, chillies, kerosene and cotton clothes.

They used to collect the costs in kind at the time of harvest. The prices fixed by the merchants were always high and therefore, the tribals always paid very heavily. In many cases, the produce was found insufficient for the prices charged by the merchants. This ultimately led to credit transactions, leaving the tribals heavily indebted to the merchants. The resources of the tribals being limited, their indebtedness increased day by day and finally, a situation arose when the tribals had to offer their land to the merchants. The tribals often borrowed from the merchants to meet unforeseen expenditure on account of illness, death, religious rites, etc. Being unable to repay the loans, the tribals had to offer themselves as bonded agricultural labourers in the farms captured by the merchants from their own people. Thus, their status was reduced to that of landless serfs. Once a tribal family gets caught in this vicious circle of economic exploitation, it is well nigh impossible for them to escape for generations.

Post-Independence, the Land Alienation Act declared that any sale of land by a tribal to a non-tribal without the permission of the District Magistrate would be illegal. Now, such powers have been delegated to the SDOs. The documentation of cases of illegal transfer of land has been a difficult affair for prosecution and restoration. The tribals who sell their land are reluctant to reveal their identity for fear of economic intimidation. Non-tribal buyers do not get the land recorded in their name and hold it as a usufruct. Even though some cases have been instituted and decrees obtained to restore the land to the owners, the lack of follow-up action has rendered such decrees infructuous. As a result, non-tribal merchants continue to enjoy the benefits of the land they acquired from the tribals and the latter are as impoverished as before or even worse. A study conducted by the Indian Institute of Social Sciences (IISS), New Delhi, reports that about 18 per cent of the tribal land alienation is caused by outsiders.

Government-sponsored service cooperative societies and Grain Gola societies are intended to advance loans in cash and kind separately to the tribals at the time of need. The Community Development Study of NICD, (now NIRD) Hyderabad, reveals that

> in practice, however, the cooperative societies were found to be rendering very little help to the tribal people as their management was in the hands of the local merchants who did not want to lessen their grip on the tribals. Also, due to official red tape, there was considerable delay in disbursement of loans, even when they were finally approved. Thus, the very purpose of the loan was not served and whatever was received was spent on something else. Under the circumstances, the tribals were left

with no choice than to borrow either in cash or in kind from the merchants with whom they maintained unbroken economic relationships. Further, it was observed that the cooperative society officials were involved in corrupt practices. Even though the loan repayments were received in cash or kind, it was not being entered in the register and the debtors who had already cleared all dues were repeatedly called upon to repay loans.

Another aspect of tribal exploitation even in the post community development stage is discerned by the economic studies conducted by different institutions. To protect the tribals from exploitation by the local merchants in respect of purchase of forest and agricultural produce, the Government of Orissa organised depots. But, here too, the local merchants have outwitted the authorities, intercepting a tribal going to such depots or in his village itself and procuring the produce there itself, often adopting coercive methods. The few tribals who succeeded in bringing their produce to the market centres were literally swarmed by the merchants and deprived of their legitimate income. The tribals do not dare hurt the feelings of the merchants lest they forego the financial help they get from them in times of their need, but inter-ethnic conflict is likely to emerge if this systematic exploitation is not checked immediately.

The extent of control exercised by the non-tribal money-lenders, traders may be assessed from the source and quantum of credit. The sources can be classified into two categories, viz., official and non-official, the former comprising the commercial and cooperative banks/societies and the latter, consisting of money-lenders, landlords, liquor vendors, petty businessmen, etc. It is estimated that the proportion of loans taken from the unofficial resources is about 55 per cent and that taken from official sources about 45 per cent.

Land Alienation Caused by Industrialisation

Ironically, the tribal belts of Orissa have become a zone of intense industrial and mining activities in recent decades. These belts are not only rich in mineral resources but also provide strategic locations for dams. Also being rich in flora and fauna, they are either exploited or have been reserved by the government. The Rourkela Steel Plant, Machkund Hydro Electricity Project, Talcher Coal-based Thermal Project, NALCO, a host of ancillary industries, and a chain of mining complexes, as also wild life sanctuaries have made their appearance in the tribal belts. An ancient agro-forest based traditional culture has been confronted with a modern sophisticated industrial culture. The abrupt confrontation has produced disastrous results for the tribals. There has been large-scale alienation of tribal land in favour of public and private sector industrial and mining complexes, townships, private enterprises, etc. Wild life sanctuaries, too, tend to exclude tribals from the forests they have been utilising for centuries. The tribals have not been able to secure alternative sources of livelihood. The first generation has found it nearly impossible to imbibe the skills and culture of the industrial age. It would appear that the shock impulses generated on account of imposition of modern industries have been beyond the absorption capacity of the tribal communities. In fact, for the first generation, it has been an unmitigated disaster, inasmuch as it has meant a wholesale destruction of tribal values.

Detailed data on the extent of the forest area that has been destroyed for developmental projects and the number of tribal families displaced by these projects is not available. However, some instances are cited in Table 9.1.

Table 9.1
Displacement of Tribal Families

District	Name of the Project(s)	Forest Area Covered (Sq.Km)	No. of Tribal Families Displaced
Koraput	NALCO and Other Industrial Projects	2,000	NA
	Machkund Hydel Dam	—	1,500
	Balimela Project	—	2,000
	Upper Kolab Multi-purpose Project	—	7,092
Koraput/ Kalahandi	Upper Indrabati Project	—	5,000
Keonjhar	Salendi Dam	—	965
Sundargarh	Rourkela Steel Plant	13,185	NA
All Orissa	Sanctuaries(16)/ Parks(12)	7,395	NA
	Mining	950	NA

The displaced tribals, already a marginalised people, have been driven to the brink of acute poverty. Traditionally dependent on natural resources, the tribals are unable to adapt themselves to the market economy into which they were thrown into after being evicted from their old habitat. This has resulted in impoverishment and malnutrition. The IISS study reveals that about 15 per cent of the tribal land alienation has been caused by developmental projects.

Land Alienation Through Cash Crop Cultivation

Mono-crop plantations also have not only displaced the tribals from their habitat, but have given them little or no benefit since the government or the company concerned takes all the profits. In 1960–61, cashewnut plantations were undertaken by the Soil Conservation Department, Government of Orissa, partly on the land used by tribals for grazing their cattle or collecting dry shrubs for use as fuel wood or even for cultivation. Tribals in Keonjhar district were similarly disadvantaged, when tea plantations were set up.

Exploitation in Non-Timber Forest Produce Collection

Although separate agencies have been created to prevent the exploitation of tribals by money-lenders/traders and to ensure better remuneration for the forest produce collected by them, the inefficient functioning and the callous attitude of government officials has put paid to such efforts. The tribals are also subject to exploitation by the state government on the collection of Non-Timber Forest Produce (NTFP) also.

Kendu leaf: Kendu leaf is one of the main NTFP items on which the livelihood of lakhs of tribals depends. Nationalised in 1973, the Kendu leaf trade has become the monopoly of the Forest Department, which has been entrusted with its collection and processing, and the Orissa Forest Development Corporation (OFDC) with its marketing. As it is lucrative, the revenue from Kendu leaf has increased over the years from Rs 3.31 crore in 1973 to Rs 124.72 crore (estimated) in 1990–91. Nationalisation of the Kendu leaf trade has, however, not eased tribal exploitation, rather it has got firmly entrenched under the iron hand of government laws and policies. A study reveals that in 1979, the purchase price of Kendu leaf was Rs 50 per quintal while its selling price was Rs 350 per quintal—a 600 per cent profit to the government. Again, while the purchase price remained unchanged, the average selling price per quintal rose further—from Rs 972.61 in 1985 to Rs 1,052.33 in 1986 and to Rs 1,082.20 in 1987. Though the purchase price has now been revised to Rs 500 per quintal, it is much less than the prices prevailing in other states.

Mahua Flower: The nationalisation of the mahua flower trade is another instance of government encroachment and exploitation of tribals. Though the government increased the purchase price to Rs 3 per kg, it never sincerely enforced it. Apart from this, payment was not done quickly and it is reported that in 1991, the Tribal Development Cooperative Corporation (TDCC) owed Rs 100 lakh to the tribals of Sundargarh for the forest produce collected from them. Interestingly, the government of Bihar pays Rs 5 to Rs 7 per kg for mahua to the tribals. The price paid for certain other produce is also very less in comparison to those given outside Orissa (See Table 9.2).

Table 9.2
Prices Paid for Forest Produce

Item	Inside Orissa (Rs/Kg)	Outside Orissa (Rs/Kg)
Kusum Seed	2.00	4.50
Kachada Seed	5.00	8.50
Karanj Seed	2.00	4.00
Char Seed	5.00	10.00

Deforestation Due to Timber Felling/Logging

Forests are the lifeline of the tribals and its destruction threatens their very existence. For industrial and commercial ventures, forests are a source of abundant natural resources that are to be exploited and consumed at a frenzied rate. But, the resultant consequences are borne directly by the tribals. The state-owned OFDC, whose major activity is timber trading, not only sells timber to the paper mills, sawmills, manufacturers of furniture, etc., but also leases out forests to various industries. For example, Mangalam Timber Products has a lease of over 90 sq. km in the Rayagada forest division. Straw Products Ltd., which is the only paper unit relying on the Forest Department for supply of wood, had a lease of 30 sq. km in 1989–90.

Bamboo nationalisation was another blow to the tribal economy. Used as a basic raw material for various artisan activities and as a construction material in all rural households, its nationalisation in 1988 made it the exclusive monopoly of the state. Though the OFDC has to supply bamboo to tribals/tribal artisans, this policy is observed more on paper. The most worrisome fact is that while the paper industries greedily swallow bamboo plantations, using unscientific methods of cutting, the bamboo reserves of the state are slowly being depleted and no attention is being paid to replacement of its stock.

Migration Trends Among Tribals

Mining and industrialisation, natural resources exploitation, impoverishment, socio-economic and cultural transformation among the Santhals and Mundas began in the early 19th century. Correspondingly, the Santhals and Mundas began migrating to the Assam tea gardens in the 1840s. Evidently, they were among the first recruits to the tea gardens. Historical records also show that the Santhals were among the first labourers of the Tata Iron and Steel Company (TISCO) plant in Jamshedpur, Bihar, in the first decade of the 20th century. By the 1930s, the Santhals of the adjoining Mayurbhanj district of Orissa migrated regularly to the Assam tea gardens. From all accounts, migration has now become a way of life among these tribals.

The other major reason for migration, besides the inducement techniques used by the contractors, has been natural disasters. For instance, the famines in 1886 and 1921 were responsible for tribal migration, which increased from 19,407 in 1917–18 to 22,753 in 1918–19 to the tea gardens. Tribals comprise a bulk of the tea garden labour even today.

From Orissa, the initial recruitment was primarily from the Mayurbhanj and the surrounding districts of the Bihar border, inhabited by Santhals and Mundas. New areas for recruitment were opened up in 1943. These included the Parlakhemundi sub-division and the nearby district of Srikakulam in Andhra Pradesh. The main residents in these areas were the Saoras. Though initially only the Hinduised mainland inhabitants of Srikakulam district joined the flow, this gradually spread to encompass Gumma, probably in the late 1950s or the early 1960s. The hill Saoras of Gumma were well known for their hard work and capacity to survive under adverse conditions.

Credit for Tribals

As commercial banks had not set up branches in the tribal areas, most credit requirements there were met by the cooperative credit system. For about 25 years after Independence, the PACSs were supposed to meet credit requirements in tribal areas as in any other part of the country. But, the intricacies of tribal credit led to the realisation that the requirements of tribals were not being met by the traditional PACSs, and specialised tribal cooperative societies combining various functions—Large-sized Adivasi Multi-purpose Societies (LAMPS)—were set up.

The operational inadequacies and the problems of LAMPS in Orissa need to be reviewed so as to offer practical solutions for strengthening LAMPS and to meet the genuine requirements of tribals. Instead of prescribing yet another specialised institution, the emphasis is on identifying the reasons for non-performance and suggesting changes where required. The accent is on revitalising LAMPS on the basis of emerging requirements and identified constraints. LAMPS need a fair chance to be made operationally viable and effective in meeting the requirements of tribals. An integrated approach for strengthening LAMPS and reducing exploitation can serve tribal interests better.

After 1947, cooperative societies were assigned the role of change agents in furthering socio-economic activities in rural areas due to their agrarian base. While these service cooperative societies lent cash and inputs, exploitation of farmers by traders and middlemen did not cease due to the absence of strong marketing/procurement agencies. Surplus agricultural produce continued to be sold at low prices. The PACSs had limited functions, relating to disbursal of agricultural credit (cash and inputs) for land improvement (including irrigation) and allied purposes as also procurement of surplus produce by linking credit with marketing and distribution of consumer articles, including on barter. The state government provided package assistance such as share capital assistance, risk fund contribution, price fluctuation compensation, managerial subsidy, etc. These were expected to strengthen the cooperative structure and make them viable. In tribal areas, the PACSs failed to have any impact due to the following reasons:

- The PACSs were meant to provide traditional credit support for farmers while in tribal areas, the land was mostly unirrigated and unscientific farming practices were resorted to, rendering traditional business unviable.

- Erratic monsoons and drought conditions resulted in reduced loan recovery. In view of the minimum loan collection stipulations for eligibility of fresh finance, sale proceeds of marketing and consumer business was siphoned away for loan repayment due to pressure from the DCCBs, resulting in non-availability of funds for procurement/ marketing of consumer operations in tribal PACSs.
- As the tribal PACSs were located in inaccessible places, the Regional Co-operative Marketing Societies (RCMS) and consumer federation did not meet their requirements, resulting in drying up of marketing and consumer business.
- While officially the PACSs discontinued procurement/marketing operations, many chief executive officers (secretaries) continued to procure surplus agricultural produce/minor forest produce (SAP/MFP) in a private capacity by giving cash advances or consumer goods on 'barter-trade'. These secretaries ran private trading operations using society funds and flouted rules for procurement and avoided taxes. Tribal exploitation continued due to inaccessibility and poor monitoring.
- The management of PACSs in tribal areas was dominated by non-tribals and vested interests, who did not have any stake in empowering the tribals. In most cases, the president and other office bearers of PACSs were non-tribals, either money-lenders or traders, who exploited the tribals.

The Need for Specialised Cooperatives for Tribals

The Fifth Five-Year Plan emphasised reorganisation of cooperatives in tribal sub-plan areas to act as centres of tribal economic activities. The aim was to avoid regional imbalances and free the tribals from the grip of money-lenders and traders. The Bawa Committee, 1971 recommended that LAMPS should be set up by amalgamating service cooperative societies in tribal areas, to give more emphasis to SAP/MFP and to provide long-term loans and consumption loans as also to undertake consumer business, including inputs supply and sales. In 1975–76, the reorganisation of LAMPS was taken up and 43 LAMPS were set up covering large tribal areas. There are now 223 LAMPS in 16 districts, covering 1,410 gram panchayats and 118 tribal blocks. Factors considered for setting up LAMPS included viability on the basis of population and potential as also compact area of operations from the communications point of view.. There are 46 block-level LAMPS, while 177 LAMPS are of smaller size. Of these, only 193 are functional today; 52 of these are making profits.

Most LAMPS were housed in one of the buildings/godowns of the service cooperative societies (SCSs) and the other SCSs in the area of operations were converted into branches or procurement/sales outlets. The recommended staffing pattern of five employees at the headquarters branch of the LAMPS include the managing director, an accountant-cum-branch manager, one store-keeper-cum-salesman, one peon and one watchman. The branches have three employees, one branch manager-cum-accountant, one storekeeper-cum-salesman and one peon-cum-watchman. Most of the employees of existing service cooperative societies instead of being retrenched were absorbed in the LAMPS due to political pressure, court orders, intervention of the Labour Department, or on humanitarian considerations. Thus, the viability of the LAMPS were doomed from inception itself due to excess staffing.

According to government guidelines, the managing director of the LAMPS was the key person to achieve the desired goal of the LAMPS and officers of ARCS rank with missionary zeal were to be posted to these sensitive posts. But in practice, unwanted ARCS were posted in one or two LAMPS while officers of SARCS rank were deputed to other LAMPS. As tribal areas did not have many infrastructural facilities or amenities, most SARCS were also not willing to work under adverse conditions without special incentives. Gradually, the SARCS were also withdrawn and today inspectors of cooperative societies or CCB employees are functioning as managing directors of LAMPS, providing poor quality leadership.

Functions of LAMPS

The LAMPS were re-designed as multi-purpose societies and could take up any economic activity. The entire tribal population was expected to be enrolled as members. In the management committee, eight out of 11 were to be tribal people and only one, a non-tribal. Consumption credit was to be given to tribals and no land mortgage was insisted upon as tribals had either no land or no record of rights. Loans could be given against personal sureties and tribal members were automatically 'A' class members while non-tribals were 'B' class members. Only 5 per cent share contribution was demanded from tribal members as against 10 per cent for others. Concessions were offered on long-term loan interest rates with longer repayment periods. Short-term and medium-term loans were given for agricultural and allied activities and also for handicrafts and cottage industries without mortgages. Block-level LAMPS were expected to disburse at least Rs 10 lakh per year while smaller LAMPS were to disburse Rs 5 lakh.

Various government agencies like ITDA, DRDA, etc., also provided financial assistance for share capital contributions up to Rs 40 per member so as to enable loan limits up to 20 times, and also gave risk-fund contributions to effect possible loans. Minimum collection stipulations were also dropped. For the first time, consumption credit up to Rs 250 was provided, repayable in 1–3 years, for medical expenses and social needs against personal surety only to those tribals selling SAP/MFP to the LAMPS, and an interest rebate of 2 per cent was also given on loan repayments. LAMPS were also appointed as collection agents for SAP and MFP on behalf of the Tribal Development Cooperative Corporation which was the sole leaseholder alongwith the OFDC.

All LAMPS branches at growth centres were to sell essential commodities and other consumer goods as also purchase SAP/MFP under the traditional barter system. LAMPS had to purchase goods only from the TDCC which was also expected to close down its procurement centres/consumer sales outlets—which it never did and offered unhealthy competition to the LAMPS. And where TDCC distribution was weak, LAMPS did not get consumer articles to sell. LAMPS, were also expected to sell agricultural inputs like seeds, fertilisers, raw materials for tribals engaged in cottage industries and handicraft activities besides small agricultural implements as the agents of the Orissa Agro-Industries Corporation. LAMPS having a good potential were encouraged to open agro-service centres and small processing units like oil crushers, huller units, etc., which could be hired on nominal charges by tribals.

The Realities of LAMPS in Orissa

Only 52 LAMPS of the total 223 are making profits and 30 are non-functional (1993–94 data). The total membership is 9.03 lakh of which 5.13 lakh are tribals, out of a total tribal population of 70 lakh. The number of borrowing members has been diminishing as is seen in Table 9.3.

Table 9.3
Ratio of Borrowing Members to Total Members

Year	Ratio of Borrowing Members to Total Members	Remarks
1980–81	30%	—
1986–87	12%	Debt-relief Scheme
1989–90	3%	Debt-relief Scheme
1994–95	6%	—

The mini-bank scheme has shown very good performance during the last two years and deposits have increased sharply. The increased aggressiveness in deposit mobilisation reflects the ability of LAMPS to change and function more efficiently.

Lending operations and recovery performance have not shown good results (See Table 9.4).

Table 9.4
Loan vs. Recovery Performance

(Rs lakh)

Year	Amount of Loan Disbursed	Recovery
1981–82	1,865	60%
1989–90	303	5%
1994–95	1,579	35%

The procurement of SAP/MFP by LAMPS has never been encouraging and has been restricted to the undivided Koraput and Mayurbhanj districts, mainly due to lack of coordination between LAMPS, TDCC and the Forest Department. This has benefited only the private traders at the expense of the tribals. Consumer business is poor, with an average business of only Rs 4 lakh per LAMPS per year. Unless a business turnover of Rs 30 lakh per LAMPS is achieved—with sale of mixed commodities including textiles, etc.—break-even business is not possible. A recent study by AFC of LAMPS in Orissa in 1996 has opined that the tangible net worth, capital funds and net working capital are negative in most LAMPS and there is no provision being made for bad debts. Even financial statements are not prepared in time and audit is in arrears for 2 to 3 years in some LAMPS. In most LAMPS, the committee members and staff are often not present; one of the reasons for poor operating results. No agro-processing of MFP is being done and private traders continue to proliferate and squeeze the tribals. There is a need for financial restructuring of LAMPS so as to make them self-supporting and viable institutions able to meet the tribal requirements. One of the factors affecting the profitability/viability of LAMPS is transportation charges for carrying goods from the purchasing centres to the inaccessible and remote tribal areas. The transportation subsidy for PDS and for Orissa State Cooperative Marketing Federation (OSCMF) supplied goods like fertilisers, seeds etc., are inadequate. The LAMPS have an uneconomic margin by way of commission after meeting all the charges for processing various materials, rendering all procurement/sales activities unviable.

Another major factor is the TDCC's unwillingness to appoint LAMPS as agents for procurement of SAP/MFP and in fact, private traders are appointed as sub-agents. Thus, LAMPS do not provide essential services and hence, the tribals do not depend on LAMPS. The share capital and managerial assistance provided to LAMPS is inadequate and there is need to restructure the share capital contribution of LAMPS members. The staffing pattern of LAMPS is not uniform and deputationists from CCBs, TDCC and Corporation Department have differing pay structures which affect LAMPS's viabilities and also staff morale and efficiency. Due to their weak financial condition, LAMPS are unable to invest in purchase of fertilisers for meeting the tribal farmers' requirements. Some LAMPS are even unable to pay the salaries of staff members. The official working hours of LAMPS are also often inconvenient to tribals and hence, business suffers.

Profitability and Break-even Levels of LAMPS

Out of the 223 LAMPS spread over different districts of the state, 210 are considered to be viable and 13 are potentially viable as per the assessment by the Corporation Department. As reported earlier, there are 9,03,000 members in all the LAMPS, of which 5,13,000 members belong to the ST community and 1,31,000 belong to the SC community. The total paid-up share capital of LAMPS is Rs 9.64 crore as on 31 March 1994. Reserves by way of apportionment of profits, made during the year as well as reserves in other forms amounted to Rs 6.51 crore. Total deposits amounted to Rs 4.23 crore and the borrowings made from higher agencies were Rs 23.56 crore. The working capital base of the LAMPS aggregated to Rs 60.95 crore. The total number of borrowers of LAMPS is estimated to be 65,000. Loan outstandings as on 30 June 1994 has been estimated at Rs 20.84 crore and the entire loan amount has been given for short-term agricultural operations. As per the latest report available on cooperative statistics, 52 LAMPS have been found in profit, making a total amount of Rs 20 lakh whereas 171 LAMPS have incurred losses aggregating Rs 3.46 crore.

In a study on the functioning of LAMPS and role of nationalised banks, made by AFC, most LAMPS have yet to attain the break-even level. For example, in case of a financial analysis carried out in respect of certain major LAMPS like Balliguda, Karanjia, Kamormunda, Patna, Udayagiri, it has been found that the net worth of these LAMPS is on the positive side, ranging from Rs 0.56 lakh to as high as Rs 10.03 lakh. These LAMPS were in profit, though marginal, as on 31 March 1994 (See Table 9.5).

Table 9.5
Details of Profit/Loss in Selected LAMPS

	(Rs lakh)
Name of the LAMPS	Profit or Loss
Balliguda	+ 1.19
Karanjia	+ 0.81
Kamormunda	+ 0.15
Patna	– 0.28

However, the low business turnover has impeded their functioning to a large extent. The average business turnover is as low as Rs 3 lakh per year. Moreover, the cost of management is found to be disproportionate to the volume of business. This needed further analysis—the ratio of cost of management to the gross income (see Table 9.6).

Table 9.6
Details of Cost of Management to Gross Income in Selected LAMPS

Name of the LAMPS	Cost of Management to Gross Income (%)
Balliguda	8.94
Karanjia	16.92
Komarmunda	4.53
Patna	18.59

Diversification of Activities of LAMPS

As a part of the diversification effort by LAMPS, some important activities like processing units in regard to agricultural produce, especially fruits and vegetables like tomatoes and mushrooms, can be given encouragement in the state.

The Regional Research Laboratory, Bhubaneswar, is equipped with the technical know-how regarding extraction of essential oils from aromatic grasses, plants and spices. This technology can be utilised by LAMPS through higher cooperative agencies under the MFP scheme.

Processing is essential to add value to the MFP, thereby benefiting the tribal people. Incidentally, most products can be processed at the primary stage right by the tribal people themselves. Very simple and less expensive decorticators are available for different seeds, such as tamarind products, sal seeds and mahua seeds. These activities are ideal for value addition. Therefore, LAMPS should diversify their activities in extending financial support to the target scheme of the population for these activities. The production of kusumi lac also has a good scope and can be given encouragement in three specific districts, i.e., Keonjhar, Koraput and Kalahandi. Lac cultivation is spread over nine districts; of them, Keonjhar and Sundargarh have already been identified as districts for lac cultivation. These activities can be further promoted with financial assistance from LAMPS.

Revitalisation of LAMPS

LAMPS have been set up with wide-ranging objectives to enable the tribal members to be self-sufficient. For the complete involvement of the tribals, LAMPS have to be restructured—both financially and organisationally in order to enable them to achieve the goals of tribal empowerment and financial stability. The manpower development and training needs of LAMPS have to be met by on-site training programmes as the tribals rarely prefer leaving their area of operations. The OSCB has already prepared a draft MoU for LAMPS and PACSs to be signed by the DCCBs and PACSs/ LAMPS so that their functioning is rendered viable and profitable. Certain practical suggestions for strengthening LAMPS and thereby empowering the tribals have been made in the Annexure 9.1. These have been made on the basis of various studies and need to be implemented on an urgent basis.

However, there are a few more suggestions for economic upliftment of the tribals using the credit-oriented process as a lever of development.

(a) LAMPS operating in tribal areas need persons who are sympathetic to the tribals and their way of life. Postings in tribal areas are generally not preferred by most officials. So implementation of a system of rewards for working in tribal areas say, in the form of weightage in promotion, educational allowance for the children, additional health and LFC facilities, extra remuneration, etc., will be a desirable step to induce quality staff. Most branches have no vehicular facility for mobility of the staff. Motorcycles or cycles should be provided to these branches on a priority basis.

(b) Lack of entrepreneurship/awareness is one of the main reasons for the economic backwardness of the tribals. Bank branches in coordination with the developmental departments of the state government/ NGOs should, therefore, undertake entrepreneurship development programmes and also provide adequate finance so that the tribals can undertake investment ventures. The bank may form farmers' clubs in the tribal areas, with financial support from NABARD under the Vikas Volunteer Vahini Programme, to further principles of development through credit in order to ensure proper utilisation of loans and satisfactory recovery.

(c) The security-oriented lending approach of banks is a hindrance in the flow of adequate credit to the tribal areas. The banks insist on security—two to three times of the loan assistance provided. While the present security norms merit further relaxation by the RBI, a system may be developed by the state government to provide guarantee for payment of interest and repayment of principal by tribal borrowers, particularly for these who do not possess the requisite ownership of land. Land records should also be set right so that the tribals can avail of loans from the banks, wherever necessary, against land mortgage.

The timing of provision of tribal credit is also an important factor. In Orissa, the tribals observe a festival called *'Nuakhai'* some time around August/September, when new clothes, new household items, etc., have to be purchased as also feasts organised. As the harvest season is only in January/February, it is not possible for banks to lend money for festival requirements against future produce. So, the tribals are forced to depend on traders/middlemen/agents who give small loan amounts against future produce/sales. Thus, the middlemen/agents/traders are able to purchase produce at very low rates. In tribal areas, the crop production loan should have three components:

- Production component in cash (30 per cent).
- Kind component (seeds, fertilisers, pesticides, agricultural components—40 per cent)
- Marketing/consumption component in cash (30 per cent) for meeting festival/social obligations.

This will enable the tribal farmers to escape from the clutches of the traders/agents/money-lenders, who are now able to exploit the tribals year after year. The third 'cash' component should be given as and when required by the tribal farmers for festival/consumption purpose under relaxed conditions.

(d) SHGs having linkages with the financing banks may be encouraged among the tribals. This innovative credit dispensation system not only reduces the transaction costs of the banks and borrowers, but also enables leadership development, meets emergent credit requirements and ensures recovery of loans. The 100 per cent refinance facility available from NABARD for financing of SHGs may be availed of by the banks.

The Sri Lanka experiment known as Community Credit Facilitators (CCFs) Scheme may be adopted in tribal areas. The scheme has enabled people in Sri Lanka to obtain loan facilities conveniently at reasonable rates of interest through the CCFs, who are appointed by the banks for routing loans through them. As the tribals are more inclined to deal with a person whom they know well rather than with banks, the CCF scheme could be ideally implemented in the tribal areas.

SHGs can be set up on a village-wise basis with the LAMPS as a federating unit.

(e) The procurement activities of line organisations need improvement to save the tribals from exploitation. LAMPS, TDCC and other agencies should cooperate and coordinate among themselves and other apex organisations in the state as also with national level federations like TRIFED and NAFED.

According to the Government, it should be ensured that LAMPS function as agents for procurement of SAP and MFP in all tribal sub-plan areas on commission basis. Funds for the purpose may, therefore, be placed with LAMPS well in advance. The State Cooperative Marketing Federation (SCMF) or the TDCC may ensure marketing of the produce collected by LAMPS on a priority basis. The LAMPS too, should properly utilise the funds given for procurement without diverting the same for meeting their administrative expenditure.

The credit support available from NABARD for the development of lac cultivation and collection and marketing of minor forest produce has not been availed of by the OSCB. As these are primarily meant for the tribals, the OSCB should take advantage of the facility.

(f) Tribals are still being caught in the exploitative clutches of traders, middlemen and money-lenders and sell their produce at prices dictated by the exploiters. Due to poor finances, the TDCC and the OSCMF are unable to procure the entire MFP/SAP and make timely payments. Both the cooperative agencies have been running on losses for the last several years. The state government should make a detailed study of the functioning of these two premier agencies and initiate suitable measures for re-establishing their effectiveness. Processing units should be set up in tribal areas taking into consideration the quantum of procurement and demand in the market. This will not only create additional employment opportunities for the tribals but also add value to their produce and fetch a better price. These processing units may be set up by LAMPS/OSCMF/TDCC and other tribal development organisations.

Issues

The economic activities of the tribals have to be linked to the restructuring of LAMPS as a first step towards the tribal people's participation in their own empowerment. Else, they run the risk of being permanently sidelined in the economic liberalisation process that has been initiated by the government without a social safety net for neglected and deprived people. An integrated approach is needed if the tribal people of Orissa are to claim their rightful place in the state's economy.

A vast chunk of the tribal population in Orissa lives in remote and hilly areas. The natural isolation has deprived them of the fruits of development, they are far behind the mainstream on social, cultural and economic fronts. Their problems are mainly due to ignorance, illiteracy, rigid adherence to traditional faiths, poverty, unhelpful terrain and lack of communications. All these combine to encourage traders and middlemen. Despite getting very low prices for their goods and being cheated in weights, a majority of tribal households continue to sell their produce to the traders/middlemen; they also buy their essential requirements from them and remain indebted.

Even after the reorganisation of cooperative societies (1975–78), creation of various institutions to serve them, initiation of several stringent measures by the state government and enforcing them rigidly, exploitation has not been checked. As a result, the tribal economy continues to be marginalised. A piecemeal approach will fetch no results; an integrated approach to develop and sustain the tribal economy is a must. Development should not be forced down their throats. The need for good-quality NGOs to take up work in these areas is felt acutely.

Annexure 9.1

Revamping LAMPS: Some Recommendations

To strengthen the functioning of LAMPS, the following recommendations may be given effect.

1. The large area of operations of LAMPS has made them less effective in meeting the demands of the tribals. Task forces, comprising DRCS/Secretary, DCCB/PO, ITDA belonging to respective districts and select representatives of LAMPS, may, therefore, be constituted to suggest the service area, volume/mix of business, margin, staffing pattern, etc., for viable and effective LAMPS. No direct or indirect recruitment may be permitted till the LAMPS are reorganised and staffing norms prescribed.

2. The pay and allowances of the staff may be made commensurate with the business level, and provide for minimum salary. Incentive schemes may be introduced for enhancing business level and recovery performance. Incentive schemes could also apply to directors and presidents.

3. Although, it is the responsibility of LAMPS to arrange for loan recovery drives, the support and intervention of state government agencies are inevitable in view of the adverse climate for recovery. The following steps need to be initiated to improve the recovery climate, which holds the key for viability:

    (a) Loan procedures and policies should be revamped to avoid delays in disbursement.

    (b) Defaults should be studied on a case-by-case basis and strategies evolved for recovery.

    (c) Supervisor-wise recovery targets should be fixed and the recovery performance be carefully monitored and appropriate remedial steps be taken for achieving the target.

    (d) The state government should not interfere in the recovery process except in declaring *'Annewari'* for rephasing/rescheduling of loan instalments in natural calamities, etc., as per the guidelines.

4. Credit discipline should be inculcated and it should be made part of all training programmes for officials. They should be exposed to training on recovery ethics, discipline and imperatives.

5. The LAMPS staff may be vested with adequate powers to handle 'execution petition' filed cases.

6. A uniform service code may be developed and implemented at the earliest.

7. Imbalances may be avoided by strengthening recovery and passing on the same to the DCCBs.

8. Audits of accounts should be streamlined and made up-to-date; an audit calendar prepared for strict compliance; and, vigilance maintained through special audit and inspection of records without prior intimation.

9. The management information (MI) system needs to be established/revamped to meet the requirement of emerging challenges. An expert in the field be identified and appointed to work out appropriate MI and accounting system (preferably computer based).

10. As a result of PDS, LAMPS are incurring small losses each year when only the revenue receipts and expenditures are taken into consideration. But when the cost of capital is also added, average annual erosion of funds per lakhs of rupees is to the tune of Rs 880 for Ganjam and Rs 723 for Dhenkanal district after accommodating consumer subsidies received by consumer societies.

11. Imposition of flat margins (Rs 15 per bag) in case of all commodities except kerosene puts far-flung and inaccessible LAMPS at a loss.

12. Most LAMPS deal only in sugar and kerosene. Wheat, rice or palmolein are seldom dealt in.

13. Most LAMPS have reported that there is always a shortage of 2–5 kg per bag in the case of sugar at the time of taking delivery from wholesalers. The latter refuse to weigh prior to purchase.

14. Transportation of commodities from the wholesaler's godown to retailing points is the responsibility of retailers. This involves huge costs as transportation facilities in rural areas are inadequate.

15. Supply of commodities by wholesalers is irregular. Different commodities are supplied at different times; nearly three times a month on an average. LAMPS thus have to pay more on transportation.

16. Some measures suggested for profitability of PDS operations of LAMPS are:

    (a) Supply to retail centres may be made the responsibility of wholesalers.

    (b) LAMPS may be permitted to open PDS accounts with CCBs and pay by cheque for the supplies.

    (c) Licensing procedures for PDS operations may be simplified. It need not require annual renewal.

    (d) Margins for sugar transactions may be increased to 28 paise per kg.

    (e) Supply may be streamlined.

    (f) Margin in case of wheat and rice may be increased to Rs 20 per bag.

    (g) LAMPS located at block headquarters may be encouraged to take up wholesale activities for PDS.

17. Human resource development in LAMPS needs the attention of policy makers. Practical training and orientation courses may be imparted to the staff as well as directors of LAMPS. Cost consciousness may be emphasised.

18. Procurement of SAP and MFP, distribution of agricultural inputs and essential consumer goods, and area-specific innovative functions need to be greatly increased. This is especially so in essential consumer goods operations in view of the potential profits.

19. As regards the deposit-tapping functions, the commission allowed to LAMPS by CCBs, may be raised to 2 per cent for savings bank and 4 per cent for recurring and fixed deposits.

20. LAMPS have inherited some bad and irrecoverable loans due to excess financing over the repaying capacity of their members. The loss arising out of bad debts need be shared by all the members of three-tier credit structure, i.e., LAMPS, CCBs and SCBs in the ratio of 60:20:20.

21. Targets for financing different schemes by the government at the state level and its compulsory implementation at the district level sometimes lead to bad finance with loans being given to the wrong persons. Before fixing targets, the felt needs of members should be ascertained and proper identification of beneficiary/loanee should be made at the level of LAMPS to avoid wrong financing and misutilisation.

22. Consumption loans must be given to meet the needs of tribals in off-seasons in the form of an advance for MFP purchase. However, LAMPS personnel should approach them for procurement of MFP early in the season, so that the consumption loan advance is recovered. Thus, a method of linking credit with marketing can be implemented and the tribals will not be compelled to go to unscrupulous traders and money-lenders. These consumption loans should be given in times of need preferably in shape of daily necessities instead of cash.

23. Credit should be available to LAMPS at the right time before commencement of rabi and kharif seasons.

24. In order to increase the working capital of LAMPS, the government of Orissa should contribute more as share capital, besides giving a working capital loan at concessional rate of interest. Soft loans should be extended to LAMPS by the state government to carry on fertiliser business and PDS business.

25. Marketing of new items like oilseeds, sabai grass, pulses, etc., may be exclusively given to LAMPS.

26. No private agent should be allowed to undertake procurement operations of SAP and MFP in tribal areas.

27. Market price should be fixed before selling the goods. Absence of sales centres at the district level sometimes creates barriers for LAMPS. District-level tribal societies may be organised to meet the need.

28. The margin available for procurement of SAP and MFP is considered to be much less in comparison to the expenditure involved in it. The margin should be increased so as to strengthen LAMPS.

29. All LAMPS should be allowed to undertake independent procurement of SAP and MFP, preferably as a lease holder. Therefore, it is suggested that the government or NCDC should provide funds at a concessional rate.

30. Small-scale units for turmeric and chilly grinding, and sal leaf and lac processing units should be set up in selected LAMPS with financial assistance from NCDC.

31. The margin fixed for LAMPS on fertiliser business is much less as compared to that for the OSCMF. Therefore, more commission should be given to minimise losses.

32. The transportation charges on fertiliser available to LAMPS is not sufficient to meet the cost. It should be increased suitably.

33. Consumer business is greatly affected by the paucity of funds. Therefore, adequate funds from the state government or NCDC or centrally-sponsored scheme may be provided to rehabilitate the weaker LAMPS.

34. The civil supplies authority should ensure timely release of stocks from storage agents and extend door delivery facilities at the retail outlet points.

35. The stock should be supplied considering the regional variation of demand in order to prevent unnecessary stockpiling in certain items and scanty supply in others.

36. Prudent funds management is necessary for restricting the diversion of funds from the consumer section; fresh financial assistance may be given to the societies for increasing their credit business.

37. Government land should be made available to the cooperatives free of cost or at a nominal price, preferably in the vicinity of the local market to open sales centres and give better facilities to consumers.

38. For the distribution of consumer goods by LAMPS at various branches, mini delivery vans or *Tempos* (luggage carriers) should be supplied.

39. The Board Management should be vested with the power to decide on clearance sale of slow moving stock and writing off of damaged stock, say at half-yearly intervals.

40. Well-trained personnel, both, in maintaining accounts and undertaking business expansion should be appointed with appropriate pay levels.

10

Credit for the Rural Non-farm Sector

The rural non-farm sector provides employment to over 45 million people and is estimated to generate a quarter of all rural employment. This includes employment for small/marginal farmers and landless agricultural labourers, especially during the non-crop seasons. Income from non-farm activities contributes about 30 per cent of the total income of rural households. With land resources being limited, especially quality arable land with irrigation facilities, and population growth estimated at 2.3 per cent every year, the rural non-farm sector has to employ a vast number of unskilled labourers and has been creating about 1.5 million new jobs every year. However, in this sector household manufacturing has been declining while transport, business and legal services, miscellaneous services and trades, and public administration are growing fast. Manufacturing activities (30 per cent), powerlooms, handlooms, agro-processing industries are the 'sunrise' industries. The services sector provides 60 per cent of rural employment.

The rural non-farm sector serves as an important safety net for many rural households in times of natural calamities. It also provides an opportunity for rural women to take up remunerative work beyond casual labour and household labour. The growth of the rural non-farm sector has had a positive impact on poverty alleviation and benefited most sections of rural society. However, wealthier rural households benefit most by way of increased non-farm incomes. This has enhanced rural income disparities to some extent. But working conditions are certainly better here than in the rural farm sector as wages are higher and child labour a lot less as more education and skills are required. As per the 1991 Census, 48.4 per cent of rural workers are cultivators and 31.6 per cent are agricultural labourers; only 6 per cent are in rural services, with the remaining in various sub-sectors of the rural economy. According to the Economic Census, 1990, there are 12.5 million rural micro-enterprises employing 29.1 million people, with 39 per cent of the units in trading, 28 per cent in other services and 27 per cent in manufacturing.

Most rural non-farm sector units are tiny but there are larger undertakings—two million rural labourers working in manufacturing establishments and another two million in factories. However, except in Punjab, which is developed agriculturally as also in the non-farm sector, there is no correlation between agricultural production and rural non-farm sector employment. Rural non-farm activities are not confined to traditional village industries but cover a vast range across the primary, secondary and tertiary sectors.

As employment and incomes in the rural non-farm sector are increasing, this sector has become economically dominant and an important part of the structural changes in the rural economy. With an increased employment growth rate of 8.1 per cent, the rural non-farm sector could create about 45.2 million additional jobs by A.D. 2001.

Rural Micro-enterprises

There is no specific definition of micro-enterprises or of rural micro-entrepreneurs but the rural non-farm sector would comprise:

- Small and marginal farmers who undertake some agro-processing activities.
- Rural artisans and craftsmen and those engaged in cottage industries.
- Units covered under the khadi and village industries boards (located in towns not exceeding a population of 50,000, involving utilisation of local labour and natural resources and with credit requirements not exceeding Rs 50,000).
- Tiny industries, with investment in plant and machinery not exceeding Rs 25 lakh.
- All IRDP (industries and small business) borrowers.
- 82 per cent of SSIs (with investment not exceeding Rs 1 lakh)

These micro-enterprises contribute about 40 per cent of the gross industrial turnover and 34 per cent of total exports. Various incentives to enhance the competitive strength of the SSI sector are given by the central and state governments, including reservation of certain items of production, lower tariffs, purchase preferences, priority in supply of credit, technology upgradation and entrepreneurial development.

By 2001, it is estimated that bank credit worth Rs 31,800 crore would be necessary for creating 45.2 million jobs in the rural non-farm sector, with 60 per cent coming from the institutional sector and the remaining from the informal sector. For such a high level of credit support, rural credit agencies would have to be considerably strengthened. There should be a congenial and productive labour climate, adequate policy and infrastructure support as also adequate linkages support.

Constraints of Micro-enterprises in Rural Areas

In a World Bank Report discussed in the Micro-credit Summit in Washington, it was mentioned that only 2 per cent of micro-enterprises in developing countries had access to financial services; others had to rely on own funds or borrow from informal sources. Various studies have analysed the problems of micro-enterprises that inhibit their access to institutional/government help as also to larger domestic/foreign markets. Some of the major constraints identified are:

- Tendency to remain small due to lack of resources.
- Lack of adequate infrastructural support in rural areas (power, communication, markets).
- Market information regarding inputs and outputs.
- Economies of scale.
- Inadequate technological transformation to meet market quality standards.
- Inability to access financial capital.
- Lack of standards and standardisation.
- Absence of 'brand equity' to enter niche markets.
- Absence of clear-cut government policies.

All these problems can be taken care of by concerted approaches by various institutions such as the government, banks, industries sector, NGOs, producers' associations and export promotion agencies. Countries such as China, Malaysia, Singapore, Thailand, Japan and Korea which have adopted this coordinated approach have been able to progress at fantastic rates since the mid-80s. A 'soft state' like India is unable to take certain 'hard' decisions on the growth model for the rural economy and hence, there is chaos and confusion on the policy front!

Credit Needs for Micro-enterprises

There are over 150,000 credit retail outlets of commercial banks (both public and private sector), regional rural banks and cooperative banks. Public sector banks are expected to provide 40 per cent of the total lending to the priority sector comprising small-scale industries, small rural-transport operators, etc., with 18 per cent earmarked for agriculture. Further, of the IRDP loans, 40 per cent is supposed to be earmarked for industries and small business. The khadi and village industries boards of different states are expected to provide concessional loans (short-term or long-term) to certified khadi and village industrial organisations.

The need for non-farm sector credit was addressed in 1982, with the creation of NABARD. The creation of SIDBI in 1990 opened another channel for SSIs. However, rural industries have not benefited much from SIDBI as its resources are cornered by urban SSI units. Both SIDBI and NABARD have a number of promotional and developmental programmes, including primary marketing support, upgrading technology and adopting areas for special development inputs. However, the village industries sector is estimated to have received only 4.1 per cent of the total outstanding of Rs 13,960 crore (end-March 1992) while bank credit for rural services aggregated Rs 5,080 crore for the same period with retail traders accounting for 51 per cent of the total outstandings. Some sections of the rural non-farm sector have had better access such as large export-oriented units, powerlooms, hosiery, ceramics, cement and plastics.

INFORMAL SECTOR CREDIT

Money-lenders rarely provide credit for capital assets acquisition. They concentrate on lending for consumption needs and social/medical contingencies while trader-lenders provide working capital. Thus, venture capital for the rural non-farm sector is generally financed from own resources and supplemented by loans from friends and relatives. The time taken for getting a loan sanctioned by a bank for the rural non-farm sector can vary from two months to 18 months. Some money-lenders do provide bridge loans to those rural borrowers who have been sanctioned bank loans but have yet to receive the funds.

INSTITUTIONAL SECTOR CREDIT

Of the total credit flow from banks to the small-scale sector during 1993–94, 1994–95 and 1995–96, the proportion of credit to the tiny sector was between 27.4 per cent to 30.0 per cent. The break-up is given in Table 10.1.

Table 10.1
Credit to Tiny Sector

(Rs crore)

Purpose	1993–94	1994–95	1995–96
Credit to SSIs	21,561	25,843	29,482
Credit to Tiny Sector	5,896	7,734	8,183
Per cent of Tiny Sector to Total Outstanding	27.4	30.0	27.8

Banks' advances outstanding for SSI sector constituted 14 per cent of total loans outstanding on 31 March 1996.

Credit Policy for Rural Non-farm Sector

In a country as vast as India, with great divergence in social and economic levels, a single strategy or approach may not be feasible. Multi-pronged strategies for promotion of micro-enterprises, including stable policy institutions, providing different types of financial products and adoption of promotional approaches (credit and non-credit), are needed. While credit by itself does not bring about economic development, it is an important input in any economic activity. The constraints of micro-enterprises and the need for looking beyond credit have to be recognised while framing appropriate policies for assisting their growth. The strategies can be summed up as:

- Target group specific approaches.
- Area or region specific approaches.
- Sector or issue specific approaches.

Policies will have to also address the need for strengthening the credit delivery system and for developing entrepreneurs/enterprises.

Credit packages have to be designed to meet short-term requirements for day-to-day operations and also term loans to meet the cost of plant and machinery and other infrastructure. Short-term loans are generally for periods not exceeding 12 months while term loans normally do not exceed 15 years. These credit packages disbursed by rural credit agencies, with the assistance of NABARD, cover the traditional sector comprising handlooms, sericulture, handicrafts, coir and modern industries. In the case of industries, credit is given for manufacturing/processing and services, small road transport operators, infrastructure and marketing development, setting up of new units, and modernisation/renovation/expansion/diversification of existing units.

Other facilities such as guarantees, letters of credit, bills purchase/discounting facilities, etc., are also provided by the banking system.

Credit Strategies for the Future

Certain credit strategies for the future will need to be prioritised.

Government Policies and Interventions

The central/state governments have to create a conducive environment for growth of the rural economy and make a conscious policy commitment for the growth of micro-enterprises. This approach has been successfully demonstrated in Italy, Japan, etc., which are strong in micro-enterprises. As this sector is financially not very strong, the state could help in maintaining high quality standards and also provide RED (research, extension and development) support to micro-enterprises to enable them to compete in developing/global markets. Developing India as a strong brand name—as has been done for say, China and Japan—also needs to be taken up so as to enable micro-enterprises to enter 'niche' markets. A number of strong brand names will have to be developed through technology promotion and high quality export products.

Assistance from Rural Credit Agencies

The credit flow for the micro-enterprise sector should have thrust, direction and a clear, long-term vision of growth. Identification of potential areas/activities and development of a sub-sectoral approach based on potential, needs to be followed up. The SHG approach to micro-enterprises, especially for rural women, tribal people and the rural non-farm sector, will be a useful supplementary channel for rural credit delivery. Banks need to adopt credit-linked promotional packages for rural micro-entrepreneurs. The use of reliable NGOs, with a good track record in serving the rural people, is a must for developing strong bank-SHG linkages which would help in timely credit delivery, drastic reduction in transaction costs and better loan repayment rates. NABARD/SIDBI may give a thrust to sunrise industries for continuous technology upgradation and technology transfer.

Role of Promotional Organisations

Development of data-based information systems and dissemination of information, especially for market identification and penetration, would benefit the micro-enterprises sector. Exchange of information on technologies/strategies between developing countries for mutual benefit should also be explored.

11

Credit for Rural Women

Given our male-dominated rural society, it is not surprising to note that prior to the 1990s, there were hardly any credit schemes designed for rural women. It is only after women-oriented studies highlighted the deprivation and struggle for survival that the concept of women's credit was born. There is growing realisation that rural women have been underestimated and discriminated against in all walks of life, despite their substantial contribution to the household economy and in turn, the national economy. The UN Commission on Status of Women observed 'women who contribute half of the world's population by virtue of an accident of birth, perform two-thirds of the world's work, receive one-tenth of its income and own less than one-hundredth of its property.' In India, women produce 30 per cent of all food commodities consumed but get only 10 per cent of the income, and own 10 per cent of the property or wealth of the country.

It is clear that provision of rights and protection from social inequalities in statute books are not enough. Women have been deprived of their economic status, especially in rural areas. Thus, the empowerment of women and improvement of their status and economic role needs to be integrated into economic development programmes.

Rural women, especially those belonging to the weaker sections of society have limited access to resources or employment opportunities that would make them financially independent. They live in conditions that do not permit them to meet bare minimum consumption needs. Even the money earned by them from hard physical labour is not controlled by them. Institutional credit is difficult to access as women rarely have any property rights to mortgage or collateral to offer, and they have to depend on rural money-lenders for their production-cum-consumption needs. This entraps them into a vicious cycle of perpetual poverty and indebtedness. The rural men do not welcome NGOs/SHGs working for the uplift of women as an economically independent woman is perceived as a threat to their male dominance. That a woman's savings/earnings are generally used for the family is conveniently forgotten!

The Tamil Nadu Women's Development Project

This project was taken up in four districts of Tamil Nadu from 1989–90 onwards with IFAD, Washington, assistance and with Indian Bank as the sole banker. Poor rural women were organised in SHGs to undertake both social and economic development activities. The main objectives of the project were:

- To ensure uplift of women, economically and socially.
- To enhance the welfare of assisted families.
- To improve the status of women in the family and community and empower them to gain access to resources.
- To foster confidence among women by organising strong supportive groups.

The project is surprisingly akin to the IRDP, but the distinguishing feature is the induction of NGOs to identify target groups and organise them into SHGs within the village, motivate and guide the rural women, and provide small amounts of credit for emergency, social or production purposes. This project was successful, with recovery levels at the rate of 80 per cent in areas where IRDP recovery was around 26–40 per cent and non-profit NGOs had recovery levels of 95 per cent. The project has largely achieved its aims, even though initially the identification of women beneficiaries was not properly done as the poorer women in the villages were excluded. However, this was rectified soon and their involvement sought. Of the over 8,000 SHGs organised by NGOs with NABARD refinance linkages, 95 per cent are women SHGs. The success of the 'participatory supervised credit model' presents both an opportunity and a challenge.

Credit for Women

So far, rural credit packages had been exclusively male-oriented and women were largely ignored. However, with various supervisory credit programmes for rural women and the number of SHGs exclusively for women, the neglect of earlier years is being slowly erased. But the economic empowerment of women can only be marginally improved upon by such programmes. Certain other production-oriented programmes like women's dairy cooperatives (GOI programme since 1995–96), etc., have had a positive impact in states like Orissa and Bihar.

A large number of case studies on women SHGs reveals that individually these women had accepted their poverty and miseries as due to divine fate or destiny and had little hope of improving their lot in life. But, the formation of SHGs has led to a growing awareness, education and availability of information has led to confidence-building and the ability to handle complex issues. Those very same women are now able to deal with banks, government officials and NGOs, very successfully.

Various case studies in Orissa show that there is a positive correlation between credit availability and women's empowerment. Rather than concentrating on a fragmented approach for savings or credit only, an integrated approach for development of women offers greater scope. NGOs keen on forming women SHGs should have expertise in education, rural health and hygiene, tribal development, etc. Savings and credit functions should be developed along with the other capabilities of members so as to provide a framework for economic activities.

Government Programmes

The Development of Women and Children in Rural Areas (DWCRA) programme has been an important adjunct to the Integrated Rural Development Programme (IRDP), which was launched in 1980. The IRDP is a unique programme in view of its vast coverage, but it does not target women specifically. In 1996–97, women covered under IRDP credit were about 34 per cent of the total.

For example, the SEWA Bank is a cooperative bank for women who are poor and self-employed, operating in Ahmedabad. The clientele is serviced through a team of mobile workers visiting specified collection areas, on specified days. Transaction costs for bank loans, which are as high as 24 per cent for women elsewhere, are only 1–8 per cent of the loan amount. The SEWA Bank emphasises that poor women can also serve and be good borrowers despite their erratic income pattern. Other NGOs like PRADAN, MYRADA, CDF, etc., have formed SHGs exclusively for women which have been highly successful. The DWCRA ensures that women are organised in some production activity of their choice and then are provided training. Funds (part loan and part subsidy) are given on soft terms for tools or asset creation with a revolving fund for ensuring production and marketing. The Prime Minister's Rojgar Yojana (PMRY) is also an important poverty alleviation programme though women are not a specific target group.

Group Financing

Credit for women is a concept which has come to India only in the late 1980s and suffers from the rural problems of screening, monitoring, enforcement and bias. One novel solution has been group lending with joint liability. Group credit schemes involve borrowers to form homogeneous groups which reduce transaction costs both for the lender and the borrower. Group credit also reduces monitoring costs by involving group members to monitor loan usage and repayment. If any member defaults, it leads to denial of further credit to the group members. However, joint asset management is a risky concept as there is no ownership by individuals who ensure proper use and repair of assets.

Group lending has proved that credit worthiness is critical in reducing default risk. However, group formation risks are high and a period of loan amortisation is needed for better repayment.

In contrast, the SHGs set up by NGOs, with the assistance of bank linkage, ensures individual loans for women beneficiaries and individual/joint liability for repayment. The stress is less on asset creation and more on production-cum-consumption loans, ensuring quicker repayment and less borrower fatigue in loan repayment. The repayment rate is much higher in SHGs as there is no subsidy involved.

Cooperative Development Foundation, Hyderabad

The Cooperative Development Foundation (CDF) has supported over 95 women's thrift cooperatives in Warangal and Karimnagar districts of Andhra Pradesh. It offers savings and credit services to members. Besides it promotes urban and rural, workplace and neighbourhood women's and men's thrift cooperatives in Andhra Pradesh, Karnataka, Goa and Tamil Nadu. It has formed regional associations and federates these for common financial services. There were 21,170 members of the women thrift societies with total savings of Rs 130 lakh (on 31 March 1998). Loans outstanding are over 86.2 per cent of the loanable funds. Overdues contributed only 1.32 per cent of total funds while average loan size was Rs 1401. There were 54 men's thrift societies, with 9,608 members and savings amounting to Rs 55.19 lakh. Overdues are only 1.07 per cent of total loans outstanding at Rs 65.61 lakh. Average savings per member was Rs 574 and the average loan size was Rs 1,748.

The Cooperative Revolving Fund increased to Rs 308 lakh and is used by production cooperatives for the purpose of agro-processing, marketing, acquisition of equipment and asset building, on-lending as also equipment and asset building for cooperative thrift and credit systems. There is no bank linkage at all envisaged in the programme and the stress is on self-sufficiency. CDF believes that the cooperative form of organisation when successful, results in increased income and savings for families, increased purchasing power and increased employment opportunities for rural people.

MYRADA, Bangalore—Alternate Credit Systems

The preferred mode of credit and other institution-building activities had been through cooperative societies based on the success stories of the Tibetan Cooperative Societies organised during the 1970s. But the accidental break-up of a cooperative society at Kadiri into 14 small groups due to mutual distrust led to better functioning. Initially, working capital loans were permitted. From 1984–85, MYRADA built up village development groups for poor families which were large in size, and a conscious decision was taken for women's groups which were small-sized and participative in nature. The major purpose was to inculcate the savings habit with regular meetings every week, literacy and numeracy being taken up and minimum attendance at 75 per cent. Bank books, such as attendance registers and minutes books were maintained, prepared by the group. These voluntary savings groups were small, homogeneous and voluntary in nature and succeeded in empowering the poor women from rural areas. Since 1987, NABARD actively assisted these efforts and considerable Government aid was also received. Loans given were very tiny in a majority of the cases. MYRADA emphasised in the groups that savings come from essentials not from surplus; daily savings were encouraged. The project has been successful in Tamil Nadu, Karnataka and Andhra Pradesh.

SEWA, Ahmedabad: Beyond Survival

The poor need to move beyond the struggle for survival by building structures and mechanisms that will increase their assets and economic security. The poor need assets if they are able to break the cycle of subsistence, deprivation and survival. Poor women need to be able to borrow and save so that they can have economic independence. The SEWA Cooperative Bank caters exclusively to its women members and has a 96 per cent loan repayment record. Women with assets are able to fight poverty and exploitation better. Asset ownership is also safer in the hands of women than men. Men spend 45–55 per cent of their income on themselves while women spend less than 5 per cent of their income on themselves. SEWA also has a social security system for poor women and believes in empowerment of women through democratic processes.

Credit for Women Entrepreneurs

Some banks notably SBI have formulated specific schemes for women entrepreneurs and have specific training course for developing their skills. But in many cases, it is husbands of the women entrepreneurs, who may be employed elsewhere, who are the real beneficiaries and decision-makers while the women take a back-seat once the loan is sanctioned. However, this is true more for large loans for SSI ventures. The needs of rural women entrepreneurs are limited and the micro-credit approach would be more useful for them. The potential for small savings should be utilised and their production-cum-consumption needs are much less and especially in the SHG system, rarely misused. In fact, the income from the micro-enterprises is generally used for the betterment of the families, especially children. Thus, there is a need to target the flow of credit to women SHGs and rural women entrepreneurs.

The experience of women SHGs in Orissa linked with bank finance is that transaction costs are reduced for both the rural banks and the rural women borrowers, repayment exceeds 95 per cent and credit is available on time. Women are able to manage their credit operations very practically and are able to face the future with a greater degree of confidence. Thus, banks need to reorient themselves to handle the needs of women entrepreneurs with a focus on the micro-credit needs of poor rural women.

Evolving New Strategies

There is a need for reorientation as regards micro-credit needs of rural women, using new production, distribution channels and promotional services, based on the perceived needs of women entrepreneurs in rural areas. As the need for credit is in frequent but small doses, innovative savings-linked cash credits, may be the answer as these will provide safety, liquidity and lower transaction costs. The credit programmes should be based on savings and credit alone should not be made the basis for group formation. These savings can also be used for emergent family needs such as consumption, medical needs and for social/religious needs.

Collateral should not be insisted upon for loans below Rs 1,000 if the previous history of repayment is good and the savings have been satisfactory. For loans up to Rs 5,000, the purpose of loan need not be insisted upon if adequate collateral is available. If the collateral is inadequate then a graduated system of loans with short maturity periods can be devised with the loan amounts gradually increasing. A composite loan system (including term and working capital requirements) can be devised for loans up to Rs 25,000 for women entrepreneurs running village industries so as to ensure timely credit both for assets and for working capital. Insurance needs also have to be met and rural credit agencies could provide for integration of income with credit, after discussions with insurance companies. Insurance should be required for the life of the women borrowers, for the assets purchased with the loan and for loan repayment in the event of the borrower's death. Finally, training in cash and funds management, marketing and packaging and credit management has to be provided to women micro-entrepreneurs.

12

Credit for Micro-enterprise Development

In developing countries with vast sections of the population caught up in the web of poverty, the challenge is to generate enough employment and income opportunities for the rural and urban poor, but in a sustainable manner. Micro-enterprises can play an important role in improving the quality of life and poverty alleviation. Ensuring their success is cost-effective and enables the vulnerable sections, such as women and weaker sections of society, to smooth over seasonal fluctuations in household income.

Globalisation and economic liberalisation with the doctrine of free markets, have opened up tremendous opportunities. But without a 'safety net', these economic changes are making the marginalised and poor sections of society more vulnerable. The profit at all costs approach of the huge commercial conglomerates (MNCs and TNCs) concentrates on cost-cutting through technological improvements and ignore the needs of the people. With the developed countries and institutions like IMF/World Bank increasingly dictating economic and social policies under the ploy of structural adjustments, economic transformation is being hammered through at the cost of social development.

Economic development without social development can only increase tensions and friction within any society. In developing countries, where only a handful are rich, ignoring the poorer sections of the population, is a sure recipe for disaster. In our country, if civilised society is to be maintained, all development efforts have to be people-oriented. After many years of centralised planning, it is clear that employment cannot be ensured by the government. The industrial and agricultural sectors are unable to absorb the growing labour force. Micro-enterprises, whether in the informal or organised sectors, provide opportunities for gainful employment while preserving the social structure.

Characteristic Features

Micro-enterprises are all pervasive in the large informal sector but invisible in terms of their contribution to the growth of any economy. Micro-entrepreneurs need to be fully aware of laws and regulations, credit and finance, marketing and environmental concerns. Micro-enterprises would be more robust if their emerging needs are addressed effectively, and in time. Rapid changes are expected to continue and a sense of impermanence will also grow for the micro-enterprises sector as we enter into the 21st century. A major challenge facing this sector is the compulsion to become self-supportive and self-reliant given the phased dismantling of protective business. The sector has to build up its capacity to compete more effectively in the context of the emerging economic environment. The government should create a conducive environment for the overall growth of micro-enterprises.

The areas of concern for micro-enterprises are:

- Identification of demand-led potential.
- Timely supply/availability of raw materials.
- Technology/skills upgradation.
- Access to market information.
- Availability of proper supportive infrastructure.
- Other backward and forward linkages.

Another area of concern is the non-availability of adequate and timely credit. Banks need to develop new financial products and adopt innovative approaches to meet the growing financial requirements of micro-enterprises. Banks should recognise this emerging business opportunity and make adequate preparations for servicing the credit requirements of this sector. Self-employment has now become a necessity rather than an option. Micro-finance in rural areas is meaningful only if the poor are empowered with crucial skills to run micro-enterprises successfully. Long-term entrepreneurial education, access to cheap loans and the formation of SHGs will enable the poor to fight poverty with dignity and build up various skills. However, lower subsidies, product orientation with appropriate technology inputs and payment by results are increasingly critical.

The Micro-credit Summit, Washington (February 1997)

The Micro-credit Summit was hosted by the Government of Bangladesh, sponsored by the World Bank and other organisations and attended by over 2,600 delegates. The summit formally launched a global campaign for micro-credit with lofty aims like credit for self-employment and business to reach 100 million of the world's poorest families, especially women, by the year 2005. The summit aimed at eliminating extreme poverty by the year 2005. Some of the concepts relating to micro-credit discussed at the Summit are:

The poor are as good a credit risk as anyone else.
International and national financial institutions should specifically plan for micro-credit.
High repayment is a sign of a well-run micro-credit programme.
Micro-credit by itself is not sufficient for development to take place.
The focus should shift from micro-credit to micro-finance and then to micro-enterprise development.
Beneficiary participation is required to manage micro-credit programmes.
Training of staff and beneficiaries is an important factor in successful micro-credit enterprises.

The Declaration of Support adopted at the Micro-credit Summit by the participants is:

- Build institutional capacity to reach very poor people in developing countries by strengthening existing institutions preparing new practitioners through training programmes and promoting appropriate policy, legal and regulatory changes.
- Similar measures to reach the very poor in industrialised countries and economies in transition.
- Institutions should develop an Institutional Action Plan outlining how they could contribute to the goal of the Micro-credit Summit.
- Enlist others in the campaign to meet the goal of the Summit, promote a learning agenda, encourage institutional action plans.
- Work with the media to expand awareness, fuel implementation and enlist new participants in the campaign.

Operational Guidelines for Micro-credit Groups

At an international seminar on Micro-credit Groups conducted by CENDERET, XIM, Bhubaneswar, between 25–29 March 1996, draft guidelines for ensuring smooth operations of micro-credit groups (for credit purposes or for income-generation activities) were framed. These are set out in Annexure 12.1. While these guidelines are simple and user-friendly, they can always be improved upon or modified to meet the needs of micro-enterprises or SHGs. Some flexibility should always be permitted so as to suit local needs.

Future Needs

Surprisingly the Micro-credit Summit in Washington did not set out the agenda for linking up with the formal institutional credit delivery system. It did advocate a networking of NGOs and SHGs, federating at appropriate levels and building a cross-cultural network, transcending international boundaries. If these micro-credit activities grow into a well-coordinated movement, they will have to be integrated with the formal credit structure, in view of the volume of funds required in developing countries. There is no need to build separate structures if the process of bank linkage is coordinated with that of SHG formation. Developing another set of institutions and bureaucracies is not the answer.

Annexure 12.1

Draft Guidelines for Small Credit Associations and Income-Generating Activities

Introduction

The growing population pressure as well as extreme poverty in the Third World has brought about a situation wherein the means available with the poor are not sufficient for them to live a normal human life. Despite considerable efforts in the last three decades to overcome widespread poverty and economic stagnation, a majority of the population still has little access to the market economy to support their private initiatives. In order to address their state of poverty and marginalisation in South Asia, social movements in the form of labour unions, cooperatives and community organisations have taken shape. These provide considerable social protection and income opportunities to their members. These organisations have sought to explore new ways and alternatives, based on values such as mutual aid, cooperation and solidarity and by establishing an organising system that introduces new types of relationships and takes into account the social and economic aspects of collective living.

As a valuable alternative to the public and market sector, during recent years partners of WSM have undertaken a lot of initiatives in the field of social economy. Although the activities vary from social movement to social movement and priority to priority, the essence is same.

When BSSF in Bangladesh is running a cooperative of rickshaw pullers and income-generating activities for women, National Workers Congres and Solidarity Organisations for Foreign Employment in Sri Lanka have a rotation fund for fisheries and migrant workers, respectively. In the Philippines, the Federation for Free Workers is engaged in the Dapla Salaza Resettlement AGRILEND Project and income-generating activities; YCW is engaged in consumer cooperatives. The situation in India is similar. The Orissa Rural and Urban Producers Association (ORUPA) is promoting credit and savings cooperatives for artisans in Orissa and the Dindigul Multipurpose Social Service Society (DMSSS) in Madurai is involved in income-generating activities (gems cutting) for unemployed women and credit unions respectively.

The activities being implemented generally relate to marketing of products, granting of credit, cooperative training and technical counselling for augmenting the income of the members of the social movement.

In order to intensify the social movements in developing a socio-economic sector, the following guidelines have been developed to strengthen credit associations and income-generating activities with an overview of strengths and weaknesses of various social movements.

Like most jargon, savings and credit run the risk of being overused and underdefined. Savings is not just another sectoral add-on, like micro-enterprise development, gender development or advocacy. Savings and credit or income generation requires a holistic approach to human development which ultimately leads to community development. Human factor plays a decisive role in this endeavour since only better human relations will generate conditions favourable to the quality output. It is high time people discarded elitist concepts and gave due weightage to human relationships in the community. Only then, the ideal conditions of people's belongingness to the community would improve.

Such a movement should aim at self-reliance. Therefore, attention needs to be placed on:

- Creating awareness at the people's level
- Identification and development of Internal Resource Persons (IRPs) to work as key resources.

Simultaneously, groups could be formed by involving the community of their respective functional groups. Suggestions for improving people's economic condition, health and motivational climate can be discussed in a free, frank and forthright manner so that concrete plans are developed and implemented.

The groups need to be self-motivated wherein attitudinal and behavioural changing programmes are undertaken. This group may be a sub-system as a part of the whole system.

Responsibilities could be:

1. At the group level: Leadership, supervision, generation of ideas and opinions.
2. At the technical level: Self-upkeep of assets and area, self-process control and self-quality control.
3. At the organisational level : Guidance, supervision, follow up, collection and dissemination of information and external networking.
4. At the client level: Marketing information, marketing segmentation, marketing expansion/creation/retention, taking up promotional measures.

The gains could be:

1. At the group level: Strong groups, group decision-making, leadership creation and unity.
2. At the technical level: Better quality, higher output and lesser dependency.
3. At the organisational level: Ideal monitoring and information system, better documentation and networking.
4. At the client level: Better marketing, better products and service. Consistent

and continuous efforts are required for the creation and retention of effective demand for products. Such a situation will lead to the generation/formation of self-motivated workers where human factor plays the most predominant role.

It would be prudent to adopt an approach which would facilitate a gradual bottom-up, phased initiation of the programme without a top heavy organisational structure.

Thus, in the programme initiation phase, the following aspects should be checked with respect to process design and layout planning:

- Community is more effective in proper utilisation and better repayment of loan amounts.
- Basic business unit's viability is a reality but after few years of operations.
- Repayment of non-economic or consumption loans is possible.
- It is possible to bank profitably on a clientele drawn from amongst those below or at the level of subsistence.

Based on the above criteria, the objectives of the savings and credit movement have been drawn as follows:

Objectives

- To develop an uniform ideology in creating a movement for people who do not have access to the formal banking system. To enable them to set in a process of an alternative bankable credit and savings system.
- To bring in group cohesiveness among the people for facilitating income-generating and economic activities from available resources.
- To enable the people to develop skills for managing savings and credit, and economic, programmes.
- To enable the process to take constant recourse to the maxim, 'Banking with the poor with near 100 per cent recovery'.
- To enable people to form a socio-economic alternative sector.
- To develop human resources above any other resources.
- To move towards sustainability.
- To develop an egalitarian and just society irrespective of caste, creed, race or religion.
- To enable people to live with dignity and self respect.
- To develop universal brotherhood among the people.

Target Population

Before fixing the target groups, there is a need to identify the groups by carrying out a survey with peoples' participation projecting their income, expenditure and various types of cash drains (in terms of interest payment, distress sale, purchase of consumer goods for want of local consumer, cooperative stores, etc.). Based on the survey, the target population may broadly comprise the following groups or sub-groups:

- People who are considered as socially ostracised such as:

  1. Scheduled Caste people
  2. Indigenous people
  3. Refugees
  4. Displaced people

- People who are considered economically downtrodden such as:

  1. Agricultural labourers
  2. Marginal and Small farmers
  3. Non-farm wage earners
  4. Women
  5. Unemployed
  6. Migrants
  7. Any other disadvantageously placed groups like rickshaw pullers, coolies, poor fishermen, petty traders, porters and craftsmen.

Activities

AWARENESS CREATION

- Making them aware of their deplorable condition
- Making them aware of the reasons of such a condition
- Making them aware of the exploitation by landlords and money-lenders.
- Making them realise their strength (unity, skill, individual capability)
- Making them aware of the need for community organisation
- Making them aware of the importance of savings
- Making them aware of the scope of credit and income-generating activities.

COMMUNITY ORGANISATION

- Bringing all the people under one roof
- Identification of common issues/needs
- Decision-making based on common issues
- Creating local leadership
- Exploring the possibilities of solving issue-based problems leading to issue-based movements.

FORMATION OF SAVINGS GROUP

- Encouraging savings among the group members
- Encouraging formation of cooperatives for undertaking income-generating/economic projects.

FORMATION OF CREDIT UNION

- Building a local network of credit groups
- Promoting income-generating programmes
- Monitoring the savings and credit activities of the group
- Identification, initiation and promotion of similar activities in adjoining villages/areas.

FORMATION OF CREDIT ASSOCIATIONS/FEDERATION

- Strengthening the credit unions
- Networking of credit unions
- Liaisoning with parent body and other agencies, both governmental and non-governmental, having similar objectives.

TRAINING

- General Training
  - — To savings and credit groups
  - — To cooperatives
  - — To credit unions
  - — To associations/federations
- Specific Training

  In addition to the categories mentioned under general training, the extension workers of the implementing organisation would be included.
  - — Job-oriented training

    This will be imparted to the staff and workers of the implementing organisation.
  - — Employment-oriented training

    This will be given to the members of the cooperative undertaking or those wanting to undertake income-generating/economic activities.

Other activities include monitoring and follow-up, community welfare and evaluation (both formative and summative).

Availability of Resources

HUMAN RESOURCES

- Mostly from the group
- From the organisation
- Local area

FINANCIAL RESOURCES

- Mostly from peoples' savings
- From the delivery system
- Occasionally from donor agency(ies) through the implementing organisation

Expected Outcomes

- Savings habit will be promoted for people's own development
- Loan facilities will be available through an alternative credit system (for production as well as consumption)
- People will avoid borrowing money from outsiders like money-lenders or landlords at a higher interest rate.
- People will be self-motivated to evolve a peoples' bank
- Collective thinking and its execution will emerge within the members.
- People will develop leadership qualities within themselves.
- Societies formed will shoulder and solve the problems independently after a certain stage.
- Local resources will be exploited for enhancing employment and income generation.
- Will develop skill in administration and effective management
- Will strengthen the web of group solidarity.

Organisation and Management

LOCATION

The process of savings and credit may be restricted to distinct areas. While the process could be centrally co-ordinated, area offices may be located at the block level. The rationale underlying special choices are based on:

- The need to gauge the probable effect of highly diverse socio-cultural conditions on borrowers' behaviour.
- Choice of an area with little banking infrastructure and predominantly inhabited by the downtrodden and others living at or below the level of subsistence.

- To chalk out 'regional' typicalities pertaining to borrowing and saving habits.
- To take advantage of operating in a geographically contiguous region from the point of uniformity.
- Fair understanding of the area chosen with respect to its geography, demography, economy and socio-cultural profile. To study the impact of, or alternatively the reaction to, an uniform system/set of procedures pertaining to savings and credit delivery in different villages.

STRUCTURE

Each group area would be viewed as a strategic unit and viability at this level would be the key performance indicator. Groups would be functionally autonomous in all respects and should be responsible for:

- Identification, orientation and growth of groups and their evolution towards sustainability.
- Quality of service in respect of approval and speedy disbursement of credit and relationship with members in general.
- Monitoring of savings, disbursement of loans, recovery of loans and interest mobilisation.
- Routine reporting to the coordination units at different levels with detailed information on progress and performance.

The coordination units, in addition to their support and monitoring role, would undertake to:

- Manage funds flow to groups so that they never go 'dry'.
- Manage funds in hand profitably
- Plan and organise training needs and programme
- Analyse and provide feedback, both routinely and upon urgency
- Constantly review progress internally
- Liaise with the implementing organisation

The organisation structure would remain a four tier one, the critical fourth tier being the interface with groups and therefore, not a part per se of the implementing group, although an integral component of the system. Manpower requirement/staffing therefore, could be planned at two tiers, i.e., the first and the fourth tier.

The structure has been planned with a view to have an effective savings and credit system linked with income generating and other socio-economic activities. The major thrust revolves around the group, the unions and the federation so that the initiative undertaken gradually spins off into a solidarity movement.

Tier 1 (Group)
The groups formed would be independent in all respects with regard to decision-making pertaining to all major activities at the group level. There may

be more than one group in the same village/area. However, they would operate independently.

Tier 2 (Union)

The president and secretary would automatically qualify for membership in the credit union formed at the gram panchayat or cluster-level administrative unit as the case may be. The credit union will have elected members, who will be responsible for networking and monitoring, providing feedback and maintaining savings and credit flow in that particular administrative unit.

Tier 3 (Association/Federation)

The president and secretary of each of the credit unions would automatically qualify for membership in the credit association/federation. The federation will focus on networking, monitoring, providing feedback, and liaisoning with external agencies and the implementing organisation. One of its major roles would be to influence policy matters.

Tier 4 (Implementing Organisation)

This would comprise the implementing organisation's processes for achieving the objectives of the movement. This may have a structure so developed so as to cater to the needs of not only the savings and credit programme but also its inter-linkages with income-generating and socio-economic activities.

A schematic representation of the organisational structure is given in annexure (a).

STAFFING

The staff to group ratio in the first tier could be kept at 3:1. They may comprise one accountant, one storekeeper and one marketing worker. Initially, the project implementing organisation would pay the honorarium to these staff. In course of time, with the strengthening of the groups and increased turnover in its operations, the groups would take over the responsibility. The accountant should be responsible for accounts relating to the savings, credit interest calculations, repayments and cooperative activities. The storekeeper will be responsible for maintaining the stock pertaining to the economic and marketing activity. The marketing worker would be solely responsible for assisting the group in procurement of raw materials and marketing the products of the cooperative or of an individual member, if required.

At the fourth tier, the staff to group ratio could be kept at 1:6. This is assumed to be a reasonable average in the face of ground realities and the objective of 'regular savings and credit with near 100 per cent recovery'. The workforce of the fourth tier in the long run would serve as the core group for the expansion phase which is supposed to spiral off as a sequel to the process.

While there are strong grounds for phased, gradual initiation, it must be noted that the programme must be launched 'laterally' within an area.

Savings and Credit Management

FORMATION OF GROUP

The implementing organisation should identify, develop and motivate various categories of societal agents, collective and individual, to serve as the critical interface between community and the proposed savings and credit delivery systems. These are referred to as groups.

Being essentially born out of community, group and inter-personal dynamics are likely to tend towards a certain robustness. Given this, they would evolve over time and become capable enough to conduct community banking functions and cater to credit requirements with small injections of external resources.

As listed under the activities, people are made aware of their condition and the importance of savings and credit. With the assistance of the key personnel of the organisation, groups should be formed in villages. Before forming a group, the following guidelines should be kept in mind:

- Only the targeted people should be the members of a group. The group should be homogeneous in terms of the members' income, sex, social status, place of residence and like-mindedness.
- Gender bias may be avoided while forming the group. Wherever possible, efforts may be made to initiate women groups. This is being suggested in view of the successful stories of women savings and credit groups all over the world.
- Household should be a unit of the group. In other words, only one person from one household should be a member of the group.
- A group may be constituted of not less than 50 and not more than 100 members. However, the members could be fixed as per the existing local situation.
- If in a village, the number of interested persons exceed the upper ceiling prescribed by the group, then they should wait till they reach the minimum number to form a second group in the same village.
- A member should have attained the age of 18 years but should not be older than 60 years.
- Each member must be willing to accept the objectives of the group.
- Memberships should be accepted only after the group unanimously agrees. Filling up the membership application form and depositing required entrance and membership fees as per the decision of the group should be mandatory. Membership can be accepted at any time subject to the approval of the group.
- All the members will automatically get voting rights to elect an executive body. The term of the executive body may continue for at least three consecutive years or as decided by the group.

- The executive body may comprise president, vice-president, secretary, asst. secretary, an accountant and executive member(s), depending upon the size of the group. In other words, each of these office bearers may represent at least 10 member-households/units.
- The chief functionary and the accountant should have basic numerical and writing abilities.
- The executive body should be ready to assist group members in identifying and initiating income-generating activities and identifying different avenues for marketing the products and procuring raw materials through group ventures or cooperatives.
- Income-generating activities may be undertaken by a cooperative formed by members of the group.
- The cooperative should manage its affairs under the guidance of the executive body of the group. Day-to-day functions would be administered by the members of the cooperative.
- The cooperative should undertake all economic group ventures.
- The group may appoint a storekeeper and a marketing worker immediately before the cooperative starts. Both must be members of the credit group.
- The accountant who maintains the group's accounts may also maintain the accounts of the cooperative.
- The group should be ready to bear the honorarium of the workers in due course of time, i.e., when the implementing organisation gradually withdraws itself. This expenditure should be remunerated from income earned from credit flow and marketing activities. Expenditure should be earmarked for this purpose by the group.
- After the formation of the group, the members should select a name by which the group can be identified.
- They should develop the bye-laws of their group and get it registered in due course of time.
- Regular weekly/fortnightly/monthly meetings should be held in which attendance is to be compulsory. The time and place of the meeting should be fixed and any member coming late or remaining absent should be fined.
- The group should immediately open a savings account in the bank as decided by the group with at least three signatories—president, secretary and accountant.
- All transactions need to be approved in the group meeting through a resolution.
- The amount spent towards administrative costs and bank charges should be met out of the savings and accordingly, recorded in the accounts register.
- Put in place appropriate internal systems for routine reporting pertaining to financial matters, progress and unit performance at the implementing organisation level, group and community levels.
- Collation and interpretation of information at the various coordination units with routine and emergency feedback systems should be evolved.

FORMATION OF CREDIT UNION

- The president and secretary of each credit group will automatically become the member of the credit union at the gram panchayat/cluster level.
- They should democratically elect the president, vice-president, secretary, asst. secretary and two to three members from among them.
- The credit union should be responsible for overall supervision, guidance and monitoring of the groups.
- All conflicts and problems arising in any of its member groups should be resolved by the union.
- Call for executive body meetings every quarter and accordingly take decisions on policy matters.
- Attempt to maintain uniformity in the functions of the groups
- Initiate expansion of the movement in new areas
- The executive body should hold its position for three consecutive years or as decided by the groups at the first tier.

FORMATION OF CREDIT ASSOCIATION/FEDERATION

The elected president and secretary of each credit union would automatically become members of the general body of the credit association/federation at the block level. They should then elect a president, vice-president, secretary and asst. secretary along with two to three members of the federation. The term of the office bearers would be as per the decisions of the groups and the union.

The responsibilities of the federation could be:

- Network between the various credit unions
- Meet every quarter
- Attend to the needs of the credit unions
- Liaison with the delivery system and credit unions
- Call for a general body meeting once in a year. This meeting should be attended by members from all tiers.
- Ensure that the credit operations spiral into credit movements.

This is an important deviation from the Grameen Bank approach, where village-level centres do not tend towards functional autonomy. Although, the inherent tendency to move towards self governance would not be observed in the first year, one could be optimistic in presuming that this is likely to occur since the intermediary is dynamic.

Growth and viability would need to be looked at over a period of at least five years. Given the proposed approach, it is strongly felt that the reach in terms of number of members and the quantum of credit flow would multiply at a very brisk pace with little necessity for fresh capital expenditure or increased spending on manpower and other overheads from the second year onwards.

In effect, the groups themselves would constantly evolve and gradually emerge as alternatives of the implementing organisation following its gradual withdrawal, thus contributing substantially towards increased savings and credit turnover. In fact, large amounts would require to be revolved to sustain 'actual' credit operations.

Savings and Credit Operation

SAVINGS

- The weekly/fortnightly/monthly contribution of each member should be fixed by the group, as compulsory savings. There should be compulsory savings by all the members for a period fixed by the group (at least for 2 years).
- Each member should save regularly in every week/fortnight/month which will prevent accounting complications.
- Voluntary savings should be encouraged and the ceiling should not be fixed.
- The savings contribution could be in the form of cash or kind (which has an immediate market value). The group would convert the kind into cash in order to maintain an uniform accounting system.
- Nobody should be allowed to withdraw his/her membership before the said period.
- Receipts should be issued against each deposit.
- All collections should be made during the meetings.
- Savings should be deposited in the bank through the accountant within three days of the collection.
- Individual pass books should be issued to each member by the group.
- The pass book should be entered at every meeting after the collection is made
- Defaulters should be charged a fine.

CREDIT

With the mobilisation of savings collected from the members for a period of six months or as fixed by the group, the savings and credit committee of the group should fulfill the needs of the members by disbursing small loans on an experimental basis to observe proper usage of the loan and whether members are prompt in loan repayment .

- Develop systems for making available, and recovery of, credit and implementation thereof.
- The amount should not cross the limit decided by the group.
- Loans should be disbursed to an individual member or to a group of members (if five to six members like to initiate a collective programme).

- A loan application along with description of the purpose for which the amount will be utilised and the estimated budget should be submitted to the group.
- Scrutiny of the loan application will be done by the credit group's executive body and the members' consent will be duly taken. Priority will be given based on regular savings, repayment capacity and purpose of the loan.
- During the loan period too, one has to pay the monthly contribution of savings. Savings should not be interrupted.

PURPOSE

Loans should be disbursed to the members for:

- Rural non-farm activities: which may include all sorts of small or large self-employment schemes.
- Farm-based activities: agriculture, animal husbandry, fishery, sericulture, apiculture, etc.
- Credit needs of the urban informal sector, i.e., small production units in the slums.
- Consumption needs arising during the investment period in the process of a productive activity.

HOUSING LOANS

- Social needs which include expenses like marriage, funeral, etc.
- Education of children and health expenses
- Emergency needs subject to approval of the office bearers, which should be resolved in the meeting falling immediately after the approval.

AMOUNT

- The group should fix a ceiling on the loan for each of the activities.
- In the first year, the ceiling should be fixed irrespective of the type of activity.
- The savings to loan ratio could be 1:2 or more as per the ceiling fixed.
- The group should see that no sort of guarantee is undertaken. This is because the group in itself should evolve as a cohesive force wherein mutual trust and faith should be the key factors in its operation.
- Keeping movable and immovable properties as security against the extra amount of loan should not be encouraged.
- The loan amount may be increased every year.
- The loan amount should be kept within the ceiling; 80 per cent of the total savings amount may be disbursed in the first year of loan.
- From the second year onwards, after keeping aside the administrative and emergency loans, the total savings may be disbursed.

- While the average loan size can increase in subsequent borrowings, the total number of members in the group may be kept constant.
- If the need of any one of the members exceeds the ceiling amount and is found genuine by the group, an amount equal to the ceiling may be sanctioned. For the balance amount, the group would forward its recommendation to the credit association/federation executive body through the credit union. After proper assessment, the executive body would forward it to the savings and credit coordinator of the implementing organisation. A matching grant amount should be parked with the implementing organisation and may be used for meeting the additional requirements. This process can be continued till the groups become financially sound and are capable of dealing with larger amounts. Even if the group has the capacity to meet the excess loan amount, it should not do so because this will debar other members from availing loans. The project coordinator should sanction the amount in consultation with the credit association executive body. The whole process should be expedited within seven days from the date of submission of application. The extra amount should be given to the member only through the group.
- The loan amount may be paid in cash or kind by the group. In the case of loans in kind, the same should be given to the member through the cooperative.
- The money should be utilised for the said purpose within 15 days of the receipt of the loan.

REPAYMENT

- Loans to other members would depend upon regular repayment of instalments by the loanee members. Thus, the repayment schedule should be strictly adhered to.
- In order to increase the volume of the group fund, a certain rate of interest should be fixed by the group in order to make it financially viable.
- The repayment period should be scheduled for each loanee based on the nature of activity he/she undertakes. However, for the first and second year of credit operations, the repayment period should be one year or less.
- Total interest against the principal amount for the specified period should be calculated and repaid by the member in monthly or weekly, equal instalments as decided by the group.
- If any member wants to repay his loan, s/he may be allowed to do so and accordingly, interest should be calculated.
- If the group decides, in case of loans pertaining to farm-based activities like agriculture, pisciculture, etc., the principal amount along with the interest should be repaid within one month after the harvest.
- Fines should be charged to the member who violates the repayment schedule.

- If the group feels that the default has been due to genuine reasons, then it may provide a grace period for repayment.
- Rules for repayment and interest calculation should be uniform irrespective of the category of loan one has availed.
- Under no circumstance should the rate of interest vary from member to member, or loan to loan.
- Repayment should be made only by cash.
- Producers who want to repay their loans in kind must sell their products to the cooperative if the cooperative deals in such a product or in the open market.
- Other than the loanee, members of the group could also sell their produce to the cooperative. The cooperative should take the responsibility to pay immediately at the selling rate of the producer.
- The cooperative should make its own arrangement for marketing of the products through marketing worker.
- In case of joint loan (from the group and the implementing organisation), the loanee has to repay the total instalment to the group. The group would transfer the organisation's share every month.
- The group should be fully responsible for the recovery of loans.
- If any member of the group does not repay the loan taken from the group, then all the group members will have to bear the repayment.
- Till the total repayment is made, any member or any executive body member may have access to inspect the loanee's activity from time to time, and the loanee must extend his/her full cooperation.
- If a member wants to leave a group, he can do so, but only after clearing the dues.

INCOME-GENERATING ACTIVITIES

- Members intending to undertake income-generating activities may do so through the cooperative.
- Identification of activity and market feasibility should be made in consultation with group members.
- Assets required for any income-generating activity should be purchased through the cooperative/group.
- The cooperative should assess the feasibility of the activity before approaching the group for credit assistance.
- The cooperative within itself should segregate all its internal functions. A group of members could be made responsible for specific functions like activity viability, production, consumer cooperative, accounting, etc.
- It should be ensured that all functions of the cooperative are documented and reported in the group meetings.
- At times of crisis or problems, the cooperative should immediately consult the executive body of the group for guidance.

INCOME

- The income earned by the group throughout the year by way of interest, donations, marketing, subscriptions, etc., should be divided in the following manner:

  —Training of the group members
  —Community welfare
  —Honorarium to the credit group staff
  —Administrative cost and stationery
  —Dividend to the members (to be pumped back into the individuals' savings)

- Paying dividend to the members would not only create interest by way of increased benefits, but would also increase the savings and credit turnover in the succeeding years.

Emergency Fund

- Apart from regular savings, the group should constitute an emergency fund at par with 25 per cent of the monthly savings contribution and deposit it in a special account.
- Money accumulated in this fund should be spent for arranging insurance for different purposes:

  —Life saving
  —Crop saving
  —Cattle life saving
  —Health

Money from the emergency fund should be spent only on the basis of the decisions taken by the group. The operation of the emergency fund should be made by the group simultaneously.

The group should also contact various insurance companies and deposit the premiums for various insurance categories.

Training

Successful credit delivery systems worldwide show that a qualitative work force is a critical component on the list of contributing factors. The training methodology has been drawn after studying such programmes. In essence, the staff will undergo two types of training; informally, on the job, so as to provide hands-on experience of grassroots realities; and, formally, through a structured curriculum combining theory and practice and conducted by experts. For greater exposure, the staff would be taken to various successful, ongoing programmes on alternative credit systems.

In addition to the skill and motivational aspects, there is need to clearly lay down job descriptions, responsibilities and performance indicators.

Development interventions can be delivered through the means of technical, advisory, on-the-job training or formal class room training courses. Training should be imparted at all levels to make the total programme a success.

In order to maintain uniformity, the implementing organisation should prepare training manuals on the subjects mentioned under the following heads:

TRAINING FOR CREDIT GROUP MEMBERS

- Savings and credit
- Community organisation
- Leadership
- Motivation
- Group Behaviour
- Methodology of the Credit Association Movement
- Procedure and criteria to form savings and credit groups
- Rules and criteria for managing the savings and credit fund
- Formation of village cooperatives and its functions
- Rules and criteria for utilising the emergency fund
- Numerical and writing ability
- Preparation of loan proposal
- Rules for filling up the loan contract
- Utilisation of loan amount
- Supervision of utilisation of the loan amount
- Procedure and criteria to form savings federation
- Role of the group leaders in resolving conflicts and other problems of the members.
- Basic accounts-keeping
- Resource planning and utilisation
- Organisational management
- Organisational development

PRODUCTION AND INCOME-GENERATING ACTIVITIES

- Skill formation
- Skill development
- Identification of economic activity
- Resource identification
- Production techniques
- Simple finance management
- Costing and pricing
- Marketing

TRAINING FOR ACCOUNTANTS

- Book keeping
- Maintenance of weekly/monthly registers
- Regular pass book entry
- Loan register
- Consolidated monthly savings and loan ledger
- Bank operation
- Repayment register
- Expenditure register
- Cooperative training
- Cooperative management
- Organisational development
- Finance management
- Resource identification
- Activity identification
- Production process
- Marketing
- Costing
- Packaging

TRAINING FOR CREDIT UNION AND FEDERATION MEMBERS

In addition to the concerns mentioned under training for group members, the following training programmes should be conducted for credit union and federation members.

- Community organisation
- Organisational management
- Organisational development
- Leadership
- Motivation
- Financial management
- Resource management/development
- Networking and liaisoning

Monitoring and Supervision

SAVING AND CREDIT OPERATION

Monitoring and supervision would be based on the information flow system. The nature of the project warrants a bottom-up approach and hence, the information flow should emerge from the group level without pressure from above. The 2nd, 3rd and 4th tier would function as levels from where guidance and feedback would be provided. The system would be targeted at people's involvement in the movement where importance would be given to their participation and decisions.

The system would allow the levels to monitor one another's functions. Hence, although the hierarchy will be laid down, it should be considered as a hazy one except under exigencies.

REPORTING

Tier 1 (Group)
The members and the cooperatives would make available their progress of activities to the group in group meetings once a month. The group would consolidate the reports and forward them to the union.

Tier 2 (Union)
The union would consolidate all reports received from its member-groups and would forward the same to the association/ federation.

Tier 3 (Association/Federation)
The association/federation would consolidate all reports received from its member-unions and would forward the same to the implementing organisation for information.

The association/federation, in consultation with the implementing organisation, would assess the strengths and weaknesses of the groups, the unions and itself.

If the association/federation feels that intervention is required in certain levels, the implementing organisation may be asked to intervene.

Tier 4 (Implementing Organisation)
The implementing organisation would conduct periodic reviews and assess whether the units are moving in the right direction or not. Accordingly, it should develop its strategies.

A schematic representation of the savings and credit flow is given in annexure (b).

FEEDBACK

Tier 4 (Implementing Organisation)
The implementing organisation would place its staff at all levels for monitoring and supervision of the total credit movement. The staff should operate more as facilitators rather than implementers. Based on the information available through the staff at the various levels, strategies should be developed to enable the three levels to have a system directed towards sustainability. Thus, more emphasis should be laid on training members at all levels to build up their capacity.

Tier 3 (Association/Federation)
The association/federation would provide feedback to the groups through the respective unions. Further, the association/federation would also provide

information gathered through its efforts. This information flow would be both directly to the groups and to the unions. This is being suggested in view of time management and faster flow of information.

Tier 2 (Union)

The union provides feedback to the groups based on the feedback received from the association/federation. However, for certain functions, if the union is able to give direct feedback to the groups, it may do so.

Tier 1 (Group)

The group would share the feedback received from the other levels with all members and get their response.

A schematic representation of the monitoring and supervision of savings and credit activities is given in annexure (c).

INCOME-GENERATING ACTIVITIES

When the loan is received by the member, the credit group executive body should ensure that the loan is being used for the purpose it has been sanctioned for. It should review the plan and implementation of the activities. The group should see that the member embarks on the activity right away.

Follow-up visits should be conducted by the credit group executive body, credit union executive body and extension workers at least once in three months. This would help the member in adhering to his/her schedule of work and help him/her to overcome the problems confronted.

Extension workers as well as members of the credit association executive body should inform the loanee about their availability besides the regular visits, especially during crisis, which may affect the production activity.

During the follow-up, emphasis should be directed towards the development of the member's family in terms of improved living conditions, positive work habits and attitudes, improved capacity to participate in community activities, improved capacity to utilise community services and to live with dignity.

The group should keep updated monthly progress reports of each of the loanee members. This would be one of the component for the evaluation of the loanee members and the credit groups as a whole.

General

In order to simplify the monitoring system, formats for reporting should be adopted. These formats should be simple in nature such that the members don't find it difficult to fill in. Sample formats are given in annexure 12.2.

(a) SCHEMATIC PRESENTATION OF THE ORGANISATION STRUCTURE

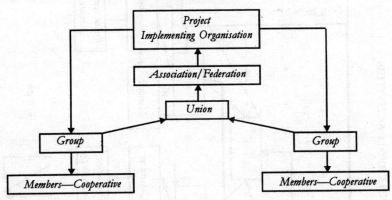

(b) SAVINGS AND CREDIT FLOW

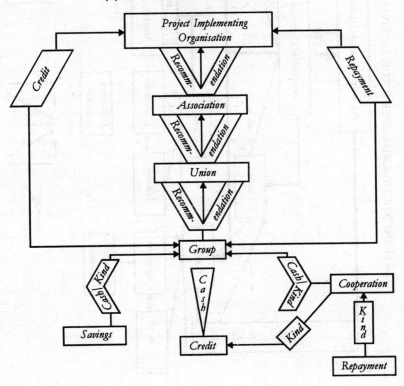

(c) MONITORING AND SUPERVISION OF SAVINGS AND CREDIT ACTIVITIES

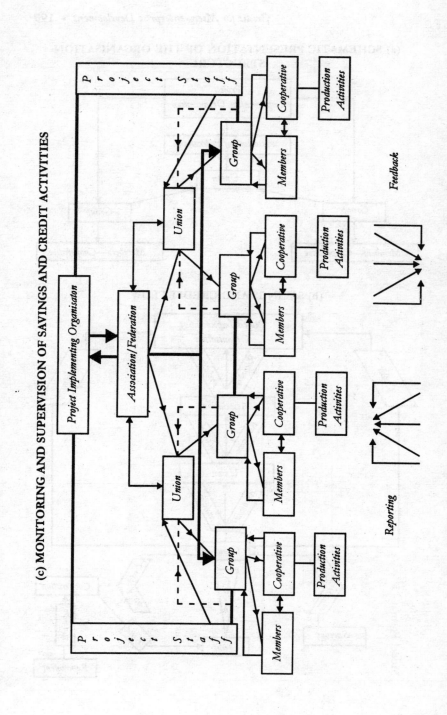

Annexure 12.2

Model Format - I

Individual Savings and Loan Ledger

Week/Month : _____

Group Name : _____

Group Code : _____

Name of Member	Savings				Loan							Repayment			
	CS	VS	Late Fine	Others	Total	Produc- tion	Consu- mption	Emer- gency	Housing	Socio- Cultural	Others	Total Outst.	Inst Amt. of Prin- cipal	Int. Repay- ment	Total Repay- ment	Balance Outsta- nding

Model Format - II

Consolidated Savings and Loan Ledger

Union Name : _____

Union Code : _____

Week/Month : _____

Name of the Borrower	Savings				Loan							Repayment			
	CS	VS	Late Fine	Others	Total	Produc- tion	Consu- mption	Emer- gency	Housing	Socio- Cultural	Others	Total Outst.	Inst Amt. of Prin- cipal	Int.	Total Repay- ment	Balance Outsta- nding

Model Format - III

Loan Application Form

Personal Information

Applicant's Name: **Code :**

Group Name :   **Code :**

Village :

No. of Family Members :

Occupation :

— —

About the Loan

Purpose : _____ Amount Request : _____

_____

_____

Expected Period of Repayment : _____

APPLICANT'S SIGNATURE   **DATE**

— —

To be filled by the Group Representative

1. Sanctioned/Deferred/Rejected :

2. Amount Sanctioned :

3. Repayment Period :

SIGNATURE OF THE SECRETARY   **DATE**

SIGNATURE OF THE TREASURER   **DATE**

Model Format - IV

Receipt

Received an amount of Rs._____ (Rupees _____
_____) as a loan with _____ % flat rate of inter-
est to be repaid in _____ instalments.

I promise to repay the amount with interest in _____ instalments.

SIGNATURE OF THE APPLICANT

Model Format - V

Clearance

This is to certify that _____ does not have any out-
standing loans or balances with the savings and credit programme of the group.

SIGNATURE OF THE ACCOUNTANT

Model Format - VI

Pass Book

Group Name : _____

Group Code : _____

Date	Savings	Accumu-lation	Loan Outst.	Principal Repayed	Interest Outst.	Interest Paid

PART III

Role of Self-help Groups

13

Self-help Concepts

Financial Requirements of the Rural Poor

The information, resources, skills and technology base of the poor are very weak and the scales of their operation, irrespective of the economic activity pursued by them are, therefore, small. Their credit needs arise due to growing family size and societal obligations, for example, expense on marriages and deaths, medical treatment, and to bear market and climatic uncertainties. The need to expand or diversify operations places tremendous strain on the existing family income, which is barely adequate to meet routine production and consumption requirements. Such additional demands are, however, rarely out of proportion; the line dividing production requirements from the conveniently termed 'consumption' requirements, seems to be rather thin as the latter has as vital an impact on economic activity as the seemingly direct 'productive' requirement.

In times of such emergencies, there are no credit institutions to fall back upon and they are forced to rely on credit supplied by bigger landlords, traders and money-lenders at high rates of interest. This is notwithstanding the threat of losing their means of production, indebtedness and sometimes even bondedness—an indication of their struggle to survive against all odds. The fact that they are generally able to repay their high interest loans only exemplifies their tremendous risk bearing capacity, exceptional ability to optimise on their frugal resources, the 'real' potential of their meagre income generation and the possibilities of mobilising 'tiny' savings.

The primary objective of the 'informal' money-lender is to set up an economic relationship with such terms and conditions that the borrower is squeezed for repayment and if the income situation worsens, the supply of cash is tightened and interest rates (representing higher risk cost) are raised. The terms of further loans are set such that the borrower is never able to repay the principal and as a result loses the collateral, making him ready for another loan to service the 'eternal debt'. As financial institutions do not cater for consumption loans for the poor, this market has been controlled by money-lenders.

However, financial institutions have not entered this particular credit market for certain reasons. The existing framework of rules/guidelines do not permit meeting such requirements. Also, branches cannot directly supervise or service borrowers in vast, scattered areas because:

- Staff is limited.
- The staff is not 'oriented' to such 'marginal' operations.
- Their functional style is not cost-beneficial for generating 'viable' operations.
- There is too much work involved (documentation, follow-up visits for monitoring operations, etc.).
- Lack of 'viable' schemes for implementation unless a target is imposed (IRDP, etc.).

The Rural Poverty Syndrome

There are various shades of rural poverty but among the poorest of the poor are those termed as 'landless'. They are also termed as 'marginal farmers' or 'agricultural labourers' who have no land and depend only upon their physical labour. As these 'landless poor' operate from a very slim economic base, a great transformation in their economic base and mobility is possible if they had access to financial resources to support their physical labour resource.

Within the existing system, availability of credit resources is restricted to the few who are able to have recourse to credit under various government-sponsored programmes like IRDP, PMRY, JRY, etc. The majority of the rural poor is unable to avail the benefit of these credit programmes due to past indebtedness, lack of sufficient knowledge about these schemes, inability to interact with bank/district officials, etc. Besides, the banks do not provide credit to meet the real urgent needs of the poor. Their income levels thus, stay at such a low level that very little can ever be saved and invested to let the economic base expand.

The poor are not unproductive. Infact, by virtue of sheer numbers and labour potential, they are one of the more productive segments of the population. However, their labour does not yield adequate returns; control over financial resource is in the hands of the better-off segments. The ideal way out would be a credit programme for the poor, so that genuine credit needs are met. A poor person who takes a loan may continue to do just what he has been doing before. However, there is a significant difference in income, as he would be able to retain a greater part of the profits. The common reservations against a credit programme for the poor are:

- Credit alone is useless unless packaged with training, marketing, transportation facilities, technology, education, etc.
- Credit to the poor is counter-productive as it imposes the burden of loans on the poor who have no repaying capacity.
- The consumption and social needs are so pressing that any loan will be diverted from production requirements.
- Chronic poverty has a crippling effect on the mind and aspirations of the poor and this shackles the poor to lower levels of living.
- The rural power-structure is too powerful and entrenched to allow such a credit programme for poverty alleviation to succeed.
- By encouraging the poor to take up independent professions, a shortage in wage labour will be created. This results in higher wages, increasing the cost of agricultural production.
- Credit programmes for the poor will be highly inflationary and cause imbalances in the rural economy.
- By extending credit to women, the traditional place of women in the family will be disturbed.
- Credit helps the poor only temporarily and does not achieve an equitable restructuring of production relations.
- Success of credit programmes depend on wider national economic policy issues. If the terms of trade for food and cash crops between rural and urban areas are biased against the rural poor, credit programmes will have limited impact.

While designing an appropriate programme, sound financial principles as also clear social objectives must be kept in mind. The problem is not fulfilment of these objectives but multiplicity of objectives and sense of priorities, which become an excuse for poor performance. There have to be productivity and profitability improvements for the poor. A key factor is their participation in programmes for poverty alleviation especially those in the agricultural and rural development sphere. In addition to increasing agricultural productivity and promoting non-agricultural enterprises in rural areas, there need to be activities that enhance inputs of production. These inputs are:

- Natural resource management
- Human resource development
- Rural infrastructural development
- Savings and credit programmes

Success is possible if the poor participate in the process of their poverty alleviation. The four kinds of participation sought are:

- In decision-making, identifying problems, formulating alternatives, planning activities and allocating resources.
- In implementation, carrying out activities, managing and operating programmes, partaking of services.
- In economic, social, cultural or other benefits, individually or collectively.
- In evaluation of the outcome of the activity and provide a feedback for the other aspects.

Need for SHG Formation

Individually, a poor person tends to be rather tentative, uncertain in his behaviour but group membership smoothens the rough edges of his behaviour pattern, making him more reliable as a borrower. A poor person feels exposed to all kinds of hazards; he requires guidance and advice from people he knows and can trust. Membership in a group gives him a feeling of protection. Thus, formation of a group would ensure the best participation of the poor in a credit programme.

The approach towards poverty alleviation should be self-help. Others should help the poor to help themselves. It is felt that individual effort is too inadequate to improve their fate. This brings about the necessity for organising them in a group by which they get the benefit of collective perception, collective decision-making and collective implementation of programmes for common benefits. The organisation holds power and provides strength; it can be an antidote to the helplessness of the poor.

The multiplier effect of investment can be vividly demonstrated in a credit programme for the rural poor through the continuous expansion of their economic base. Incomes also rise with additional investment through borrowing. The vicious cycle of low income/low savings/low investment/ low income/can be broken by injection of credit in the cycle. Credit/more investment/more income/more savings/more investment/more income is the result that is sought through credit intervention.

It is assumed that those who save and those also borrow are two different groups of people. Savers stash away deposits in banks while borrowers go to the bank and borrow the savings of others at a price. However, a saver can himself be an investor, as is usual in the case of the poor. His investment is calibrated in very small steps and any small savings can be ploughed back into investments at any time. Subtle, at times not-so-subtle, peer pressure keeps the group members in line and contributes to the collective strength of the group.

Group savings serve a wider range of objectives other than immediate investment:

- It imposes discipline on group members in developing savings habit.
- Savings enhance the self-confidence of the individual as it is a sign of group encouragement.
- Savings cover the individuals' risk against normal business risk, normal variations of income, natural calamities like floods, drought, cyclones and diseases. Investments of a riskier nature can also be considered because of the savings cushion.
- Group savings of the poor can demonstrate the strength of unity of members.

Savings plus credit can then be a good starting point for group formations called Self-help Groups (SHGs). There is a great incentive to form a group if people feel that it is the only way to have access to credit. The size of the group should be restricted to less than 30 members divided into 5–6 sub-groups so that members have better access to information, better cohesion and interaction. Smaller groups would also reduce the concentration of power in a single person.

Credit groups should be allowed to come up on their own or through the intervention of voluntary agencies (NGOs) rather than being formed by officials of financing agencies. If the group takes shape on its own, interaction and group dynamics ensures that group solidarity and a group 'consciousness' is fostered.

For self-reliance and reduced dependence on financial institution, a strong savings programme is essential. This is not because the savings programme will enable the group to avoid taking loans from the financial institutions but because existence of a common fund enables the members to acquire expertise in money management and financial discipline. The acquired experience also encourages the group members to take up larger projects, on a collective basis in future.

Aspects of SHG Formation

Given an opportunity to keep their small thrift amounts safe during normal periods, their tiny economies would perhaps manage their emergent needs themselves—individually, or perhaps, collectively. It is this understanding, which prompted many voluntary agencies to promote SHGs among the rural poor with the aim of helping them save, collect and manage their funds, and help one another by way of credit from their own funds. Even in cases where the SHGs have come up primarily for taking up economic activity, savings mobilisation has become important.

As creation of awareness and non-formal education is integral to the activities of any voluntary agency, SHGs not only provide the members with an opportunity to carry out economic activities but also discuss and analyse their social and economic situation to arrive at the root causes of their problems, and strive to find and implement solutions. SHGs, therefore, become a forum for the collective voice of the poor against common oppression and exploitation, to understand individual and common problems and improve their skills and capacities to manage resources.

SHGs work on the same principles as cooperatives, but have the chances of becoming much more successful than the formal cooperative structure as far as the poor are concerned. This is because SHGs are highly cohesive entities; for example, they may be of women only, the members may have the same occupation, they may belong to the same caste or sub-caste, they may be living in the same village, and so on. Admittedly, different situations require different forces to bind the people together and there can be no generalisations. But the common feature of the SHGs, irrespective of their organisational character, is their participatory nature as they are often small in size (their membership varying from 20 to 60). In fact, large SHGs often break into smaller ones as members, due to their caste, occupation, etc., get 'ignored' and lack 'participation' or 'voice'. Advantages of individualistic needs and group cooperation balance each other so as to lead to a functional size and character of the group. Voluntary agencies also help enhance 'participation' by assigning responsibilities to passive members; no one is encouraged to 'become a leader'.

It is these very factors which are found missing in formal cooperative structures, which are too large and dominated by the non-poor. At times these are even, exploitative. The interests of the non-poor clash with those of the poor and the poor are generally not allowed any say in the working of the cooperative.

Besides, the formalities and interference by officers work as deterrents. Thus, the poor, even in a successful cooperative perhaps get loans or deposit savings, sell products and get raw materials, but would never learn to analyse their own situation, take decisions, manage larger resources and become a collective force. They would become 'members', but not 'cooperators' and would continue to live on the decisions made by others— something that the SHGs help them break away from.

There are three types of situations in which the poor members of SHGs may take up economic activities.

- They may take up individual activities like farming, animal husbandry, artisan work, petty trade and wage labour.
- They may also come together to own common investments, for example, a common well or a common agro-service centre, by sharing the capital and operating costs. In such an event, however, their principal activity (farming in, this case) is individual-based.
- They may take up joint activities like social forestry, etc., which are run by the entire group with various responsibilities divided between the members.

Financial Requirements of SHGs

Although small groups help enhancement of managerial skills through active participation of members in all the activities of the group, it also results in the disadvantage of a very small resource or capital base as the members are all poor with capacities to save very small amounts. Often, the concerned voluntary agencies supplement the resources of the SHG by providing some seed capital, in the form of grant or interest-free loan, to be used as a revolving fund by the SHG. This enhances the SHG's capacity for providing small loans, both for production and consumption, as formal institutions do not play any significant role. In the process, they successfully eliminate exploitative sources like money-lenders. Voluntary agencies, however, survive on donor assistance which is always limited and uncertain. In providing seed capital to SHGs, their funds also get locked up for a long time. Their capacity to support SHGs on a large scale is, therefore, limited.

Normally, financial institutions find it difficult to provide credit to the very poor due to reasons which are as varied as the target group members lacking legal status as land owners or tenants, or not having no-dues certificates, being victims of *benami* transactions, their requirements not matching the 'approved' unit costs, sizes and norms for viability, and so on. Even if these procedural constraints are overcome, the bank staff available in a typical rural branch would be too insufficient to identify, appraise and service such tiny loans for a large number of people. Provision of more staff would render the entire operation non-viable for the bank. Similarly, even if the poor overcome the long distances separating them and the bank branches, the banks would find virtually impossible to service the high volume of tiny savings/loan accounts. Thus, even if banks realise the importance of mobilising tiny thrift amounts, the cost of mobilising them through the normal banking system would be prohibitive enough to keep them away.

Cost-effective innovations, both for linking thrift and small savings as well as consumption and production credit needs of the poor with banks are, therefore, imperative. Some formal institutions did come out with innovations in savings mobilisation. For example, 'savings stamps' for tiny amounts like 10 to 25 paisa could be bought from the village post offices (who also manage savings) and pasted on a special pass book till it became a 'respectable' figure of at least two rupees when it would be entered in the regular pass book. This is a highly simplified version of the savings stamps scheme of the post office. But, one was required to go to a post office every time one wanted a savings stamp. The Syndicate Bank introduced the 'Pygmy Deposit' scheme with a 'part-time banker'—a person the villagers could trust, say the village priest or school teacher—going door to door and collecting tiny savings keeping their accounts, etc. This, however, had the limitation of the thrift collector visiting only on specific days. The necessity of having an easy access to a safe deposit, therefore, still remained.

SHGs fulfil this role of the omnipresent savings collector without the bank being required to pay even the meagre honorarium to the part-time collector. The groups pool the savings and deposit the pooled sum with the bank. No doubt, individual members are denied the benefit of interest in this process. Considering, however, that the funds with the SHGs are generally lent to the members at substantial rates of interest, the returns to the members, whenever distributed would far outweigh the interest earnings foregone from the bank.

Similarly, in order to reduce the cost of servicing a large number of borrowers' accounts, banks have come out with innovations that have externalised some of the functions and thereby, costs. For example, Syndicate Bank floated a farmers-based subsidiary named Syndicate Agricultural Foundation (SAF). SAF promotes 'farm clinics' which are small attachments to rural branches and are manned by carefully selected local youths who act as a bridge between the bank and the villagers by making them aware of credit possibilities and helping them with the formalities.

Some other banks have associated themselves with voluntary agencies which identify prospective borrowers, appraise their requests and forward viable proposals to the bank. After the loan is sanctioned, voluntary agencies (sometimes through SHGs promoted by it) also help in providing necessary training to the borrowers, in maintaining assets, in monitoring loans and recoveries. Some voluntary agencies also help farmers by accepting recovery in kind.

The banks, therefore, successfully cater to the requirements while saving their costs on three counts:

- They save on appraisal costs of totally non-viable cases which are not forwarded to them.
- The appraisal by the voluntary agency provides them with adequate material for their own appraisal.
- The voluntary agencies help in monitoring and recovering.

These experiments are, however, limited to loans under existing banking norms. And, a relationship of dependency continues between the voluntary agency and the borrowers. The borrowers do not mature into analysers of their problems or enhance their managerial capacities, not to speak of the absence of adequate group pressure and support of SHGs. The positive feature is that the resources of the voluntary agency are not locked up in the form of seed capital to the SHG. Moreover, transaction costs of NGOs are high in setting up and maintaining SHGs.

14

Self-help Groups in India— An Assessment

The expansion of the rural credit delivery system since 1947 has not changed the dependence of the poor on money-lenders and commission agents/traders. The population per branch ratio has been brought down from 65,000 in 1969 to 12,000 in 1992. But this impressive growth in branch network has been uneven; in many under-developed areas, there are no branches within 10–20 km. Given the poor rural transport system, day-to-day banking transactions are negligible and the transaction costs for borrowers and bankers are also rather high. Further, the poorest of the poor (about 30 per cent of those below the poverty line) have been excluded from bank finance.

This appears to have led voluntary organisations to promote the formation of informal groups and encourage them to save small amounts for their future needs. The outcome has been the evolution of various methods of organising, collecting, managing and utilisation of funds that are collected largely by the poor themselves. The Seventh Five-Year Plan (1985–90) had emphasised the need to closely associate NGOs with rural development programmes, particularly poverty alleviation.

The London-based Barnes Institute carried out a study (May 1990) in 11 countries, including India, proving that the poor are creditworthy if credit can be chanelled to enterprising individuals and small groups through non-banking organisations. Credit schemes are founded on the basis of solidarity and loans are given to individuals in a group (between 10 and 30 people) who are also borrowers and act as co-guarantors for loans. NGOs, besides facilitating the creation of SHGs also discuss a whole range of rural problems, including social, political and personal. In several cases, after the success of the villagers' own credit efforts, commercial banks give follow-up loans without asking for any guarantors for the member of a credit group. This represents an alternative development effort.

In Karnataka, the Coolie Credit Fund was formed by landless labourers in Bagepalli Taluk, Kolar District with the help of ADATS (an NGO). It has initiated several income-generating activities since 1985. These have weaned the labourers from landlords/money-lenders who charged interest rates as high as 1 per cent per day and also prevented many from being relegated to the state of bonded labourers.

The proportion of all rural households borrowing from formal credit agencies has been steadily increasing, as revealed in the All India Debt and Investment Survey Reports (1951,1961, 1971 and 1981) set out in Table 14.1 (from 7.2 per cent in 1951 to 11.3 per cent in 1961 to 29.2 per cent in 1971 and to 61.2 per cent in 1981). Also, the percentage of non-cultivator borrowers depending on non-formal sources of credit (agriculturist money-lender, professional money-lender, landlord and trader) continued to be above 50 per cent. The dependence of the rural poor on non-institutional sources of credit is one of the causes that perpetuate their poverty and restrict surplus generation to maintain their meagre economic activities and households.

Table 14.2 shows a clear inverse relationship between the incidence of poverty reflected by asset-holding of the households and the need to incur debt for household expenditure. There is also a positive relationship between the wealth of the household and the debt contracted for productive purposes (crop loans, etc.)

Credit has been an important element in linking the factor and commodity markets in rural areas, especially where the poor are concerned. Institutional rural credit agencies lack the required mechanism to assess the credit needs of the poor and meet their specific requirements at specific points of time and hence, are at a considerable disadvantage. The emergence of SHGs in partnership with the banks, has been encouraging. The main features of these SHGs are:

- The line dividing consumption and productive credit needs is blurred when economic operations are at a subsistence level.
- Consumption credit needs for the poor are very important and also determine productivity.
- The consumption/productive credit needs of the poor have to be met

Table 14.1
Share of Debt of Rural Households: India

Sl. No.	Year/Kind of Debtor	Govt.	Coop.	Banks	Relatives and friends	Landlords	Agriculturists Money-lenders	Professional Money-lenders	Traders and Commission Agents	Others	Total Debt (Rs. Crore)
1.	1951/										
	Cultivators	3.9	3.7	–	11.4	3.2	25.2	46.8	4.7	1.1	–
	All families	3.7	3.5	–	11.5	3.5	25.2	46.4	5.1	1.1	–
2.	1961/										
	Cultivators	6.7	11.4	0.3	5.2	0.9	48.1	13.8	7.1	6.5	3126
	All families	6.6	10.4	0.3	5.8	1.1	47.0	13.8	7.5	7.5	3610
3.	1971/										
	Cultivators	7.1	22.0	2.6	13.1	8.1	23.0	13.1	8.4	2.6	3292
	All families	6.7	20.1	2.4	13.8	8.6	23.1	13.8	8.7	2.8	3754
4.	1981/										
	Cultivators	3.9	29.8	29.5	8.7	3.7	8.3	7.8	3.1	5.2	2164
	All families	4.0	28.6	28.6	9.0	4.0	8.6	8.3	3.4	5.5	2336

Source: All India Rural Debt and Investment Survey Report, 1981.
Note: Includes insurance and provident funds.
At 1970–71 wholesale prices.

as and when they arise so as to prevent dependence on non-institutional credit sources.

A flexible credit strategy which meets the needs of the poor to rise above the subsistence level of living, needs to be implemented.

SHG strategies will be analysed in-depth later.

Table 14.2
Percentage Distribution of Cash Dues Outstanding
by Asset Group and Major Purposes for Rural Households

Asset Group	Capital Expenditure	Current Expenditure	Household Expenditure
Up to Rs 1,000	5.7	3.8	79.1
1,000–5,000	12.5	9.4	59.3
5,000–10,000	19.7	8.8	44.6
10,000–20,000	24.4	20.4	34.6
20,000–50,000	35.8	19.1	27.2
50,000–1 Lakh	42.6	22.0	19.2
1 Lakh–5 Lakh	54.3	19.8	10.1
5 Lakh and Above	79.4	4.0	1.6
Total	42.4	17.6	22.4

Source: All India Rural Debt Survey Report, 1981.

Credit for the Rural Poor

The earliest form of SHGs was the cooperative credit system which aimed at bringing together poor people by promoting small savings and mutual self-help concepts. But over the years the vested interests have ensured that the cooperative institutions became bureaucratised and politicised to safeguard the narrow self-interests of a few. Though the lending performance of the cooperatives has been impressive, deposits mobilisation has been neglected. Deposits of PACS recorded an increase from Rs 15 crore in 1960–61 to Rs 1,227 crore in 1988–89 with a compound growth rate of 17 per cent a year. The management and decision-making has been passed on to a socio-economically heterogeneous group of people and effective communication has been lost, making participative management difficult. The self-help character of these institutions has been lost and overdues has been disappointing, increasing from 20 per cent in 1960–61 to 39 per cent in 1988–89. The failure and weaknesses of the cooperative system led to the growth of the commercial banking system in rural areas.

The nationalisation of 20 major commercial banks (first in 1969 and then in 1980) has seen the number of rural branches increased from 1,832 in 1969 to 32,498 in 1989. Rural branches constitute 57 per cent of the total number of branches while RRB branches have grown from 6 in 1975 to 13,920 by 1989. The main aims for this large-scale expansion were:

- Monitoring the stagnant rural economy.
- Meeting the credit needs of the rural poor.
- Bringing down the population per branch ratio from 65,000 in 1969 to 11,000 in 1992.

A large number of rural branches also had to be opened to meet the credit needs of the rural poor. This enhanced transaction costs as a disproportionately large number of small credit accounts had to be serviced. The ACRC Report (1989) observed the following major defects in the rural credit delivery system.

- The bulk of rural lending (exceeding the stipulated 40 per cent of total advances norm) is to the priority sectors; a large number of small advances is to borrowers in far-flung areas with community facilities being non-existent.
- Sanctioning and monitoring these loans is time consuming and requires more manpower as in certain areas, field officers cover 1,700 accounts each (as against the norm of 750 accounts per field officer). This has led to a dilution of loan supervision norms.
- Staff tended to accord priority to routine housekeeping functions and returns submission, and this led to poor loan recovery and reduced profitability.
- Controlling offices tried to economise on costs in rural branches and cut down staff, thereby further reducing profitability.

Government programmes like IRDP, Rural Labour Employment Programme (RLEGP), Self Employment for Educated Unemployed Youth (SEEUY), Self Employment Programme for Urban Poor (SEPUP), etc., have also not been very useful to the poor. A large number of poor families are not prepared by way of skills, attitudes and enterprise to manage activities involving relatively large financial outlays. This explains the relatively low level of loan amounts disbursed per beneficiary under the IRDP programme. The average credit disbursed per assisted family averaged Rs 2,566, Rs 2,289 and Rs 2,880 in the primary, secondary and tertiary sectors, respectively as against the maximum limit ranging from Rs 3,000 to Rs 9,000 (NABARD study–IRDP 1985). Also, a large number of the rural poor has remained outside the purview of the formal credit system.

The experience of other Asian countries has been the same; programmes for amelioration of rural poverty based on cheap credit availability, liberal institutions, etc., have not been successful. The premise that the poor are unable to save or organise themselves and need cheap credit is now being examined afresh. A report on 'Linking Self-help Groups and Banks in Developing Countries' (APRACA/GTZ Deutsche Gesellschaft fur Techniche Zussammenarbeit, German Technical Co-operation 1989) has pointed out that interest rates were set below market rates; the cost of funds inhibited banks from covering a large number of the poor; and, the lending portfolio remained limited as local resources were not mobilised and the programmes depended on foreign aid. A significant point made was that the credit programmes were not linked to a savings component which led to poor repayment performance.

Mounting international debt, shortage of internal resources and growing dissatisfaction with state-nurtured and largely ineffective credit programmes have led to changes in developmental policies and now, concepts such as self-help, self-sufficiency and self-reliance are being explored. In 1984, these issues were discussed at an international conference organised by the United Nations. At the APRACA Regional Workshop in China (May 1986), a coordinated programme for the promotion of linkages between banks and SHGs for savings mobilisation and credit delivery to the rural poor, was agreed upon.

Financing Informal Groups

In recent years, several voluntary agencies working for the development of weaker sections through social organisations, informal education, skills improvement programmes, etc., have sought to widen the access of groups to formal credit institutions so that they can widen their production base. Apart from persuading bankers to extend credit to such groups, based on their own formal or informal guarantees, a major initiative undertaken by some of the voluntary agencies has been to form groups comprising the underprivileged rural poor and assist them in promoting savings and credit activities. The groups have been encouraged to practise thrift and the small savings collected are lent to individual members to meet consumption needs.

Such group formation can not only help impart credit management skills to individuals but also lead to better end use of credit and prompt repayment due to group pressure. If proper linkages are established with groups, bank financing could lead to lower transaction costs and systematic credit supervision—resulting in the improved cycling of funds. There is a growing feeling that closer interaction between SHGs and banks resulting in the area of group financing may possibly lead to improved access of formal credit for the rural poor.

The credit needs of members are usually assessed in periodic (monthly) group meetings where competing claims on limited resources are settled by consensus and dues from members are collected. The surplus, if any, is deposited in the savings accounts with banks or post offices. There is usually little or minimal documentation between the borrowing member and the group. Defaulters, either in loan repayments or non-participation in group meetings, usually face stiff penalties but such occurrences are rare.

Certain features of the SHG experience are relevant for devising future credit strategies for the poor. Crossing the poverty line by particular families is possible only when the poor socio-economic situation is realised by the family and depends on the enterprise and ingenuity shown by the family. While not denying the need for technical support services and other guidance, the SHG studies stress that the poor themselves are likely to have a better appreciation of their socio-economic situation, the micro-enterprises that can come forth and the necessary support required for the same. Official agencies, including credit agencies, could strive to create conditions whereby responsible self-management by the poor is fostered.

Another aspect relates to the perceived low or negative profitability of lending to the poor and the problem of high overdues of the formal credit structure. The nearly cent per cent recovery rates of SHGs stand out in sharp contrast. The underlying reasons for the high overdues of the formal structure are usually classified into those which are internal to the banking system and those which are external. The internal factors comprise defective loan policies and procedures involving under/over financing, improper choice of beneficiary and activity, inability to link credit with marketing, non-recognition of the need for consumption finance, especially, to the poor end of the beneficiary spectrum and ineffective credit supervision. The external factors relate to the weaknesses and uncertainties of the agricultural and rural economy, natural calamities leading to losses in enterprises, the vitiating impact of target pressures and subsidies, and the politicisation of the rural credit delivery system.

Some of the internal factors are effectively countered through the SHG concept. SHGs have a better appreciation of the enterprise and willingness of its individual members to undertake specific economic activities. The ability of the member to bring forth his own resources and the extent of external credit support is better assessed by the members of the group. The diversion of finance and the income generated from the activity can not be hidden from the rest of the group. And the very proximity of the group ensures the recovery of the dues. Certain SHGs like those promoted by the Aga Khan Rural Support Programme in Gujarat undertake pooled marketing of their produce or its processing. As the entire credit cycle of assessment of need, appraisal, disbursement, monitoring, supervision and recovery is closer to the scene of action under the SHG model, the consumption requirements of members are also better taken care of.

The external causes involving politicisation of the credit business and environmental encouragement of default are better answered by the SHG concept. According to one of the liberal estimates of the ACRC drawn from a sample study, nearly 50 per cent of defaulter borrowers could be classified as wilful defaulters. Conversely, if credit finance is seen as the management of one's own funds and enterprise, a feeling of responsibility in the borrower would be generated. SHGs generate such a feeling of ownership and self-management; they also inculcate in the member borrowers, the concept of recycling of credit resources.

In many respects, there is considerable commonality of principles between PACSs and SHGs. SHGs are not a channel of credit competing with cooperatives. The experiences of SHGs indicate that they have usually worked with sections, especially the poor, that are neither served by cooperatives nor are their emergent needs covered by formal credit agencies, including the PACSs.

Differences between the PACSs and SHGs are:

- Cooperatives tend to be large and formal reducing the participation of individual members. The typical size of an SHG would be around 20 members.
- In cooperatives, in spite of the one-man-one-vote principle, the needs of poor borrowers get marginalised because of the stronger economic and political status of the vested interests. Typical SHGs consisting of poor members having homogeneous socio-economic backgrounds, are likely to serve the credit needs of the poor better.
- The cooperatives tend to get dominated by the vested interests. The SHG working is managed through consensus of all members during periodic, usually monthly meetings.

Historically, cooperative credit institutions represented the earliest form of self-help initiatives. Over the years, their self-help character has declined due to various reasons. However, if democratic participation in management, decision-making and self-help values are resorted to, cooperative credit institutions with their well-entrenched network would be able to greatly improve the access of the rural poor to formal credit. with regard to banks, experience suggests that the scope to lend further to the production-cum-investment of dry land areas also appears best amenable to the group approach. The group approach has also been adopted in implementing the DWCRA—a sub-component of the IRDP—to bring women together for pursuing economic activities. Thus, it appears that recognising the importance and merits of group lending, banking institutions have made a fresh beginning to dovetail in their credit strategy, the group approach in lending to the rural sector.

The difficulties in establishing linkages between SHGs and banks still persist. The problem in lending to such groups arises mainly on account of the absence of legal status. The other problem faced by the banks is that of high demand for consumption loans. The legal problem could be overcome if the NGO that has promoted the group is registered, and is willing to act as a guarantor. The banks, in such cases, could finance NGOs for on-lending to the members of the group. But if the NGO is not registered, then the banks find it difficult to establish credit linkages. In such a situation, there is a need either to simplify the existing documentation procedures as done in the case of the DWCRA experiment or to evolve a guarantee mechanism by way of establishing a suitable risk fund, at least in the initial stages of this experiment.

Collateral Security Needs of Banks

One finds different interpretations of the term collateral under different situations in different countries. Even though security lending in Indian banking has been followed for a long time, the norms have been relaxed for financing marginal and small farmers as also for small enterprises. The bank lending norms as per the guidelines followed at present in respect of a loan for Rs 15,000 or more—for acquisition of movable farm/non-farm assets require additional collateral by way of mortgage of land and/or third-party guarantee. However, for land-based immovable farm activities, loans above Rs 5,000 require security by way of mortgage of land.

Even though security has not been insisted upon for providing loans to the weaker sections, their access to institutional credit is very limited. From the banker's point of view, they are not able to meet the demand of loans for weaker sections because of the large clientele. Further, their financial requirements are small and quite frequent and that too, for consumption needs. Bankers also have reservations on whether these small borrowers will repay their loans without any security. This situation warrants the need for grouping the rural poor, which would facilitate gaining a collective moral/social strength either to meet their needs or to avail loans from banks. Here, group pressures, assurance and peer-pressure act as collateral security and experience highlights that they can do better in groups rather than individually. Under the present situation where security lending has not shown encouraging performance in recovery, considerations of group pressure are more realistic and appropriate. Group pressure and moral/social security have been considered as collateral substitute for financing micro-enterprises of the rural poor.

One of the disquieting features of financing by rural credit institutions to small and medium enterprises is huge defaults in repayments resulting in poor recycling of funds and reluctance to lend further. Surprisingly, the recovery performance is bad in cases where banks had taken primary/collateral securities and where security norms were relaxed as per government/RBI directions. In fact, even after spending large amounts on legal proceedings, banks have often not been able to enforce securities or recover any substantial amount. It is, therefore, being realised more and more that while financing small and very small entrepreneurs, it is not the availability of security that will ensure repayments but winning their confidence, organising them properly, guiding and monitoring them. Perhaps, that is why loans to small entrepreneurs to or through SHGs are being regarded as more suitable by banks as well as NGOs. The results of a study conducted by S.C.Wadhwa ex-General Manager from NABARD are given below:

Performance of a Bank Branch in SHG Lending

a) The performance of the Indian Bank branch at Thalli village, Dharampuri district, Tamil Nadu, has been analysed with regard to SHG financing and the results have been tabulated:

- Staff strength—4 officers, 5 clerks and messengers
- Service area—10 villages, 7,350 households
- Performance indicators—given in Table 14.3.

Table 14.3
Performance Indications of Selected Bank Branch

(Rs lakh)

Year	Deposits	Advances Outstanding
1988-89	62.10	70.94
1989-90	81.67	77.52
1990-91	111.58	77.77

Note: Mainly priority sector advances (2,018 a/c.).

b) SHG project particulars

- Implemented in 1989—22 SHGs with 274 members
- Amount advanced in 1990–91—Rs 90,109 (13 per cent of total priority sector advances)
- Loans given for purchase of dairy animals, sheep, sericulture, consumption, non-farm activities, without security as per existing RBI norms.
- Repayment performance of branch in priority sector advances—43 per cent (1990–91).
- Repayment performance of branch in SHG loans—87 per cent (1990–91).

c) Average cost of lending per account—is given in Table 14.4.

Table 14.4
Average Cost of Lending per Account

(Rs)

Particulars	SHG Members	Non-SHG Members
Salary & Allowances		
(incl. Travelling Expenses)	81	135
Estimated Expenses	8	8
Other Expenses	14	14
	103	157

The average lending cost of a bank for an SHG loan is two-thirds of other loans due to less follow-up and savings in manpower and travel expenses.

If all priority sector lending is through SHGs, monthly expenditure of branch reduces to Rs 1.09 lakh and profits are enhanced threefold.

d) The recovery performance for SHGs is clearly outstanding. The recovery performance for 1990–91 is given in Table 14.5.

Table 14.5
Recovery Performance of Selected Bank Branch (1990–91)

(Rs lakh)

Particulars	Current Demand	Collection	Balance	% of Recovery
1. Branch Level				
i) Direct Lending	32.80	13.95	18.85	42.53
ii) SHG Lending	9.02	7.83	1.19	86.81
2. Selected Villages				
i) Non-SHG	66.00	25.00	41.00	37.88
ii) SHG Beneficiaries	26.00	24.00	2.00	92.30

Lending through SHGs—Borrowers' View Points

a) The performance of the Manjunatha Mahila Sangha (1989), a women's SHG (with MYRADA assistance) in Gumalapuram village, Dharampuri, district was studied. The village has 140 households, with landholdings between half an acre to five acres, of which 15 per cent are landless agricultural labourers. MYRADA has been working with the villagers for several years and has been able to convince them about the need for forging small homogeneous groups for solving mutual problems, for thrift savings and for more power. The selected SHG has 19 members with seven having marginal landholdings of half-an-acre to three acres. Twelve members are agricultural labourers. The secretary and president's posts are rotated among the members every year and they conduct meetings and banking operations. An educated member of the group records the procedures of weekly meetings, maintains accounts and is also the animator on behalf of MYRADA (with a stipend of Rs 150 per month). Members contribute between Rs 5 and Rs 7 per week; the total savings is Rs 8,120 and Rs 2,150 is the interest earned by the SHG.

b) A break-up of the resources of the SHG is given in Table 14.6.

Table 14.6
Resources of Selected SHG

(Rs)

Source	1989	1990	1991	Total
Savings	1,120	2,172	4,828	8,120
MYRADA Contribution to Crop Loan(currently rotated)	–	1,500	3,000	4,500
Interest Income	46	570	1,534	2,150
Total	1,166	4,242	9,362	14,770

Loans are recovered within six years and the group decides on who is to be given a loan, the rate of interest and the quantum of the loan. Interest rates vary from 12 per cent for loan for health purposes to 48 per cent for festivals and social functions.

c) The lending pattern of the SHG is given in Table14.7.

Table 14.7
Lending Pattern of Selected SHG

(Rs)

Purpose	No.of Loans Issued	Amount Lent	Average Loan Disbursed
Health	11	5,472	497
Consumption	6	3,200	533
Marriage	4	2,880	720
House Repairs	1	960	960
Agriculture	1	320	320
Sericulture	1	628	628
Total	24	13,460	561

The average loan amount is Rs 561. Members generally keep the loan amount low, as they have to repay the loan. Capacity to repay is one of the important factors for getting a loan.

d) Linkage with banks

The Indian Bank branch at Thalli has provided loan assistance for nine members (IFAD Project) for cows/sheep totalling Rs 64,000 (average Rs 7,111) with 10 per cent interest. The group's recommendation is very important but an additional appraisal is done by the bank. Bank officers made 4–5 initial visits for confidence-building measures and also attended weekly meetings as observers prior to the linkage. There was 100 per cent loan utilisation and the repayment performance for 1990–91 is given in Table 14.8.

Table 14.8

Recovery Performance in Selected SHG

(Rs)

	Particulars	Demand	Collection	Balance	% of Recovery
1.	Bank Loan to SHG Members	13,976	13,043	933	93
2.	SHG Loan	4,675	4,462	2,133	95
3.	Bank Loan for Non-SHG Members	21,315	8,526	12,789	40

Recovery rates for SHG members average over 93 per cent but for loans in the same village to non-SHG members, the recovery rates are around 40 per cent with loan utilisation at only 50 per cent. Bank officers were pleased with the SHG loan performance. As a result, group members could get Rs 64,000 in loans (5 times the funds collected through SHG deposits). Thus, the SHG has been useful for the bank and the borrowers. However, bankers were apprehensive of loans to defaulters of earlier bank loans who were now SHG members. SHG group pressure forced three defaulter-members to repay earlier bank dues. This has generated greater trust in SHG activities among bank officials. SHG formation has been useful both for the members and the bank, and should be replicated all over the country.

Impact of Financing Through SHGs

In a micro-economic context, SHGs have been beneficial to its members, giving them access to timely credit that is less costly than credit from all formal or informal sources depending on the risk perception. Before advocating a parallel system for credit intermediation through SHGs, it would be necessary to study in depth, the macro-economic and the conceptual issues involved. Some of the conceptual issues for in-depth analysis are:

- Whether adding SHGs to an already-complex rural credit delivery system would merely add another tier or reduce transaction costs, achieve better loan recovery and mobilise low-cost deposits?
- Whether adequate number of quality NGOs exist for channelising formal rural credit?
- Whether RBI/NABARD intervention would be necessary to provide

low-cost funds to SHGs through banks to sustain or expand their operations?
- Whether external funds made available to SHGs, disproportionate to members' own savings will dilute the principle of self-help propagated by SHGs?
- Whether concessional funds are necessary to sustain SHG lending or whether commercial/cooperative banks could provide funds from their own lendable resources (without cheap refinance)?

These issues are important especially if the SHG model is to be replicated without adding to the stress on the existing rural credit delivery system.

Objectives of SHG Linkage

It is necessary to note down the objectives of the linkage programme. These are:

- To evolve supplementary credit strategies for meeting the needs of the poor by combining the flexibility, sensitivity and responsiveness of the informal credit system with the technical/administrative capabilities and financial resources of formal financial institutions.
- To build mutual trust and confidence between bankers and the rural poor.
- To encourage banking activity in both the thrift and credit aspects in a segment of the population that formal financial institutions usually find difficult to reach.

SHG Models

Due to the flexibility of the programme, different SHG models can be experimented with. These different models are:

- Banks deal directly with the SHG, providing financial assistance for on-lending to individual members.
- Banks give direct assistance to the SHG while the NGO provides training and guidance to the SHG for effective functioning.
- The NGO can be a financial intermediary between the bank and a number of SHGs, with the NGO accepting the contractual respon-

sibility for loan repayment to the bank and the linkage between the bank and the SHG is indirect.

Banks give loans directly to individual SHG members on recommendations of the SHG and the NGO. The NGO assists the bank in monitoring, supervising and recovery of loans.

A conservative banker will start with the third model and depend on the NGO while a good banker–NGO relationship would start with model two or even model one. However, the general evolutionary process is to move from model three to model two, then to model one and finally, to model four wherein individuals have direct access to the bank.

SHG Functions and Characteristics

SHGs are mostly informal groups where members pool savings and re-lend in the group on a rotational basis. The groups have a common perception of need and improvise towards collective action. Many such groups formed around specific production activities, promote savings among members and use the pooled resources to meet various credit needs of members (especially consumption needs). Where funds generation is low in the initial phases due to low saving capacities, this is supplemented by external resources loaned/donated by NGOs. Thus, SHGs have been able to provide primitive banking services to its members that are cost-effective, flexible and without defaults. Based on local requirements, SHGs have evolved their own characteristics of functioning:

- Group members usually create a common fund by contributing their small savings on a regular basis.
- Groups evolve flexible systems of working (sometimes with the help of NGOs) and manage pooled resources in a democratic way.
- Loan requests are considered by groups in periodic meetings and competing claims on limited resources are settled by consensus.
- Loans are given mainly on trust with minimum documentation and without any security.
- The loan amounts are small, frequent, for short duration and are mainly for unconventional purposes.
- The rates of interest vary from group to group and the purpose of loan. It is higher than that of banks but lower than that of moneylenders.
- At periodic meetings, besides collecting money, social and economic issues are also discussed.

- Defaults are rare due to group pressure and intimate knowledge of the end use of credit.

Bank Linkage Scheme of NABARD

India has over 150,000 credit outlets including cooperatives in the rural institutional sector. In 1993 outstanding bank loans for agricultural purposes amounted to Rs 340 billion. In spite of this, rural people still depend on money-lenders for consumption purposes. Such dependence is pronounced in resource-poor areas and in the case of marginal farmers, landless labourers, petty traders and artisans belonging to the socially and backward classes, and the tribal population. The core problem of rural finance is the high transaction costs of a large number of small but frequent borrowers for consumption/production needs. Transaction costs for IRDP loans have been assessed at 24.6 per cent. Transaction costs of operating a savings account with a bank was as high as 10 per cent of the savings (assuming one transaction per month). (DEAR Study Report on SHG, NABARD News Review, November 1997.)

To develop a supplementary credit delivery system to reach the poor in a cost-effective and sustainable manner, NABARD introduced a pilot project for linking up SHGs in 1992. The targets/achievements for this project are given in Table 14.9.

Table 14.9

Targets and Achievements in NABARD's Pilot Project on Bank–SHG Linkage

(Rs lakh)

Targeted No. (SHGs)	March 1994	March 1995	March 1996	March 1997
Targeted No. of SHGs	500	2,000	4,000	8,000
Achievement in No. of SHGs Linked	620	2,122	4,757	8,598
Of Them, Women SHGs	332	1,850	3,496	6,569
Bank Loan	84.20	244.49	605.84	1,183.62
NB Refinance	45.93	229.34	566.12	1,064.95

The broad principles were followed under the Linkage Scheme were:

- Savings first, no credit without savings
- Savings as partial collateral
- Bank loans to the SHG for on-lending to members

- Credit decisions for on-lending to SHG members
- Interest rates and other terms and conditions for loans to members to be decided by the group
- Joint liability as a substitute for physical collateral
- Ratio between savings and credit contingent upon credit worthiness and could increase over a period due to good repayment record, if needed.
- Small loans to begin with and different credit cycles clearly defined.

To review the linkage process, various studies were carried out by NABARD. The findings confirmed the following:

- Large participation in the project by women, particularly in resource-poor regions.
- Membership in SHGs mostly came from the poorest sections of society.
- Demand for credit is frequent, for small amounts, at unpredictable times and not necessarily for purchasing income-generating assets.
- Even the very poor are able to save and savings increased with addition to their incomes.
- SHG intermediation led to reduction in the time spent by the bank staff on identification of borrowers, documentation, follow-up and recoveries. This resulted in 40 per cent reduction in transaction cost which could increase further with increase in loan sizes.
- SHG intermediation significantly reduced transaction costs of the borrower due to elimination of cumbersome documentation procedures, time spent and costs incurred on repeated visits to banks, etc. The reduction was estimated to be 85 per cent.

Seeing the success of the linkage scheme, NABARD decided to intensify the programme so as to improve the outreach of the formal banking system in a cost-effective manner. The aim being to enhance the quality of credit in rural areas and promote people's participation in self-help and grassroots institutions. The initiatives taken by NABARD for SHG formation are:

- Providing policy inputs in coordination with RBI
- Coordination with banks
- 100 per cent refinance facility at 6.5 per cent interest per annum to banks
- Training programmes for bank/NGO officials at CAB, NIBM, XIM
- Exposure programmes at district level for bank/NGOs.

Alternative System or Supplementary System?

The poorer sections of rural society have not benefited from various government programmes nor have they access to the formal banking system. Besides high transaction costs, the perception of risks in financing small borrowers—who are unable to offer physical collateral, articulate their wants or submit proper loan proposals—the urban orientation of bank staff and lack of flexibility in operations are all factors which add to the physical and social distance of poor people from banks. Also, banks do not give money for consumption needs. The informal banking system in rural areas comprising money-lenders, shopkeepers, friends and relatives are willing to lend money, without lengthy documentation and collateral but at very high interest rates (3–10 per cent per month) and at terms loaded in favour of the lender, such as purchase of raw material from a supplier with deferred payment or pre-harvest sale of a crop with immediate payment.

The availability of alternative financial services could do much to improve the welfare of the rural poor and their families. The NGO–SHG–bank linkage seems to offer an alternative.

The number of NGOs registered in the country are numerous but their interests vary. According to CAPART estimates (see Table 14.10) most are keen on social welfare, many on environmental issues, some on gender issues, a few in education and some are political activists; only a very few are interested in rural development or thrift issues.

Table 14.10
Particulars of Selected NGOs

	Orissa	All India
i) No. of NGOs	5,817	23,780
ii) Of Whom Interested in Rural Development/Thrift	105	1,999
iii) Linked with Banks and SHG Programme	9	57

NABARD, Bhubaneswar, has been having regular state/district-level seminars in which all NGOs in the state are being regularly invited. Many NGOs have participated in the discussions but the actual number of NGOs that have been linked up in over three-and-a-half years (1992–95) is only nine. A few NGOs who have SHGs are not keen to act as facilitators but do wish to accept loans on behalf of SHGs, for on-lending purposes. Most major banks in Orissa like SBI, UCO Bank, Andhra Bank etc., have not entered into the linkage phase yet, due to their reservations about NGOs. Thus, the linkage process is an uphill struggle; the success rate among NGOs is about 10 per cent and among banks 20 per cent.

The formal banking system, despite having over 150,000 credit outlets, does not meet the credit requirements of the rural poor especially as the population per branch ratio is over 11,000 and there are large areas in the country exceeding 300 sq. km where there are no bank branches. Thus, it is clear that the SHG-based linkage programme can play a supplementary role in areas where good NGOs are functioning and which believe in the system of credit linkage with banks. In Orissa, NABARD has conducted over 24 exposure programmes and nine orientation programmes for banks/ NGO officials in various districts since 1992. Despite the sustained efforts over three-and-a-half years, the number of NGOs who have established SHGs with bank linkages has been only nine. A total of 404 SHGs were setup. Between October 1992 and October 1995, NABARD, Bhubaneswar, convened nine three-day SHG state-level workshops which were attended by 200 participants, including 81 NGO representatives. During that same period, 24 district-level meets were held, attended by 1,114 participants, including bankers, government officials and 343 representatives from 100 NGOs.

However, there has been poor response from many major banks and NGOs. In certain states like Maharashtra and Bihar, bankers have refused to allow SHGs to open accounts for purpose of bank linkages and need specific RBI instructions for the purpose. Many NGOs get foreign funds in large amounts and do not encourage SHGs or are wary of the banking system, which is seen to be 'exploitative' or 'callous'. Conversely, many banks are wary of dealing with NGOs whom they perceive as 'indisciplined' and 'uncontrolled' elements who are against the banking system. Only four RRBs (out of nine RRBs), four commercial banks (out of 28 commercial banks) and one CCB (out of 17 CCBs) have set up SHGs. Thus, the SHG linkage programme with banks and NGOs can never be an alternative system; at best, it can be a supplementary system.

At an all India level, only 57 NGOs have been involved in the bank linkage programme in 11 states. NABARD has initiated a dialogue with NGOs for reviewing the slow progress. Some of the reasons identified were:

- The concept of linkage has not percolated down to the branch level, with each bank having its own guidelines.
- SHG lending is not perceived as normal lending activity but is seen as a special concessional dispensation.

- Most banks do not favour direct SHG linkage but prefer linkage through NGOs. Many NGOs are not in favour of this as it would dilute their focus on developmental work.
- Many NGOs view this linkage only as a pilot project and not as a general purpose of extending credit facility. NGOs favour the direct SHG-bank linkage.
- Many banks/branch officials do not favour the SHG approach.

Also, in Punjab, Haryana and Western UP, where the number of people below the poverty line is lower, there is no enthusiasm to promote SHGs. Further, in the north-east, a different approach is needed due to socio-political factors. Group-based savings in southern India has been traditionally popular but SHGs have failed to make much headway in Bihar, eastern UP, MP, Rajasthan and West Bengal.

NABARD sent a questionnaire to 95 NGOs in 20 states who were known to be involved in credit/thrift activities but without any bank linkage, to find out the reasons for lack of enthusiasm. Only 22 NGOs replied. Of these 11 NGOs were working with village councils (gram sabhas) while a few promoted SHGs with specific activities like irrigation, handicrafts, etc. Several organised Mahila Samitis or SHGs to carry out women-oriented development schemes and social activities. Only a very small number were engaged in promoting group-based thrift and credit activities. They felt the following constraints:

- Expert manpower has to be committed by the NGO in nurturing SHGs in the initial stages.
- SHG committee members have to be trained to maintain records and loan accounts.
- SHG formation is relatively easy, the major problem is establishing linkages with banks.
- People do not voluntarily organise themselves into groups except in times of crises. SHG formation will take time and effort.

It may also be noted that certain NGOs thought it appropriate to organise separate banks/cooperatives to take care of the credit requirements like World Women Federation (WWF), Madras, and SEWA, Ahmedabad.

Thus, due to the non-congruence of goals between NGOs and banks, there is no chance of the SHG linkage programme developing into an alternative rural credit delivery system. At most, this programme will emerge as a cost-effective supplement to the existing rural credit delivery system. However, prudent linking of SHGs with banks could increase the demand for credit without commensurate increase in costs.

Concessional Funds for SHGs

The rural credit delivery system has been weakened by the poor recovery of loans, high operating cost of cooperatives and commercial banks, burden of subsidised interest rates and loan write-offs. Small farmers, agricultural landless labourers, rural artisans, rural women, SC/ST people, etc., have suffered from the non-availability of timely credit as most of the concessional credit is cornered by the wealthy farmers and the politically well-connected sections of rural society.

Improving the outreach of our banking system and deepening of rural credit by introducing a viable supplementary rural credit delivery system for the poorer sections of society is thus, a felt need. The SHG–bank linkage programme with the assistance of NGOs seeks to meet this long-felt need.

The use of concessional refinance for SHG linkage does not ensure cheap funds for the borrower as SHGs charge high rates of interest ranging from 10 per cent to 24 per cent, depending upon the need and risk involved. Concessional refinance is a tool to ensure that banks are involved in the programme. The volume of concessional refinance from NABARD for the rural sector and that given for SHGs, is given in Table 14.11.

Table 14.11
Concessional Refinance from NABARD

			(Rs crore)
Year/Refinance Purpose		*1993–94*	*1994–95*
1.	SHG	0.76	2.29
2.	ST(O/S)	4,168.18	4,564.88
3.	LT	2,745.00	3,010.75
	Total Refinance	6,913.94	8,597.92

SHG refinance as a percentage of total refinance for rural agencies is totally insignificant and cannot be expected to replace the present rural credit delivery system. But, it can be a useful supplementary for ensuring prompt credit for the really poor, with hardly any transaction costs for the banks and borrowers. The emphasis is on thrift as a major precondition for SHG linkage with banks. A few case studies of the level of savings and the extent of credit linkages with banks would be useful.

Case Studies in Bank Linkage Programmes in Orissa by NABARD

A study on the SHG linkage programme was carried out in June 1995 as regards the need for funds by the SHGs, the extent of savings and the demand for loans. Five NGOs which had set up SHGs, were studied (see Table 14.12). Of them, three had set up linkages with banks while the other two did not contemplate bank linkage. The data for all case studies is as on 31 March 1995.

Table 14.12
Details of Selected NGOs and their Areas of Functions

Sl. No.	Name of the NGO	Areas of Functions	Date Set Up	Date SHGs Set Up
1.	Fellowship	Bhadrak	1987	1993
2.	PREM/UMSBSMS	Ganjam, Koraput, Gajapathi, Rayagada, Puri	1984	1992
3.	India Development Project	Keonjhar	1989	1993
4.	United Artists Association	Ganjam	1966	1989
5.	Gopinath Yuvak Sangh	Puri	1983	1994

Fellowship Sponsored SHGs Linked with Balasore Grameen Bank

Fellowship set up five SHGs in Jan–Feb 1993 on receipt of RBI/NB circulars relating to SHGs. Sixty-eight members jointly saved Rs 29,470 and took a bank loan of Rs 19,200. Thus, the average savings over nine months was Rs 433 per person. Out of 68 members, 21 were borrowers and the average loan taken by each was Rs 2,318 but the actual loan amount varied according to the productive activity. If the bank loan had not been taken, then the average loan for each of the 21 borrowers would have been only Rs 1,403 and would not have met their production credit requirements. These SHGs had been functioning well and repayments were good. This encouraged the NGO to set up linkages for 14 more SHGs that were about 10 months old.

The 14 SHGs had 196 members who together saved Rs 36,975 and took a loan of Rs 66,785. The average savings per person was Rs 189 and the average loan taken by each borrower was Rs 1,789. There is no obvious link between savings and loan taken, and each SHG decides as to what will be the quantum of savings and loan amount sanctioned. If the loan amount from the bank had not been sanctioned, the average loan per borrower would be only Rs 638, too low for the production credit needs of the borrowers. While the first five SHGs linked up and took loans in the ratio 2:1, of the next 14 SHGs, 11 took loans in the ratio 1:2 and three took loans in the ratio 1:1. Availability of concessional funds did not mean that the borrowers took recourse to loans indiscriminately. Loans were taken on the basis of members' needs. In the first batch, 27.6 per cent took loans (see Table 14.13).

Table 14.13

Fellowship Sponsored SHGs—Balasore Grameen Bank, Jaganathpur, Bhadrak (All Women)

(Rs)

Sl. No.	Name of the SHG	Savings	Bank Loan	No. of Members	No. of Borrowers	Date of Establishment
	20-Oct-1993					
1.	Subhadra	7,270	7,270	16	8	08-Jan-1993
2.	Bhadrakali	4,800	2,400	10	3	09-Jan-1993
3.	Sagar	5,000	2,500	13	4	16-Jan-1993
4.	Sahini	6,400	4,000	14	3	29-Jan-1993
5.	Janani	6,000	3,000	15	3	20-Feb-1993
	5	29,470	19,170	68	21	
	31-Mar-1995					
1.	Jagasakti	4,410	8,820	16	6	01-Apr-1993
2.	Trisakti	1,880	3,760	15	3	24-Oct-1993
3.	Gaspabe	3,125	6,250	12	6	04-Jan-1994
4.	Champua	1,170	2,340	14	4	04-Jan-1994
5.	Laxmi	3,220	3,200	12	3	08-Jan-1994
6.	Jaydurga	1,850	3,700	16	4	10-Jan-1994
7.	Tarini	2,680	5,360	13	4	10-Jan-1994
8.	Maa Tharapith	3,945	3,945	14	4	08-Feb-1994
9.	Noor	3,660	7,320	16	5	12-Feb-1994

Table 14.13 Cont.

Sl. No.	Name of the SHG	Savings	Bank Loan	No.of Members	No.of Borrowers	Date of Establishment
10.	Tiranga	1,280	2,560	13	3	16-Feb-1994
11.	Sultania	5,090	10,180	14	6	10-Apr-1994
12.	Milan	1,080	2,160	14	3	20-Apr-1994
13.	Gauria	2,325	4,650	15	4	02-May-1994
14.	Mansoor Baba	1,260	2,520	12	3	20-May-1994
	14	36,975	66,765	196	58	

Source: Field Survey by NABARD Bhubaneswar, 1995.

PREM–UMSBSMS Sponsored SHGs Linked with Canara Bank

About 800 thrift groups were set up by UMSBSMS, an affiliate of PREM, operating in Southern Orissa over six districts in February 1992. These were converted into SHGs on receipt of RBI/NABARD instructions. They were apprehensive about the credit-linkage programme and proceeded very cautiously. It was decided that only those SHG members who saved a minimum of Rs 10 per month for 24 months, would be considered for loans. Further, the progress of each of the 800 SHGs was watched. Only 308 SHGs, which were functioning well, were selected for bank linkage (see Table 14.14). The savings were poor as the SHGs were set up amongst very poor people. The total of 16,381 SHG members collected Rs 1,42,145 over two years, averaging Rs 87 per SHG borrower.

The NGO (PREM) kept a deposit of Rs 14 lakh with Canara Bank, as collateral and took a loan of Rs 18.24 lakh for 3,513 borrowers who qualified for loans. Even though the borrowers needed about Rs 1,000 each towards small production loans, the NGO decided that the first loan would not exceed Rs 500 per borrower and the interest charged was only 9.5 per cent.

PREM requested NABARD to bear the printing and other operational expenses for the SHG linkage, amounting to Rs 1,15,000; NABARD reimbursed Rs 57,500. SHG members wanted more loans and the NGO promised to consider Rs 1,500 per borrower in the second loan cycle. If there was no bank linkage, the borrowers would have got only Rs 404 on an average. Recovery rates have exceeded 100 per cent in the coastal areas due to advance repayments but in the hill areas, repayments have been poor due to the non-availability of income-earning opportunities.

Table 14.14
PREM–UMSBSMS Sponsored SHGs—Canara Bank, Berhampur (All Women)

(Rs)

Sl. No.	Name of Blocks	No. of SHGs	Total Members	Total Deposits	Bank Loan	No. of Borrowers
1.	Mohana (BKGs)	82	5,333	373,640	384,000	768
2.	Brahmagiri (VV)	89	1,817	163,295	525,000	1,050
3.	Gopalpur	15	950	141,530	128,500	257
4.	R.Udayagiri (JJ)	19	312	89,795	99,500	199
5.	Konark (CPDA)	11	354	61,175	180,000	225
6.	Rayagada (KSD)	24	1,114	96,140	150,000	300
7.	Nuagada (PV)	0	2,097	145,995	0	0
8.	Gunpur (CD)	27	758	60,980	150,000	300
9.	Padampur (PP)	26	663	43,290	128,000	256
10.	Daringbadi (SSS)	0	1,190	92,625	0	0
11.	Sorada	5	579	42,660	20,000	40
12.	Khemundikhol (JJ)	10	539	34,915	59,000	118
13.	Brahmunigaon	0	609	41,195	0	0
14.	Raikia (S)	0	325	10,860	0	0
15.	Mandasoor	0	541	22,580	0	0
		308	17,181	1,420,675	1,824,000	3,513

Source: Field Study Survey, 1995.

The NGO was unsure of the repayment performance and hence kept the interest rate of the ultimate borrower very low (9.5 per cent) keeping no margin for operating expenses. Also, the loan amount was only Rs 500 when the requirement was Rs 1,000. It is apparent that the slender savings of the SHG members have to be augmented by the bank linkage process. However, the loan cycle is linked to the economic activity and repayment performance is carefully monitored.

India Development Project Linked with Bank of India

The NGO set up nine SHGs with 136 members (averaging 15 members) in the poor district of Keonjhar. The members saved Rs 5,325 over 12–14 months, averaging Rs 136 per member. Given the low savings and 1:1 linkage, the average loan amount per borrower was only Rs 64 and members needed it for bidi-papad making. The loan amount is clearly inadequate for meeting the credit requirements. However, the SHG loans are a very important avenue for augmenting their incomes of the tribal women who utilise the loan amount for purchasing raw materials. Without a bank loan, the average loan amount would be only Rs 32. Hence, bank linkage is very important here as it supplements the loanable funds by 100 per cent (see Table14.15).

Table 14.15
India Development Project, Keonjhar—Bank of India, Ghatagaon (All Women)

(Rs)

Sl. No.	Name of SHGs	No. of Members	No. of Borrowers	Amount Saved	Bank Loan	Date of Establishment
1.	Mahalaxmi M.S.	16	3	700	700	07-Nov-1993
2.	Tarini M.S.	19	2	1,050	1,050	30-Nov-1993
3.	Sibani M.S.	13	1	150	150	11-Dec-1993
4.	Mahashakti M.S.	14	2	400	400	17-Jan-1994
5.	Kalyani M.S.	15	1	375	375	17-Jan-1994
6.	Maa Mangala M.S.	16	3	1,000	1,000	30-Jan-1994
7.	Parbati M.S.	11	2	600	600	12-Feb-1994
8.	Barijar M.S.	17	2	800	800	07-Mar-1994
9.	Dharitri M.S.	15	2	250	250	16-Mar-1994
		136	18	5,325	5,325	

Source: Field Study Survey, 1995.

United Artists Associates

United Artists Associates was started in 1966 for social and economic development and covers 15 community development blocks in Ganjam and aims at savings, credit and income generation. There are 100 groups with 911 members, covering 2000 families. Total savings amounted to Rs 83,715; saving per group was Rs 838 on an average and the average loan amount per member was only Rs 95. The maximum loan amount per member was only Rs 300 though there is need for more loans. Loan rationing was resorted to and in spite of the credit groups functioning since 1966, not much economic progress has been achieved.

Bank linkage and the resultant boost available to economic activity has not taken place. Only marginal economic activities are being continued while income generation has obviously not been an important part of the SHG experiment though savings generation has been taken seriously. Interest rates are 2–3 per cent per month. The weakness is that savings are very small and the credit needs of members remain unmet. Various attempts by NABARD for credit linkages with banks have not met with success. The major demand for funds came from goat rearing units, small business, fish vending, dry fish making and vending, crop loans, artisans and consumption loans. Weekly savings ranged from Rs 2 to Rs 20. The United Artists Associates strongly believes that NGOs should not act as intermediaries but more as facilitators; that NGOs should not stand as guarantors to SHGs as it would weaken the SHGs who would depend unduly on the NGOs.

Gopinath Yuvak Sangh

Various SHGs have been started to encourage savings by women and for collective income-earning activities by women. The 28 SHGs set up by the Gopinath Yuvak Sangh were able to mop up substantial deposits and did not require any bank linkage. The area is experiencing a boom thanks to prawn farming. In fact, the SHGs were unable to invest the substantial deposits collected from household savings. Small income-generating activities were frowned upon; the conservative village society did not permit ladies from the upper social strata to earn a living. Many members have used part of their savings for leasing out and improving ponds for carp culture and for protecting women who have been victimised, through legal action.

The societies are well run with frequent meetings and do not need bank linkage programmes just for the purpose of accessing cheap funds. Women were given loans at 24 per cent interest which was lower than the money-lenders' rate of 36 per cent. The 955 members saved Rs 69,100 within one year with some SHGs saving about Rs 28,000 or more within 12–15 months of functioning (see Table 14.16). There was a move to link up with NABARD/banks; but, as their funds position was adequate and there was little scope for income-generation activities by ladies, the linkage process was not really necessary.

No subsidy is contemplated and each SHG is free to charge a higher annual rate of interest ranging from 18 per cent to 36 per cent per year. The bank charges a lower rate of interest (9.5 per cent) and a 3 per cent margin is available to the NGO to meet transaction costs. No concessional lending to the SHG borrower is contemplated in the scheme as it would dilute the 'self-help' process and provide only temporary crutches for the poor to lean on. One of the findings of the SHG linkage study was:

> There are a few NGOs who have started saving and credit programmes among marine fishing folk through SHGs. For lending they rely mainly on mobilisation of savings. But the amounts being very small, credit based solely on the savings of the community is not adequate to meet the requirements, particularly for assets. (ODA sponsored study conducted by Sri Vijay Mahajan, May 1995).

Table 14.16
Gopinath Yuvak Sangh, Brahmapuri, Puri District

(Rs)

Sl No.	Village	SHG	No. of Members	Saving up to 30 April 1995
1.	Natia	Indira	42	6,000
2.	Dadara Kunda	Mangalei	35	1,600
3.	Harichandanpur	Bhubaneswari	19	700
4.	Salepur	Harachandi	19	700
5.	Bhubanpur (B)	Basantei	22	4,500
6.	Gokhara	Parvati	30	1,200
7.	Balisahi	Adimata	24	8,000
8.	Barapada	Nadiakhai	38	2,000
9.	Bhubanpur (A)	Gamvikash	27	1,500
10.	Goudakena	Subarnamukhi	33	4,500
11.	Hasinipur	Birakama	52	6,000
12.	Sahajanapur	Janakalyan	26	9,000
13.	Machia Diand	Brahmani	26	10,000
14.	Mudiretha	Jugulei	40	7,000
15.	Badabena Kunda	Kalika	61	8,000
16.	Karimpur	Jogamaya	32	18,000
17.	Barakudi	Mangala	31	6,000
18.	Baghalanji	Sarvakalyan	28	5,500
19.	Keutakudi	Harizan	34	1,200
20.	Khatia Sahi	Mangala	34	2,500
21.	Gopinathpur	Hengulai	75	13,000
22.	Jadupur	Ramachandi	51	3,000
23.	Panda	Kalijai	22	2,500
24.	Gola	Maralika	107	3,000
25.	Parvatipur	Budhima	21	3,000
26.	Mirzapur	Raghunathdev	35	2,200
27.	Gavakunda	Vikashmukhi	62	5,500
28.	Panapasapada	Harachandi	28	3,700
			1,054	139,800

Source: Field Study Survey, 1995.

15

The BAAC System in Thailand

Introduction

Thailand's economy is basically dependent on agriculture with about 76 per cent of its population (total population 50 million) engaged in farming. The major crops are rice, maize, tapioca and sorghum. Oil seeds comprise soyabean, peanut and oil-palm and fibre crops are cotton and kenaf. Other crops are para-rubber, sugarcane, coffee, all kinds of vegetables, fruits and flowers, etc. The year 1988 was regarded as a golden year for the Thai economy, which registered a record growth rate of 11 per cent. Overall agricultural production increased at a rate of 8.6 per cent. The economy was currently witnessing a period of stable interest rates, increase in flow of foreign capital and growth in all key sectors of economy like agriculture, industry, investment, tourism and export. Exports from Thailand have been growing continuously in volume and value especially in farm products like rice, tapioca, maize, para-rubber, frozen shrimps, etc. Total exports increased 35.9 per cent in 1988.

From 1916 onwards, Thailand has been experimenting with various institutional frameworks for providing cheap credit to the rural sector. Farmers were encouraged to set up cooperatives for easy access to loans from government agencies through the cooperative structure. The predictable results were a high default rate and choking of credit availability. The BAAC (Bank for Agriculture and Agricultural Cooperatives) was set up in 1966 for direct loans to farmers as well as to cooperatives. By 1974, the BAAC opened branches in 58 out of 71 provinces.

In 1975, the democratic government withheld funds to develop rural areas and the Bank of Thailand instructed all commercial banks to lend 5 per cent of their total loans/advances to the agricultural sector. A short-fall in the targeted amount would invite 12 months deposit (at a pre-deter-mined rate and interest to the extent of the shortfall) with the BAAC. Further, the BAAC was requested to enhance its loan portfolio from 2.65 million baht to 3.50 million baht. As both commercial banks and the BAAC found it difficult to expand their loan portfolio, the BAAC expanded its deposits base. The rural credit delivery system was totally changed as de-tailed in Table 15.1.

Table 15.1

Rural Credit Delivery System—Thailand Commercial Bank and BAAC: 1975-86

(million baht)

Year	Target	% of Advances	Total Agri-cultural Loans	BAAC's Total Agri-cultural Loans	Commercial Banks' Deposit with BAAC
1975	4,333.3	5	3,904.4	4,556.1	1,670.8
1976	6,139.0	7	6,971.5	6,554.6	3,160.6
1977	9,647.0	9	10,419.8	8,280.2	
1978	11,771.9	9	13,610.9	10,207.8	
1980	19,208.7	9	18,553.4	13,448.3	
1983	35,330.0	9	37,419.2	18,271.4	
1986	60,347.6	9	50,794.5	-	

Source: Bank of Thailand.

In 1990, the percentage of advance to be maintained, was 20 per cent. The share of cooperatives has been poor and averages around 20 per cent of credit disbursed while informal lenders contribute about 50 per cent (a reduction from 90 per cent in 1974). Interest rates for the formal lender vary from 2 per cent to 3 per cent a month in commercialised areas to 10 per cent a month in remote areas. The rural credit delivery system depends on BAAC performing its task of disbursing rural credit.

The rural credit system in Thailand comprises commercial banks, the BAAC and cooperative institutions both at the apex and intermediate lev-els. Farmers' cooperatives are organised under the names of 'agricultural cooperative societies' and 'farmers associations', etc. Thrust is now being placed on the formation and development of autonomous informal Self-help Groups (SHGs). The BAAC plays an important role in dispensing rural credit and undertaking various operations that connected with such credit extension.

Profile of BAAC

The BAAC provides financial services to about half the farmer households in Thailand and is a state-owned enterprise. The chairman of the board of directors is the finance minister. BAAC's objectives among others are to promote occupation of farmers to ensure adequate incomes, to raise their living standards and to develop agriculture as a key sector in the national economy. The BAAC's operations are controlled by its charter (BAAC Act of 1966).

The BAAC operates through 118 branches spread all over the country and 604 field offices.It undertakes banking operations such as acceptance of deposits, issue of remittances and demand drafts, while its lending operations are confined to the agricultural sector and other agricultural credit-linked operations only.

The BAAC is a conglomerate of the national bank, commercial banks including RRBs, and the apex state cooperative institutions, if a comparison is made with the Indian context. The BAAC is an example of a single window concept in agricultural lending; in that sense, it resembles a large-sized RRB.

Commercial banks in Thailand, under a persuasive directive from the Bank of Thailand, are expected to channel credit to the extent of 20 per cent (14 per cent for farmers and small industries in rural areas and 6 per cent for agribusiness including rice mills) of their loans, to finance agriculture and other related activities. If commercial banks are not able to attain the above percentage in any particular year, the shortfall should be kept as a deposit with the BAAC. The BAAC pays an annual interest at the rate of 10.25 per cent p.a. on such deposits, which is less than the current market rate of 12.5 per cent. At end-1989, the BAAC had a total of 14,395 m.bt. in deposits from commercial banks representing 35.95 per cent of their total operating funds. Though commercial banks have been able to increase their share of lending to the agricultural sector over the years, they have not been able to reach the mandatory percentage due to a poor branch network in rural areas and lack of personnel for supervision of agricultural lending. As a result, commercial banks find it convenient to keep the required deposits with the BAAC and honour the central bank's directives. The rate of interest on such deposits is fixed by the Government of Thailand in consultation with the BAAC.

The BAAC is an autonomous corporation responsible to the finance minister for its policies, operations and other matters. Though the Bank of Thailand makes a line of credit available to the BAAC for various purposes, it does not intervene in the BAAC's operations or the policies pursued by the BAAC. While the Bank of Thailand monitors commercial banks, the BAAC has the prerogative to frame agricultural credit policies, open branches and devise ways and means to translate such policies into activities. Further, the BAAC is empowered to fix interest rates on various agricultural lending operations in consultation with the Government. The BAAC also functions as an agent of government in undertaking various activities like building linkages, provision of infrastructural support, procurement of foodgrains, etc. The BAAC carried out, as and when called upon to do so, procurement operations to maintain the floor prices and help in avoiding distress sales by farmers.

BAAC's Organisation and Branch Network

The BAAC is managed by a board of directors, under the chairmanship of the finance minister of the government of Thailand. The bank has a full-time president and executive vice-presidents to oversee its operations.

The BAAC has 118 branches and 604 field offices. Unlike a branch, a field office is an extension office wherein a team of two to three officers (mostly those who are assigned with field-level functions) canvass applications, follow up accounts and ensure required documentation. They come under the control of branch managers. The field offices do not transact any banking business.

Resources of BAAC

The BAAC's resources comprise share equity of 321 m.bt. (8.41 per cent), deposits from general public (33.24 per cent), deposits from commercial banks (30.17 per cent), borrowings mainly from overseas financial institutions (17.07 per cent), borrowings from the Bank of Thailand (8.96 per cent) and other liabilities (2.15 per cent). The BAAC obtains soft loans from foreign donors and can rediscount its bills with the Bank of Thailand at rates between 3.5 per cent and 5 per cent per year. The BAAC makes a small profit by setting interest rates according to its average cost of funds; interest rates vary between 12 per cent and 14 per cent per year. Having obtained subsidised funds from the central bank and foreign donors, funds mobilisation has not been taken up seriously by the BAAC in view of its limited network of branches.

Some Features of BAAC's Operations

Certain features of the BAAC's operations deserve to be emulated. The BAAC lends directly to individual farmers and farmers' institutions to promote agricultural occupations. Farmers' institutions comprise agricultural cooperatives and registered farmers' associations. The credits extended by the BAAC to individual farmers are in both cash and kind. Agricultural cooperatives and registered farmers' associations enable the farmers to hold equity in their organisations and attempt to improve the living standards of their members. The BAAC extended credit to 1,84,910 individual farmers through 1,45,098 joint liability groups as at end-March 1990. Credit to 812 cooperatives with 8,33,771 farmer-members and 551 farmers' associations having a membership of 84,145 was also extended.

Types of loans extended by the BAAC were mainly short-term loans for purchasing farm supplies and agricultural machinery, for purchasing and marketing of agricultural products, loans against pledge of farm produce, etc. Medium and long-term loans were for investment in agricultural fixed assets. Long-term loans for refinancing of old debts or for land redemption were also made available to individual farmers. The BAAC also gives loans for construction of houses.

There is no form of transparent subsidy (either capital or interest) available to Thai farmers. However, under government directives, the BAAC may charge lower rates of interest than its cost of capital. Recently, the BAAC had introduced a paddy pledge loan scheme wherein the annual rate of interest on the principal was kept at 3 per cent as against 12.5 per cent on short-term agricultural loans. The Bank of Thailand subsidised the BAAC to the extent of 9.5 per cent. The bank renews the loans wherever needed. (Known as 'novations'—in the event of the death or other inability of the client and any other person in his family undertaking for redeeming the outstanding debt to the BAAC). Postponement on account of drought/floods and other natural calamities, etc., are, though accepted in principle, seldom practised. The general feeling is that such concessions would vitiate credit discipline.The BAAC appoints one field officer for every 500 clients on an average. This norm is similar to what was envisaged initially. Functions of the field officers are similar to those of commercial banks. It is now felt that the norm of 500 borrowers should be increased to 750. Field officers, however, do not attend to any house-keeping functions in the field-office/branches (like maintenance of ledger accounts, etc.). The BAAC does not have branches at the village level. Commercial banks also do not have branches at these levels. Thus, farmers have to go to the province/district headquarters to obtain credit from banks.

The role of the informal sector (including private money-lenders) is still prominent. It was reported that about 51 per cent of farmers are still indebted to the informal sector. The rates of interest charged could be as high as 60 per cent per annum. The BAAC is currently concentrating on lending through autonomous informal groups (SHGs). This is still in the pilot stage. There are more than 8,900 SHGs with a membership of 5,74,000 in Thailand and many of them issue loans for agriculture and other productive activities; the rates of interest on these loans range between 18 per cent to 36 per cent.

BAAC's Credit Operations

The BAAC issues loans to client farmers, agricultural cooperatives and farmers' associations. As mentioned above, these loans could be for short-term (SAO) operations and working capital loans for crops, managing livestock, etc. Medium- and long-term loans are also issued for creating assets/investments in building and for acquiring other fixed assets for agricultural operations. Cash credit loans could be utilised for both production and assets creation.

During 1988–89, the bank issued loans of 29.74 billion bt. to client farmers, 3.65 b. bt. to agricultural cooperatives and 0.21 b. bt. to farmers' associations. Percentage-wise, 82.90 per cent of the loans issued by the BAAC during 1988–89 were for client farmers, while cooperatives accounted for 16.9 per cent. The share of farmers' associations was barely 1 per cent of the BAAC's lending. The reasons for this are not far to seek. The recoveries from these types of clients are stated to be poor. During 1987–1988, the repayment performance of agricultural cooperatives was 57 per cent, (recovery as percentage of demand with only principal included) while that of farmers' associations was 67.68 per cent. In contrast the recovery performance of individual client farmers was about 80 per cent.

The mode of the BAAC's lending to client farmers (individual farmers) is by 'group lending' and is commonly known as 'joint liability groups'. These groups comprise six to seven persons who execute a joint and several liability to the BAAC, which entitles each one of them to secure a loan of 30,000 bt. and liabilities of up to 2,10,000 bt. depending upon the number of members and total individual borrowings. The client farmer is also at liberty to produce two guarantors. It is important to note that neither the joint liability group nor the guarantors can be changed during the life time of the borrower. Loans over and above 30,000 bt. are secured by mortgaging of property.

Recovery Performance

The recovery performance in respect of loans extended by BAAC for the three-year period ended March 1988, is indicated in Table 15.2. Recoveries in respect of individual client loans are very encouraging. In respect of cooperatives and farmers' associations, recovery rate is relatively poor. One reason could be that the type of group lending that is practised for financing individual client farmers is absent here. This forced the BAAC to shift its thrust from the farmers' cooperatives/associations to individual client lending. Its current emphasis on financing of informal SHGs is also born out of this experience. As against 1,370 cooperatives with a membership of more than one million farmers, the BAAC lent to only 785 cooperatives during the year 1988–89. In regard to farmers associations, as against 4,000 farmers' associations, the BAAC had financed only 460.

Table 15.2
Study Report on BAAC, Thailand—BAAC's Recovery Performance

		(Percentage of Recovery to Demand)		
		1986	*1987*	*1988*
Client Farmers	Short Term	79.71	80.14	82.08
	Medium Term	70.96	57.28	50.22
	Long Term	89.02	71.24	78.05
All Loans		80.41	76.67	79.37
Cooperatives		45.28	48.94	57
Farmers' Association		41.12	53.48	67.68

Loan Procedures and Policies

The loan procedures and policies of the BAAC are flexible and are mostly tailored to suit the requirements of individual needs. The BAAC does not stipulate any scale of finance or suggest any unit costs for various types of investments. With regard to various technical parameters in respect of the schemes to be financed as also those to be taken up by individual farmers, the BAAC, by and large, goes by the advice of the concerned government departments. The various extension agencies and government departments in Thailand, which are charged with the role of provision of infrastructure and creation of required facilities for overall development of the agricultural sector, play a vital role in project formulation, provision of technical data, etc. The BAAC, therefore, does not maintain separate technical staff but uses those in government departments to conduct technical appraisals of schemes. Further, these government agencies formulate separate programmes for the development of agriculture and rural industry which are, in turn, posed to the BAAC for financing. In this way there is greater coordination between government agencies and the BAAC in implementation of programmes.

The rates of interest vary according to the terms and conditions of credit and type of borrower. As the BAAC has a virtual monopoly over the formal agricultural credit system, the negotiability of the rates of interest is made easy. Despite such a position enjoyed by the BAAC, it only caters to about 49 per cent of the total number of farmers. The informal sector, in which money-lenders play a significant role, still has a share of 51 per cent (of the total number of farmers availing of credit). Though the BAAC has defined a small farmer, no target is indicated or followed by the bank for channelising credit to this category. The BAAC only stipulates three conditions: (a) annual net farm income of 10,000 bt. or less, (b) land-holding less than the average of that of the province in which the farmer is located, and (c) landless farmers and labourers. The average size of land holding in Thailand is 4–4.5 hectares.

The BAAC implements a number of schemes with financial assistance from the international financing agencies. These are mainly area-specific projects and the rates of interest are decided by contractual obligations. Centralised procurement of paddy by establishing a paddy market and marketing assistance for other crops are recent ventures that are predominantly non-credit oriented. While the Government of Thailand is keen to give more facilities to the farmers and bring more and more farmers into the credit fold, the BAAC is facing a difficult financial position imposed by low margins. A summary of its financial position and the net margin available to it is shown in Table 15.3, which indicates a downward trend in its net profits as percentage of capital employed. The BAAC's staff cost is continuously on the rise; more than 7,000 staff cater to the various credit and non-credit requirements of farmers. A plus point is that the average loan outstanding in the BAAC is 15,000 bt. as against 1,00,000 bt. of commercial banks.

Table 15.3
Profitability of Operations—BAAC

					(Billion Baht)
	1985	1986	1987	1988	1989
Average Total Loans Outstanding	22.96	25.43	27.45	28.63	32.24
Interest Earned on Loans	13.51	12.28	11.8	11.86	11.68
Cost of Funds	9.44	8.29	7.78	8.2	9.01
Less Interest on Short Term Deposit and Misc. Income	(1.51)	(1.48)	(1.33)	(2.06)	(3.01)
Net Cost of Funds	7.93	6.81	6.45	6.14	6
Spread	5.58	5.47	5.35	5.72	5.68
Operating Cost	4.95	4.78	4.62	4.95	4.86
Net Profit	0.63	0.69	0.73	0.77	0.82
Net Profit as Percentage of Capital	5.46	9.41	10.06	6.87	6.57

Critical Analysis of BAAC

The BAAC's method of administering credit by means of the group loaning method has ensured a high rate of loan repayment. While cooperatives also embody the idea of group responsibility and peer monitoring, the BAAC's success lies in the small-sized groups of 8–15 people. Also, the the BAAC has earned the rural people's goodwill and besides meeting the farmers' needs, has become a reputed institution. The BAAC charges an additional 3 per cent interest per annum as personal charges and does not permit new loans to delinquent borrowers until all loans are cleared. The high repayment rate has been acheived at a small cost. Administrative costs are reported to be around 5 per cent of the outstanding loans while about 3 percent of the outstanding loans are eventually written off. The marginal cost of funds was 12–13 per cent. The BAAC would lend without any collateral to the rural sector at 20 per cent. However, the BAAC credit has a number of disadvantages, including a higher transaction cost of about 4 per cent. Thus, the collective interest cost would be 29 per cent which is below the interest rates in the informal markets. The BAAC has been useful in making available short-term working capital loans to a large number of people but is not able to expand its scope to poor farmers or in riskier areas or even to expand its scope of activities.

While the BAAC's operational policies do not hold many lessons for replication in India, its primacy in all matters dealing with agricultural credit, needs to be emulated by NABARD. There is no interference either from the government or from the central bank in Thailand. Also, there is no imposition of CRR/SLR on rural credit agencies. These need to be emulated in India.

16

The Grameen Bank in Bangladesh

Rural Credit in Bangladesh

Past attempts to make credit available to the rural poor have failed as most agricultural credit schemes do not cover half the population which is female and, therefore, thought not to be farmers. This point certainly seems to have been missed as also the lack of support and involvement in non-farming schemes. This also encourages informal credit use from suppliers, purchasers, friends and money-lenders.

In a 1983 report from IFAD, a review of 27 credit projects financed by it was undertaken. Eleven were solely concerned with providing credit, and 16 incorporated credit within a wider array of agricultural and rural components. Of the 11 credit projects, only the Bangladesh Grameen Bank appears to seriously target those who are not farmers or those who intend to use funds for non-farming activities. The report covers projects in South America, Africa and Asia—the degree and severity of landlessness obviously varies among these countries.

The interest rates charged by money-lenders in Bangladesh, average around 10 per cent per month. A recent World Bank study has listed the following influences on the interest rate:

— relationship of loanee to lender
— dependency of loanee on lender if loan given
— urgency of need
— amount of loan
— time of loan

— availability of funds
— extent of monopoly power of lender

It is interesting to note that concepts of risk, profitability, project collateral, etc., are rarely mentioned. These are common considerations in western financial theories, but do not have the same significance in rural Bangladesh. Indeed, the study goes on to say that marginal farmers are often refused loans because they have some land. They are forced to mortgage their land, at 50–70 per cent of true value, and then the lender takes a very relaxed attitude to repayment. The motive is clear; to allow the loan to become so indebted that land ownership eventually passes to the lender. This is one of the major causes of the increasing number of landless rural families.

Given these conditions in the existing rural credit market, it is hardly surprising that conventional banking mechanisms are irrelevant to the needs of most people in Bangladesh. A bank that successfully functions must consider the competition, the money-lenders, and the issues of far-reaching rural poverty.

The challenge is, therefore, to devise a system that offers credit to the poor, to people without land or any collateral, but not to seek the subservience that money-lenders demand. The five rules for a successful rural lending scheme which are observed by money-lenders are:

1. Avoid insistence on productive use of loan. This will not achieve the desired effect, but only serve to drive away the ill-informed and illiterate.
2. Accept a wide range of securities.
3. Be prepared to extend loans when reasonable requests are made.
4. Maintain interest rates at realistic levels with no subsidies.
5. Keep tight control on bad debts and maintain overall good recovery rates.

The Grameen Bank passes on most points. The choice of activity is left to the loanee and to some extent, new ideas are encouraged. Although each loanee has to state what the loan will be used for, i.e., if it is an income-generating activity, no formal check is made. In a recent study, 20 per cent of male loanees diverted the loan amount for other purposes. The group fund, however, can be used for non-productive uses, i.e., consumption needs. Group responsibility and unity is used in lieu of formal security. Whilst the rules clearly state that repayment has to be made in one year, there is no formal demand for repayment when the year has passed. Instead, the loans are rescheduled and the manager will assist with advice and help, if necessary. Interest rates were increased from 13 per cent to 16 per cent in 1983 and is now 18 per cent. Regular contact ensures that the bank manager is aware of repayments falling behind schedule. Overall recovery rates are very high. Comparison with other banks in Bangladesh might help to judge the success of the Grameen Bank. A report in the *Bangladesh Observer* on 22 April 1985 compared the performance, using recovery of loans as criteria, of three specialised banks in Bangladesh. The Shilpo (Industrial) Bank had a low recovery rate of 10 per cent; the Krishi (Agricultural) Bank 48 per cent; and, the Grameen Bank a high rate of 98 per cent. Even allowing for inaccuracy and exaggeration, the differences are dramatic. It is paradoxical that the poorest groups in Bangladesh are the most reliable to lend to. The richest, those who have sufficient social, technical, economic and political power to obtain industrial loans, appear to be the worst.

Origin of the Grameen Bank

The Grameen Bank owes its origin to the concern felt by its founder, Dr Mohammed Yunus, at the pitiable condition of landless women labourers, who were exploited both by their masters and in their own families. Dr Yunus felt that if these women could work for themselves instead of working for others, they could retain much of the surplus generated by their labour, currently appropriated by others and benefit their families. Other reasons for selecting rural women especially, as the target beneficiaries, were to elevate their social status within their own families so as to reduce male domination in a tradition-bound and conservative society and the conviction that womenfolk, as more responsible family leaders, were quick and sincere enough to seize opportunities for improving the economic conditions of their families. The missing ingredient was credit. Funds were required to improve their economic conditions through self-employment without government or external assistance or subsidies. The guiding concept was that the poor know best how to improve their economic conditions provided adequate credit was made available. The translation of this simple idea into practice gave birth to an imaginative project, which has grown to attract world-wide appreciation.

The initial scheme was started as a village credit society in December 1976 in Jobra, a village adjacent to Chittagong University, where Dr Yunus was a teacher in economics. At first, credit arrangements were made with one of the nearby banks and the Economic Programme of the Chittagong University under the leadership of Dr Yunus. The success of the experiment evoked interest among more banks. In June 1979, the central bank of the country, the Bangladesh Bank stepped in and organised sponsorships from several nationalised commercial banks for extension of the scheme to more areas. In 1980, the project caught international attention and financial aid started flowing in from different donor institutions like IFAD, Ford Foundation, NORAD, SIDA, GTZ, etc.

Organisational Structure of the Grameen Bank

With the Grameen Bank Ordinance 1983 (see Annexure 16.1) the project took on the shape of an independent institution as a legally constituted bank. According to the ordinance, the Grameen Bank could undertake any type of banking activity, except foreign exchange business. The striking feature in its constitution was the operational freedom given to it, with very little control exercised by the central bank. Except for requirements such as maintenance of accounts, preparation of annual audited balance sheets, lending rate and opening of branches, none of the other banking statutes apply to the Grameen Bank. At the end of December 1988, its authorised capital was taka 10 crore consisting of 10 lakh ordinary shares of tk 100 each. The paid up capital is tk 150 million; 12 per cent is held by the Government of Bangladesh, and the remaining 88 per cent by the Grameen Bank's borrowers themselves. In a sense, therefore, the Grameen Bank is a cooperative venture but outside the purview of the Cooperative Societies Act as well. Of the 12 members on its board of directors, the chairman, managing director and six other members are appointed by the government while the remaining four are elected by borrowers. Eight of the 12 directors as at the end of December 1988 were women. It is claimed that this structure protects the bank from irrational decisions; however, it is felt that the borrower board members play a passive role in approving policy decisions.

The affairs of the bank are controlled by its head office. The lower tiers are zonal offices, area offices and branches. The borrowers at the branch level are formed into 'Groups', each group consisting of five members. Six such groups federate into a 'Centre'. The field staff at the branch are designated as 'bank workers' and each bank worker has about 6 centres or approximately 200 borrowers under his charge. Expansion in new districts are effective due to the methodical replication of this technique. A new branch is opened in a village adjacent to an existing branch and expands its staff strength as and when the number of members and centres increase. As the number of such branches increase, an area office would be opened and as area offices increase, a new zonal office would be opened. Management capacity is continuously adjusted to the growth pattern.

During the early stages, all major decisions were taken by the managing director. However, with the proposal to have 14 zonal offices by 1992 and to avoid too many senior staff reporting directly to the managing director, decentralisation has been effectively introduced. Day-to-day banking operations have been delegated to the zonal offices. The present management structure ensures that the zonal manager is the crucial element in the administration and management of the bank and has a wide range of responsibilities for the area and branch offices within his jurisdiction, and also for expanding the bank's operation. A zone has about 10 area offices. Though the Grameen Bank staff increased from 2,601 in October 1986 to 3,748 in December 1987, the percentage of staff at the head office decreased from 14 per cent to 10 per cent as only 8 staff members were added to the staff strength of 354. The number of branches increased by 100 over the same period but the percentage of staff at the zonal and area offices remained unchanged at 5 per cent and 7 per cent, respectively, and the ratio of members to staff at 90:1. There are 13,000 staff members and the average age of the staff member is 22. Each area office looks after 10 branches and is a small office involved in the supervision of the branches. The bank's programmes are implemented by the branches, which are responsible for the mobilisation, supervision and development of the bank's clientele. On an average, each branch is responsible for around 40 centres with each centre having two to six groups.

Pay benefits match the official wage packet for all financial institutions except that the Grameen Bank employees do not receive housing loans. Field-level conditions are very arduous compared to commercial banks and the performance of field personnel depends heavily on their commitment, job capabilities and loyalty to the bank. All officers are employees of the bank and training policies are framed to develop commitment. All promotions are from below and reinforce the management ethos of the Grameen Bank wherein officers share the experience and needs of their subordinates. There is a carefully designed career path with elevations to the right candidates at definite intervals. Promotion is based on performance as recorded by the semi-annual performance records and competitive examinations. Recruitment is restricted to two sources—second class HSC passed candidates as bank workers and Master's degree holders as branch managers; those with higher qualifications are not given any special credit. Only 15–20 per cent of applicants are accepted for training and only 65 per cent of these enter service with most drop outs within the first month and hence, with negligible cost to the bank. To have about 7,100 officers and staff, about 11,000 will have to be recruited. However, even though 80 per cent of the bank's clientele is women, only about 12 per cent of the bank's staff (excluding peons and drivers, etc.) are women. For higher ranks, there are no prescribed educational qualifications and all managers have extensive field experience. Recruitment policies now encourage women applicants.

Transportation and field communication is a vital support facility for the field officers. For zonal managers and the zonal offices, there are no jeeps. There are auto-rickshaws at the zonal and area offices which provide low cost transport for officials. Field officers used to travel by boat. However, now bicycles and motorcycles are provided by the head office as work aids depending upon requirement or can be purchased by employees with a long-term loan.

The organisational structure of Grameen Bank (as on December 1988) is given below:-

HEAD OFFICE
ZONAL OFFICES (9)
AREA OFFICES (60)
BRANCHES (741)
CENTRES (19663)
GROUPS (98073)
MEMBERS (490303)

In June 1992, the bank's lending operations covered 12 lakh members in 28,215 villages (out of 68,000 villages in the country) through 961 branches. The bank is operating in 39 of the 64 districts in the country.

One of the strong points of the Grameen Bank is the extraordinary commitment and dedication of its field staff. As a matter of fact, from the managing director down to the bank worker, all are thoroughly rural-oriented. An extraordinary sense of discipline and dedication on the part of its staff is what one comes across during a visit to the Grameen Bank. This has become possible due to a deliberate and carefully evolved policy in the selection and training of personnel and other motivating factors in the form of clear career paths.

Lending Policies of the Bank

The lending policies of the Grameen Bank are totally revolutionary and deviate in many respects from the traditional approach. Foremost among these is the principle that 'the bank will go to the client; the client will not come to the bank'. In other words, the bank earmarked certain groups viz., landless and assetless, as its target borrowers and any one belonging to the target group could approach and obtain credit assistance. Contrary to the traditional approach, the bank identifies its beneficiaries and then proceeds cautiously in extending credit to the identified beneficiaries. Even within the target group, the bank focuses its attention on women. As at the end of June 1992, out of the 12 lakh members of the bank, 93 per cent were women members. Credit assistance was supported by other social measures to bring about self-reliance, discipline, awareness of obligations to society and even physical fitness and health care, amongst its borrowers. The compulsory savings element and the purposes for which it would be put to use, have taught the members about the importance and benefits of thrift and mutual help. The entire loan procedure is free from any rigid observance of legal procedures. Lending is not security-oriented and reliance is placed on people, not on papers. The group structure of the borrowers has not only provided excellent collateral for the loans but also facilitated loan repayment and furnished the institutional framework for organisation of joint social and economic activities. Lending, although directed towards amelioration of the poorest of the poor, is devoid of any subsidies. If there is any subsidy, it is in the form of the extraordinary dedication and hard work put in by the staff at all levels. The experiment has proved that there can be perceptible development in the economic standards of those below the poverty line, even with small doses of credit, totally free from external doles, provided the right path is taken. The maximum loan per account is tk 10,000 but the average loan per borrower is tk 2,000.

Identification of the Beneficiaries

Credit assistance is extended by the bank only to the target group—landless and assetless. A family is deemed to be 'landless' if it owns up to half an acre of land and 'assetless' if the value of all its assets does not exceed the value of one acre of medium type of land in the concerned locality i.e., at a cost of about tk 30,000. The bank identifies districts having a concentration of such population and extends its operation from district to district, in a phased manner. In other words, the Grameen Bank's operations did not cover all the districts in the country simultaneously.

The area offices identifies centres for opening branches on the basis of norms such as availability of large number of target beneficiaries and presence of a commercial bank branch within a radius of 3 km for availing banking facilities by the branch. After obtaining permission of the central bank, which is automatic, branches are opened. On an average, a branch covers 25 villages within a radius of 4 km. Wide publicity through local public meetings is given about the objectives of the Grameen Bank and the obligations of borrowers, as soon as a branch is opened. Thereafter, the intending borrowers are asked to form groups.

The definition of the target group covers 50 per cent of all rural households; 80 per cent of the Grameen Bank's members have no arable land and hence the value of their total assets is far below the specified values. As its resources are not sufficient for providing services to such a large target group, the Grameen Bank has established priorities for membership enrolment within the target population. The priority targets are:

- single female heads of households
  (widow, deserted, divorcee)
- persons from household not owning any land and
- persons owning a homestead but no other land.

Other criteria are:

- number of dependent children and
- access to other sources of support.

Strict compliance with these criteria explains why currently 85 per cent of the Grameen Bank's borrowers are women, who are the poorest among the rural poor and why 80 per cent have no arable land. By 1992, the Grameen Bank proposed to begin operations in all 64 districts, up from 28 districts in 1988.

Group Formation

Loan proposals are entertained by the branch only on group basis. Each group should have at least five members. The first member in the group is identified by the bank worker and thereafter, the member is expected to canvass four other like-minded members. The branch does not call for any documentary evidence to ensure whether the members of the group satisfy the definition of target group. This is left to the observation and knowledge of other members of the group. Six such groups federate into a centre and each centre has a common meeting place on a definite day and time of the week. No member can belong to more than one group and members of a group can not be blood relations. Members of a group should also belong to the same village and should not be indebted to any other credit institution. Undesirable elements are avoided.

It is only after the formation of the group that the drill of inculcating discipline in the borrowers is introduced. For the first seven days, meetings of the group are required to be held every day, when the obligations of the borrowers are explained. Each member of the group is also required to save one taka a day and at the end of week, tk 35 should be deposited by the group with the branch. Each group also elects a chairman and secretary during the period. Thereafter, the group is recognised. The responsibilities of the group chairman consist of convening meetings, collecting recoveries and contributing to various funds, recommending of loan proposals, verifying loan utilisation and operating the group fund with the branch. When the number of groups reach six, they federate into a centre. There are separate centres for men and women. The leader of the centre is called the centre chief. His duties consist of convening regular weekly meetings, recoveries and recommending loan proposals. Each centre generally has its own accommodation in the form of a simple thatched shed where its activities are conducted.

Funds

The Grameen Bank's activities attach considerable importance to self-reliance and savings. Hence, there is an element of compulsion. Each group has to maintain a group fund, contributions to which come from its members in five different forms. These are Group Tax I and II, penalty, interest and personal savings. When a member borrows from the bank, he has to contribute an amount equivalent to 5 per cent of the loan (deducted from the loan amount) as group tax I, which is credited to the group fund. A member can borrow from the group fund for any purpose, including consumption, and 5 per cent of such loan is to be contributed as group tax II, which is also credited to the group fund. Every member is required to save one taka per week as personal savings which is added to the fund. Only this part of the contribution is refundable to the member if he or she chooses to leave the group. Penalties are collected by the group chairman from members who violate group discipline. Interest on the group fund invested with the branch are also credited to the group fund.

In addition each member also has to contribute to two other funds. These are Centre Emergency Fund and Children's Welfare Fund which are maintained at the Centres. The Centre Emergency Fund is basically an insurance fund, designed to cover risks like death, permanent disability, etc., of members. The contributions to this fund come from the borrowers at 25 per cent of the interest amount paid on the loan, which is deducted at the end of the loan recovery. Lumpsum payments on prescribed scales subject to a maximum of tk 5,000 per member are made from this fund to the legal heir of the member on death or permanent disability. A weekly contribution of one taka per member is added to the Children's Welfare Fund, for meeting the expenses of the primary school run by each centre. The head office of the Grameen Bank maintains another Central Emergency Fund out of the interest earned on the investment of the emergency fund of the centres and contributions made from donors interested in economic development programmes. This fund is utilised for supplementing assistance to the group members, for the same purposes for which the emergency fund, of the centres is maintained.

Social Obligations of the Group

The essence of the Grameen Bank project is social development; credit is used as a catalyst in the process. Without the catalyst, the social development process is thwarted. The first lesson a member is taught (if he or she is not literate), is to sign his or her name. There is not a single member in the Grameen Bank who has affixed his or her thumb impression in say, attendance registers or loan proposal forms. All members of the Grameen Bank have agreed upon certain obligations called the '16 decisions' which embraces areas such as family planning, avoidance of dowry and child marriage, personal and social hygiene and health, discipline, mutual help and respect. Each of the members is fully aware of these '16 decisions' and observe them meticulously. The '16 decisions' are elaborated in Table 16.1. Periodical workshops for borrowers are held at different levels where the subjects covered range from rules and regulations regarding loans and savings, utilisation of loans to latest technologies and operational efficiencies to maximise return on investment. The bank worker meets group members under his or her charge on a fixed day in a week at the centre meeting and discusses problems, including personal ones. He guides them on aspects like health and environment. Besides, he also makes frequent visits to the residences of group members. There is, thus, very close contact between the bank worker and group members, enabling the borrowers to identify with the Grameen Bank.

Table 16.1

Sixteen Decisions Programme of the Grameen Bank, Bangladesh

1. The four principles of Grameen Bank—discipline, unity, courage and hard work—we shall follow and advance in all walks of our lives.
2. We shall bring prosperity to our families.
3. We shall not lie in dilapidated houses. We shall repair our houses and work towards constructing new houses as soon as possible.
4. We shall grow vegetables all the year round. We shall eat plenty of them and sell the surplus.
5. During the planting season, we shall plant as many seedlings as possible.
6. We shall plan to keep our families small. We shall minimise our expenditure. We shall look after our health.
7. We shall educate our children and ensure that they can earn enough to pay for their education.
8. We shall keep our children and the environment clean.
9. We shall build and use pit latrines.
10. We shall drink tubewell water, if it is not available, we shall boil water or use alum.
11. We shall not take any dowry in our sons' weddings neither shall we give any dowry in our daughters' weddings. We shall keep the centre free from the curse of dowry. We shall not practice child marriage.
12. We shall not inflict any injustice on anyone, neither shall we allow anyone to do so.
13. For higher income, we shall collectively undertake bigger investments.
14. We shall always be ready to help each other. If anyone is in difficulty, we shall all help.
15. If we come to know of any breach of discipline in any centre, we shall all go there and restore discipline.
16. We shall introduce physical exercise in all our centres. We shall take part in all social activities collectively.

Supplies and Skill Training Programmes

The Grameen Bank's economic programme is a package of measures and does not confine itself to credit activities. It undertakes a variety of supply services aimed at improving the skills of borrowers and the quality of their living standards. Seeds and saplings, power tillers, incubators, pigeon houses, pottery wheels, chicks and ducklings, etc., are also supplied to improve economic activities. Cement slabs for pit latrines, roofings and concrete pillars for houses, tubewell equipment, iodised salt, water purification, etc., are aimed at ensuring hygiene and improved quality of living. Specialised skills training is arranged but bank policy is not to push skills development but to support it when the members are ready for it. The Grameen Bank does not believe in predeciding or pre-determining skill/training needs. The needs that emerge are based on the skills which group members already possess and which need augmentation. The bank also does not provide any facility to members free of cost. They have to pay for all services, but such payments are limited to the actual cost of the suppliers. The Grameen Bank has embarked on an ambitious rural communications project involving its branches.

Kinds of Loans

The credit programme of the bank consists of four different kinds of loans. These are (i) general loan, (ii) joint venture loan, (iii) housing loan and (iv) technology loan.

Credit given for various economic activities that provide self-employment and generate income are classified as general loans. A special feature of such loans is that the bank never gives a list of activities for which it gives credit. The choice of activity is left to the borrower. The quantum of loan is also left to be decided by the group and no unit costs are prescribed by the bank. There is no practice of ensuring the economic viability or technical feasibility or the skills of the borrower, to sustain the activity or even the availability of a market for the products. These are all left to the judgement and decision of the borrower and the other group members. The bank believes in the philosophy that the rural poor have acquired sufficient 'survival skills' and they know which type of activity could assure a living. The bank has been lending for about 500 different types of activities, of which, there are 25 major activities which accounted for tk 106.41 crore, out of tk 128.04 crore disbursed during 1988. In terms of numbers, they formed 5.40 lakh loans out of 6.48 lakh loans issued during the year. The top 25 items in the order of amount disbursed are given in Table 16.2.

Joint venture loans are given to groups of borrowers and not to individuals, for purposes which require large investment. These included leasing of land and banana plantations, rice mills, etc. Such activities are operated by groups of members and the income from the joint effort is shared. Such loans are, however, small in number. During 1988, such loans were disbursed to 3,799 groups for an aggregate amount of tk 1.64 crore for 834 units.

One of the '16 decisions' adopted by members of the Grameen Bank is that they would not live in dilapidated houses and work towards building their own houses. To this end, the bank provides loans to its members. It also supplies materials such as roofings, concrete pillars, slabs for pit latrines, etc., at cost price. The loan amount is restricted to tk 18,000 per individual, with a repayment schedule of 10–15 years and carries a concessional interest of 5 per cent per annum. Such loans are generally given after watching the performance of the borrower in respect of both repayment and utilisation of other loans. The amount is adequate to construct a small but pucca and simple house for all-weather conditions. The bank had disbursed, since inception, 136,000 housing loans aggregating tk 1.33 billion, up to July 1992.

Table 16.2

List of Top 25 Items (In Order of Amount Disbursed) for which Credit was made Available During 1988

Sl. No.	Activity	No. of Loans (Lakh)	Amount Disbursed (Tk. Crore)	% of Loan Amount Total Disbursal
1.	Milch Cow	1.11	34.60	32.5
2.	Paddy Husking	1.44	2,028.00	19.0
3.	Calf Rearing	0.82	15.36	14.4
4.	Rice/Paddy Trade	0.27	5.84	5.5
5.	Bullocks	0.14	3.42	3.2
6.	Grocery Shop	0.13	3.37	3.2
7.	Goat Rearing	0.32	2.63	2.5
8.	Bamboo Works	0.13	1.86	1.7
9.	Stationery Shop	0.07	1.82	1.7
10.	Seasonal Agricultural Crops	0.06	1.61	1.5
11.	Land Lease	0.04	1.39	1.3
12.	Cloth Trade	0.04	1.36	1.3
13.	Wheat Trade	0.09	1.28	1.2
14.	Land Cultivation	0.05	1.17	1.1
15.	Poultry	0.10	1.15	1.1
16.	Mat Making	0.06	1.11	1.0
17.	Fishing Net Making	0.07	1.10	1.0
18.	Cane Works	0.07	1.00	0.9
19.	Rickshaw	0.03	0.93	0.9
20.	Vegetable Cultivation	0.09	0.92	0.9
21.	Puffed Rice	0.05	0.91	0.9
22.	Saree Weaving	0.02	0.86	0.8
23.	Vegetable Trade	0.04	0.85	0.8
24.	Betel Leaf Cultivation	0.03	0.84	0.8
25.	Sewing Machine	0.04	0.75	0.8
I.	Total for Top 25 Activities	5.40	106.41	100.0
II.	Total for All Activities	6.48	128.04	—

Source: Grameen Bank, 1989.

Technology loans involve sizeable investment. These loans are, therefore, given to groups of members or to the centres which own the assets for the common benefit of the members. Rice mills, machinery, deep tubewells, etc., fall under this category. Such loans are, however, very few in number. Besides these loans, the bank also grants loans from the group fund maintained by the members. Such loans are given for any purpose, including consumption needs. They are also available where the activity in respect of the general loan obtained earlier has failed and the borrower wishes to take up another activity or continue the same activity once again. Such loans are granted to the members on the recommendation of the group and are generally interest free. A total of tk 5.89 crore was disbursed to 51,597 loanees during 1988 under this head (see Table 16.3).

Table 16.3
Purpose-wise Break-up of Loans from Group Fund—Grameen Bank

Purpose	No. of Loans	Amount (Taka Crore)
Social and Household Needs	18,014	2.06
Health and Medical Expenses	9,449	0.86
New and Supplementary Activities	7,847	1.00
Repairing and Addition to Capital Equipment	1,783	0.23
Purchase of Raw Materials	2,478	0.27
Others	12,026	1.47
Total	51,597	5.89

Source: Grameen Bank, 1989.

Lending Procedures

The lending procedure is simple and devoid of any legal formalities. Loans are sanctioned against a loan proposal (application) form filled in by the borrower, which indicates details such as purpose, amount, etc., and is accompanied by an undertaking that the borrower would not dispose of the asset until the loan was repaid in full.

These proposals, however, require the recommendations of the group leader and centre chief. When a Group is formed, all members of the group are not entitled to loans simultaneously. The most deserving two members are first considered and the other members get assistance in a phased manner with the group chairman receiving the loan last. This practice ensures endurance and appreciation of the priorities in need of the deserving among group members. A second loan is not given to any member till the loans of all group members are settled fully. Group pressure acts as collateral for bank loans. The group's credibility and its future suffers, if there are defaults. The groups fine those members who fail to attend weekly repayment meetings and also extend financial support to the defaulting member in time of genuine financial difficulty. If a member defaults, the responsibility for payment of dues falls on the other members and if the entire group defaults, responsibility for payment falls on the centre.

A member can borrow from the group fund for consumption needs such as sickness, social ceremonies, etc., so that such expenses are not met by diverting bank funds or by taking loans from money-lenders at usurious rates (10 per cent per month). The group decides the terms and conditions of the loans, which are normally interest free. This ensures a flexibility in credit services that is valued by poor borrowers.

Investment alternatives are discussed by group members in the weekly centre meetings and when the group members and the bank worker are convinced of the viability of the loan, the centre chief initiates the loan approval process by filling in a loan proposal form and the bank worker then recommends the loan to the branch manager. After consultation and field verification visits, all such individual loan proposals are consolidated into a single proposal and submitted to the programme officer in the area office, who then recommends it to the area manager for his final authorisation. The loan amount is then disbursed with a pass-book by the bank worker in the centre meeting. The process takes one or two weeks.

Borrowers need to invest the loan amount within seven days of receipt for the purpose specified in the loan proposal. The sanctioning process starts with the group chairman, who signs a loan utilisation form and forwards it to the centre chief who passes it on to the bank worker who checks the loan utilisation and provides a written description of the asset and is responsible personally, for checking 50 per cent of the cases at random. After field visits, the branch manager signs the form and forwards it to the programme officer who is the ultimate authority for supervision of loan utilisation. The process of obtaining loans does not cause undue expenditure or inconvenience to borrowers and no security or surety is insisted upon.

Repayment of Loans

All loans (except housing loans) are repayable uniformly in 50 equal weekly instalments, at 2 per cent of the loan amount per week, irrespective of the loan amount or nature of activity. Thereafter, the interest is collected in the next two weekly instalments. The approach of the Grameen Bank is totally different in this respect from traditional banking procedure, which takes into account several aspects such as gestation period, incremental income, pattern of cash flow etc. The Grameen Bank can be different as most of the activities chosen by the borrowers are such that they generate income immediately and continuously. Most of the activities are also labour intensive, carried out in the house of the borrowers themselves and with the assistance of family members. It is, therefore, found convenient to repay the dues in weekly instalments. The bank is of the view that the system has been put to test for two decades and the excellent recovery performance proves its soundness. However, if natural or personal calamities affected the borrowers' ability to repay, there were built-in systems to safeguard the interests of the borrowers. On the recommendations of the group, the branch manager is empowered to suspend loan recovery and a second loan was also available from the group fund to commence another activity afresh. Under no circumstances is any loan written off as bad.

Recoveries are made during the weekly meetings of the group. The borrowers are expected to attend the weekly meetings without fail and bring with them the weekly repayment instalment. Absence at weekly meetings without leave of absence attracts a fine as decided by the group chairman. The recoveries made at the weekly meetings are handed over to the bank worker who remits them into the branch. Pass books are issued to the borrowers for each type of loan and entries are made therein about disbursements and recoveries.

Utilisation of Loans and Recovery Performance

Evaluation studies on the innovative experiments of the Grameen Bank by different agencies, both national and international, have shown that the investments made by the loanees have been extremely productive and have contributed to significant improvements in household output, income and consumption. In addition, there have been gains in the form of substitution of institutional credit for private sources and reduction of wasteful expenditure on social obligations. The studies have revealed that incomes increased from 60 per cent to 75 per cent over two years. The Grameen Bank rightly believes that mere substitution of institutional credit for private credit, even if nothing else happened, would generate surplus income for the loanees. Another source of income gain for borrowers is the reduction of expenditure on wasteful social obligations including avoidance of dowries, due to the social content of the Grameen Bank's programme. Group pressure and supervision, coupled with the close follow-up by bank workers ensured proper utilisation of loan. That the Grameen Bank loans have been used productively and have led to significant increases in income is further attested by the excellent repayment record of the loanees.

During 1988, the bank disbursed loans aggregating tk. 128.04 crore and recovered tk. 101.42 crore. Up to June 1992, the bank had disbursed tk. 12.28 billion and recovered 98 per cent of it. A study carried out by the central bank revealed that loan delinquency was 3 per cent in the case of male borrowers, 0 per cent for female borrowers and 2 per cent for all borrowers. Such an outstanding record of repayment, especially from poorer segments of society is unique among any development project. Not only have the loanees repaid the principal and interest due thereon but have also made contributions to various funds. Such extremely high marginal rates of savings were possible only if the investments were highly productive. The system of group and centre meetings provided a convenient mechanism for bank workers to contact the borrowers and effect recoveries. The group acted as an in-built system for bringing pressure on borrowers for prompt repayments, as it is not possible to withhold repayments on false pretexts. Group support also gave the borrowers a sense of security in time of calamities. The recovery record of the Grameen Bank's programme has attracted worldwide attention and aroused keen interest. Various countries are trying to replicate the Grameen Bank experience.

The bank has no system of maintaining demand, collection and balance registers at the branch/head office level to compute the overdues position. Instead, it related its overdues to the outstanding position. A weekly statement was, however, received from branches which indicated the position of number of loanees, the number of borrowers who repaid the loans and number of defaulters, together with the amount of instalments due and amount in default. The position was consolidated at the head office for the bank as a whole. The bank keeps a close watch and immediate follow-up action is taken on defaulters, to ascertain the reasons for default and provide appropriate support. Though the loan is required to be repaid in weekly instalments, spread over one year, a loan is treated as 'unrepaid' if the default persisted beyond one year, and as 'overdue' only after the lapse of a further year. This is, perhaps, one of the reasons for the low percentage of overdues to outstanding loans, but does not in any way diminish the bank's recovery performance. The amount 'unpaid after one year' formed only 1.6 per cent of the outstanding loans as at the end of December 1988.

Funds Management and Branch Control

The management of funds was initially controlled by the head office. Since 1987, this function has been entrusted to the zonal offices. Each branch is required to submit on a monthly basis, a fund planning report for the ensuing month, showing the likely demand of funds for the month, through the area office. Branches are required to deposit their collections on a day-to-day basis with the nearest identified branch of a nationalised bank. On each Thursday, the branch sends its 'demand' for funds to the area office and Saturdays are ear marked as disbursement days. The area office remits the surplus funds to the zonal office and the latter to the head office. When the head office provides funds to the branches, it charges interest at 10 per cent and the branches lend at 16 per cent; the margin of 6 per cent is meant for meeting the cost of the branch. This 10 per cent intra-bank rate is designed to encourage the use of members' savings and deposits costing 8.5 per cent. Branches are required to send two weekly returns—funds management return and loan recovery return—to the area office.

Sources of Funds

The Grameen Bank's resources consist of (i) share capital (ii) deposits (iii) contributions from members in the form of various funds, and (iv) borrowings from international agencies and the Bangladesh Bank. The position as at the end of December 1984 and 1988 is given in Table 16.4.

The Bangladesh government and nationaliesed banks held 12 per cent of the paid-up capital and the members held the rest. When the group fund exceeds tk. 600, each member of the group is required to contribute to one share of tk. 100. The share money is, however, paid from the members' weekly savings contribution to the group fund. The share value is not linked to borrowings and each member is required to take only one share during the life of membership. The share value is not refundable but can be transferred to another member.

Table 16.4
Sources of Funds of the Grameen Bank

Table 16.4
Sources of Funds of the Grameen Bank

	Source	1984		1988	
		Amount (Taka Crore)	% to Total	Amount (Taka Crore)	% to Total
i)	Paid-up Share Capital	2.52	6.7	5.69	3.5
ii)	Deposits	0.22	0.6	2.70	1.7
iii)	Funds Contributed by Members	3.88	10.3	29.75	18.4
iv)	Borrowings from Bangladesh Bank, etc.	17.17	45.4	1.48	0.9
v)	Borrowings/ Grants from International Agencies	13.95	37.0	121.81	75.5
		37.74	100.0	161.43	100.0

Source: Grameen Bank,1989.

Deposits are accepted only in the form of savings and current accounts and that too by certain designated branches only. Of the 741 branches, only 200 accept deposits. The deposits bear interest at rates specified in the directives of the central bank—currently, 8.5 per cent. The total savings of members were tk. 1.06 billion up to June 1992.

Compulsory contributions to the various funds of the bank by the members form the second largest source, next only to the borrowings from international institutional agencies.

The bank expects that by 1995, the fund would grow to such an extent that external borrowings could be totally dispensed with. However, this could pose some problems to the bank regarding its operational costs as it paid interest at 8.5 per cent to the members on the group fund, while its lending rate is 16 per cent. At present, the borrowings of the bank from various financial institutions are at a very low rate of interest and hence, the bank could retail a substantial margin on its lendings, to meet its high operational costs.

Borrowings from international institutional agencies at tk. 121.81 crore form the bulk, i.e., 75 per cent of the bank's resources. They are also available at incredibly low rates of interest. The credit assistance provided by foreign agencies carried lending rates ranging between 2 per cent and 3.5 per cent. A sizeable portion of the foreign assistance was also in the form of non-returnable grants. It was reported that since the inception of the project in 1976 and up to 1982, the bank did not get any external assistance. Thereafter, in the first phase, the bank received US $3.20 million at 2 per cent and US$3.20 million at 3.5 per cent. In the second phase, it received US$ 38 million at 2 per cent and in the third phase, US$106 million, of which US $10 million was at 2 per cent and the rest was a grant. The Grameen Bank has, thus, been able to successfully tap, a sizeable source of low-cost funds, which has helped in absorbing its high operational costs.

Cost of Operations

The bank's highly supervised nature of lending contributed to its high cost of operations. Of its 13,000 employees, about 12,500 were engaged in field operations. On an average, there was one bank worker (field supervisor) for every 200 members and each branch had about 1,000 members in its jurisdiction. When the number of members per branch crossed 1,000, another branch was established in the area. Although this system contributed in a big way to the success of the Grameen Bank, the pertinent point was the affordability of such high cost of supervision. A break-up of its income and expenditure for 1984 and 1988 is given in Table 16.5:

Table 16.5
Income and Expenditure of Grameen Bank

(Taka Crore)

	Expenditure			Income	
	1984	1988		1984	1988
1. Interest on Deposits	1.35	2.09	1. Interest on Advances	2.33	11.27
2. Interest on Borrowings	—	2.72	2. Interest on Investments	1.21	5.16
3. Depreciation	1.72	0.29	3. Other Receipts	0.65	3.49
4. Salaries and Allowances	—	8.11			
5. Other Expenses	—	6.59			
6. Net Profit	0.52	0.12			
Total	3.59	19.92		3.59	19.92

Source: Grameen Bank, 1989.

Salaries and allowances formed 41 per cent of the total income while interest on borrowings and deposits were 24.3 per cent. The bank's over-head expenses were also heavy at tk. 6.59 crore during 1988, forming 33.2 per cent of its income, mainly accounted for by printing and stationery, rent and taxes, training expenses, and travelling and conveyance. The net profit of tk. 0.12 crore was a meagre 0.6 per cent of its income and highly disproportionate to its loan turnover of tk. 128 crore. This, despite the fact that the bank had a high proportion of low-cost borrowings at rates ranging between 2 per cent and 3.5 per cent and it charged 18 per cent on the loans disbursed by it, leaving a substantial margin. However, interest payment on an average loan of tk. 5,000 works out to 8.12 per cent of the loan as interest is charged on the reducing balance. Thus, it would appear that the bank's impressive performance is mainly due to the low cost of funds particularly from foreign agencies. If this source dried up, the bank might face serious difficulties. The bank has an ambitious programme of branch expansion and plans to extend its network to about 2000 branches by 1995 from 961 in 1992. It was reported that it took about seven years for a branch to break even at the present cost. At the end of August 1990, there were only 86 profitable branches out of 741.

Grameen Bank's Progress

Having discussed the various aspects of the Grameen Bank's projects and the factors which contributed to its success, it is necessary to review the progress made by the bank in the short span of its existence (See Table 16.6).

Table 16.6
Progress of the Grameen Bank

	As at the End of December			1990 (up to
	1980	*1985*	*1988*	*Aug.)*
1. No. of Villages Covered	363	3,666	10,552	188,125
2. No. of Branches	25	266	501	741
3. No. of Members (in lakh)	0.15	1.72	4.90	7.90
Males	NA	0.59	0.69	0.75
Females	NA	1.13	4.21	7.15
4. No. of Groups	2,935	34,324	98,073	NA

Table 16.6 Contd.

Table 16.6 Contd.

		As at the End of December		1990 (up to
		1980	1985	1988	Aug.)
5.	No. of Borrowers				
	(in lakh)	0.12	1.52	4.72	NA
6.	Loans Disbursed	1.71	42.84	128.04	NA
7.	Cumulative Position				
	of Loans Disbursed				
	since Inception and				
	up to the End of the				
	Year (taka crore)	2.01	92.77	355.99	681.07
8.	Savings in Group				
	Fund (in taka crore)	0.15	7.14	298.74	57.45
9.	Savings in Emergency				
	Fund (in taka crore)	Negligible	1.26	5.43	11.16
10.	Loans from Group				
	Fund—Cumulative				
	Disbursement since				
	Inception (in taka crore)	NA	2.23	13.19	30.91

NA—Not Available
Source: Grameen Bank, 1990.

Critical Analysis of the Grameen Bank

The Bangladesh Grameen Bank has an unique approach to providing credit to the rural poor. It imposes a strict discipline on the borrowers as well as bank staff. The management also services the poorest of the poor in the rural areas who would, otherwise, have not been eligible for credit from other institutions. By virtue of peer pressure among its borrowings and loan supervision, the Grameen Bank has achieved a repayment record in an area in which most other credit schemes fail. An elaborate system of discipline and supervision is incorporated into loan procedures and characterises its credit operations as well as related social development ac-tivities. Individually, the procedures may not be significant but together they constitute a formidable system.

The Grameen Bank recognises that the poorest in rural areas are not the farmers but the landless, who are also excluded from the traditional rural credit projects designed for farmers and requiring collateral. The assetless/landless have been targeted by the Grameen Bank as its borrowers as they are a major productive resource in Bangladesh that has been underutilised.

However, the landless lack the basic skills to take up non-traditional activities. The Grameen Bank tries to improve upon skills and productivity by testing appropriate strategies and providing suitable training on improved technologies.

In an Islamic country, women have less rights than the men but the Grameen Bank has recognised their worth as individuals and as reliable instruments in the fight against rural poverty. When women become income-earners, the incremental income is systematically oriented towards increasing family well being, which is not true of the male earners. This feature of intra-household distribution of incremental income and well being is the basis for preference of women borrowers. However, there are few female staff members as the social constraints on employing women especially as branch managers have yet to be overcome.

In some zones (e.g., Tangail), the recovery rate has come down, even though they are still higher than those of other rural credit agencies. It has been the Grameen Bank's experience that the first-time loanee's repayment record is much better than that of subsequent time loanees. Fourth-time loanees had about 10 per cent of the overdue loan instalments compared to 0.4 per cent for first-time loanees and 1.2 per cent for second-time loanees. Thus, repeat loanees fail to maintain regularity in repayment compared to fresh loanees. Further, even among repeat loanees, the repayment performance of female loanees is much better than that of males. The Grameen Bank has to take a decision about granting loans afresh to old members who have benefited from loans and are not so poor as newer loanees. For those leaving the groups, only their deposits from the group fund can be returned. Thus, the Grameen Bank has to decide about those who no longer qualify for inclusion in the group.

The repayment performance of collective loans is not particularly good. Many members with excellent individual record of repayment do not do well when they go in for collective enterprises due to lack of management skills and wrong investment decisions. Documents regarding loan proposals are also few and may not be necessary for individual loans but are essential for collective enterprises to ensure the commitment of all involved in the project. The emphasis on working out per capita repayment and whether it can be afforded by the borrower, ensures repayment for the bank but does not ensure project viability or profitability. Loanees are aware of weekly repayments but are not aware of break even costs, daily production, costs of machinery and installation, etc. In a few cases, repayment was not possible from internally generated funds and loanees were forced to borrow from other sources. Long-term projects may not generate enough funds for repayment within the stipulated one year repayment period. The weekly instalment does not work well in case of collective enterprises such as land-lease, deep tubewells, shallow tubewells, pisciculture, etc. The Grameen Bank is trying to improve the management structure of these collective groups and to change rules. In many cases, the bank has taken over collective enterprises and is teaching loanees to run them efficiently.

The Grameen Bank depends upon the honesty and dedication of both staff and borrowers and puts a tremendous workload on the field level staff. The salaries are, however, linked to the government employees' scales who do not work as hard. A better incentive structure may be needed in future or productivity may fall. The expansion of the Grameen Bank has been rather fast and consolidation efforts, may suffer. The Grameen Bank should not expand too fast due to pressure from the government, donor agencies or the rural elite and should proceed at a manageable pace. Dependence on foreign funds (72 per cent) needs to be minimised and self-sufficiency in funds is necessary. The Grameen Bank has taken steps to mobilise borrowings from members and also accepts deposits from non members. Some group members resent the imposition of physical exercise and slogans at the centre meetings. The tendency to impose social objectives may not always be welcome.

The lack of adequate documentation especially for collective enterprises would create problems in future and due to the bank's rapid expansion and quick promotions of staff, transfers are inevitable. The lack of experience and insufficient knowledge to evaluate investment proposals at head office level is a serious liability. On-the-job training is not the method for training managers who operate technically-complex enterprises. The economic viability of these group-managed enterprises is in doubt and if after 10 years, a venture has not made profits for the last three years, it is liquidated. The loan approval committee is engaged both in providing credit and in operating the enterprises and this leads to conflict of interests. There is no marketing orientation for the group-managed enterprises and the monitoring system is the same as that for routine banking operations. All contracts entered into by the Small Industries Development Enterprise (SIDE) enterprises are made in the Grameen Bank's name which is responsible for their liabilities. In 1987, SIDE enterprises were lent tk. 6.5 million (15 per cent of the bank's capital) due to natural calamities.

A crucial factor is the high cost of supervision. The risk in this direction has not manifested so far, in view of the ability of the bank to attract large doses of financial assistance at incredibly low interest rates from foreign funding agencies. But, the bank does carry a heavy load of overhead expenses and blocked assets in the form of buildings, etc., amounting to tk. 12.66 crore. This formed 32 per cent of its own resources of tk. 38.14 crore in December 1988. Most of the activities financed by the bank are low profile and devoid of any extension facility to either improve productivity or eliminate drudgery or physical stress, through modern technologies and gadgets. Extension facilities come from the bank only when sought for by the participants. The average loan size is also small and though the bank claims that the economic conditions of the participants have improved greatly, it is certain that the nature of low-profile activities is such that a single loan would not take the participants beyond a certain economic status. The most important drawback is the absence of any effort on the part of the bank to find markets for the products of the borrowers. In the absence of collective marketing efforts, individuals pursuing economic activities are subject to the vagaries of market forces, controlled as these are by vested interests. Most of the activities are now pursued on a small scale, with local consumption as the market for the products. As and when the Grameen Bank is able to bring more rural borrowers into its fold, the ability of local markets to absorb the products will be seriously hampered, resulting in either defaults in repayments or urgent need for intervention by introducing marketing mechanisms for the borrowers' products.

Although, the theme of self-reliance through savings mobilisation is laudable, the different types of compulsory contributions are definitely a sore point in the project. The contributions to the group fund, at 5 per cent of the loan amount disbursed each time, the one taka per week to the children's welfare fund and 25 per cent of the interest amount to the emergency fund all of which can not be reclaimed by a member leaving the group, added to the costs for the borrowers, and they were, perhaps, silently accepted by them as part of the several disciplinary restrictions imposed by the bank. The vertical expansion by the bank would sooner or later be constrained by the low level of productivity of many of the activities financed by it. A study conducted by IFAD in 1990 has revealed that with an increase in the size of the loan, the rate of return decreases and that the present average loan size appeared to provide optimum returns. The joint enterprises (SIDE) encouraged by the bank for larger investment have not produced better results due to management deficiencies and the bank's policy of non-intervention in the management of such economic activities.

The driving force behind the success of the experiment was the Founder-Managing Director, Dr Mohammed Yunus. His personal touch is visible in all spheres of the activity of the bank. The bank has been in existence since 1976 and with the average age of employees being 22 there is much enthusiasm and vigour among the staff. Promotions at definite intervals has been one of the motivating factors. One should not miss the limitations in this regard in due course of time, when the bank reaches its optimum growth level. Although sufficient training was imparted at all staff levels in order to equip them to rise up the ladder of hierarchy, the success of the project was largely due to the dedication of Dr Yunus who nursed the project since its inception. Decentralisation and a distinct management style and system should be evolved to continue the progress.

The rapid expansion of the project since 1976 has demonstrated its replication potential. However, one should not fail to notice that even in Bangladesh, it has not been replicated in other rural credit agencies. This is due to the fact that the Grameen Bank started as a unique institution, different from traditional approaches in many respects and has been permitted to continue to do so. It would, therefore, be difficult to replicate its operations in other institutions.

In Indian conditions, many of the policies followed by the Grameen Bank and even its organisational structure, appear to be revolutionary. The Grameen Bank in the first instance, does not fit into any type of existing banking system. It has been created by a special legislation. It has the shades of both a cooperative venture and a commercial bank. It is exempt from the rigours of banking statutes in matters such as CRR, SLR, credit control measures, etc. Its operations even deviate from requirements such as legal documentation. The central bank exercises little supervision over it in the form of statutory returns (except annual balance-sheet) or inspection. The bank has dispensed with even the minimum documentation and collateral for its lending. In the Indian conditions, all these are considered sacrilege and to think of such an institution is itself impractical. It is often stated that the practices prevalent in the Grameen Bank has contributed to its success and not one can be discarded. It is, therefore, suggested that the scheme should either be adopted in its totality or abandoned altogether. The various practices are interlocked and replicating some of them in isolation is not feasible.

An important factor is that the bank was created under an ordinance in 1983 under martial law and has never been formally regularised by an Act of Parliament. The structure has been deliberately kept loose so that the permanent control of Dr Yunus, the founder, is perpetuated. Of the 12 members on the board, nine are members of SHGs (of whom eight are women); the other three are government officials. The majority, thus, lack practical experience of running a bank. Basically, it is a one-man show. There is no democratic control or signs of a succession plan. From the bankers' point of view, there are several areas of concern:

- A major source of funding is cheap foreign credit at very low rates of interest and favourable repayment terms.
- No charge on assets is created, only social collateral or group pressure. Hence, legally, there is no chance of recovery.
- Only tk 5,000 (maximum) can be given per borrower and a large number of otherwise viable activities are not being financed as per norms.
- Assets creation is poor as borrowers are encouraged to be dependent on the bank for consumption/production finance with repeated doses of small amounts. Families rising above the poverty line are very few.
- The income pattern of the bank reveals that 61 per cent of the income is from interest payments while 39 per cent is from grants/foreign aid that is invested with commercial banks (8–10 per cent interest spread is available).
- Staff drop-out rate is too high—over 40 per cent of the newly recruited staff drop out in the first six months.

Annexure 16.1

*(Published in the Bangladesh Gazette, Extraordinary,
dated the 4th September 1983)*

GOVERNMENT OF THE PEOPLE'S REPUBLIC OF BANGLADESH
MINISTRY OF LAW AND LAND REFORMS
Law and Parliamentary Affairs Division
NOTIFICATION
Dhaka, the 4th September 1983

No. 482 Pub.—The following Ordinance made by the Chief Martial Law Administrator of the People's Republic of Bangladesh, on the 1st September, 1983, is hereby published for general information:

THE GRAMEEN BANK ORDINANCE, 1983
Ordinance No. XLVI of 1983
An
ORDINANCE
to provide for the establishment of the Grameen Bank

WHEREAS it is expedient to establish a Grameen Bank to provide credit facilities and other services to landless persons in the rural areas and to provide for matters connected therewith or incidental thereto:

Now, THEREFORE, in pursuance of the Proclamation of the 24th March, 1982, and in exercise of all powers, enabling him in that behalf, the Chief Martial Law Administrator is pleased to make and promulgate the following Ordinance:

1. Short title and extent—(1) This Ordinance may be called the Grameen Bank Ordinance, 1983.

    (2) It extends to such rural areas as the Government may, by notification in the official Gazette, specify.

2. Definitions—In the Ordinance, unless there is anything repugnant in the subject or context:
   (a) 'Bank' means the Grameen Bank established under this Ordinance;
   (b) 'Board' means the Board of Directors of the Bank;
   (c) 'Bangladesh Bank' means the Bangladesh Bank established under the Bangladesh Bank Order, 1972 (P.O. No. 127 of 1971);
   (d) 'Chairman' means the Chairman of the Board;
   (e) 'Director' means a Director of the Bank;
   (f) 'Family', in relation to a person, includes such person and his wife, son, unmarried daughter, son's wife, son's son and son's unmarried daughter;
   (g) 'initial period' means such period from the date of the commencement of the Ordinance as the Government may, by notification in the Official Gazette, determine;
   (h) 'landless person' means any person who or whose family owns less than fully decimals of cultivable land or who or whose family owns property, both movable and immovable, the value of which does not exceed the value of one acre of cultivable land according to the prevailing market price in the union in which the person normally resides;
   (i) 'loan' includes guarantee or indemnity which the Bank may give on behalf of a landless person or any liability which the Bank may incur on behalf of a landless person;
   (j) 'Managing Director' means the Managing Director appointed under Section 14;
   (k) 'new bank' means a new bank specified in the schedule to the Bangladesh Banks (Nationalisation) Order, 1972 (P.O. No. 26 of 1972);
   (l) 'prescribed' means prescribed by rules or regulations made under this Ordinance; and
   (m) 'rural area' means an area which is not included within a municipality or cantonment.

3. Ordinance to override all other laws—The provisions of this Ordinance shall have effect notwithstanding anything inconsistent therewith contained in any other law for the time being in force.

4. Establishment of the Bank—(1) On the commencement of this Ordinance, there shall be established a Bank to be called the Grameen Bank for the purposes of this Ordinance.
   (2) The Bank shall be a body corporate, having perpetual succession and a common seal with power to acquire, hold and dispose of property, both movable and immovable and shall by the said name sue and be sued.
   (3) Subject to sub-section (4), the Banking Companies Ordinance, 1962 (LVII of 1962), and any other law for the time being in force relating to banking companies shall not apply to the Bank.

(4) The Government may, by notification in the official Gazette, direct that specific provisions of the Banking Companies Ordinance, 1962 (LVII of 1962), or any other law for the time being in force relating to banking companies shall be applicable to the Bank.

5. Head Office, etc.—(1) The Head Office of the Bank shall be at Dhaka.

(2) The Bank may, with the approval of the Bangladesh Bank, open such regional and other offices as the Board may think fit.

6. Authorised capital—(1) The authorised capital of the Bank shall be taka ten crores.

(2) The authorised capital shall be divided into ten lakh ordinary shares of taka one hundred each.

(3) The Bank may increase its authorised capital with the prior approval of the Government.

7. Paid-up share capital—(1) The initial paid-up share capital of the Bank shall be taka three crore which shall be subscribed as follows:

(a) 60 per cent by the Government or by any organisation or body set up, managed or controlled by the Government, as may be determined by it; and

(b) 40 per cent by borrowers of the Bank of which 20 per cent preferably by women borrowers.

(2) The Government may increase the paid-up share capital of the Bank from time to time.

(3) Shares held by a borrower may be transferred to another borrower of his class.

8. Direction and superintendence—(1) The general direction and superintendence of the affairs and business of the Bank shall be entrusted to Board of Directors to be constituted in accordance with the provisions of this Ordinance and such Board may exercise all such powers and do all such acts and things as may be exercised or done by the Bank.

(2) The Bank, in discharging its functions, shall act prudently with due regard to the public interest and shall be guided on questions of policy by the instructions given by the Government, which shall be the sole judge as to whether a question is a question of policy or not.

(3) Until the first Board is constituted, the Managing Director shall exercise all powers and do all acts and things as may be exercised or done by the Board.

9. Board—(1) The Board of Directors of the Bank shall consist of the followng Directors:

(a) the Chairman;

(b) the Managing Director;

(c) three persons, at least two of whom shall be in the service of the Republic, to be appointed by the Government;

(d) one woman having experience in working with landless persons to be appointed by the Government;

(e) two persons from amongst the Managing Directors of the new banks and the Bangladesh Krishi Bank to be appointed by the Government;

(f) four persons preferably including two women, to be elected by the borrower-shareholders in the prescribed manner;

Provided that, for the initial period of two years, these four Directors shall be appointed by the Government from amongst the borrower-shareholders.

10. Chairman—(1) The Government shall appoint one of the Directors, other than the Managing Director, to be the Chairman of the Board.

(2) If a vacancy occurs in the office of the Chairman or if the Chairman is unable to discharge the functions of his office on account of absence, illness or any another cause, the Government may 'authorise any other director, other than the Managing Director, to discharge the functions of the Chairman during the period for which he is so unable.

11. Term of office of Directors—(1) Appointed Directors shall hold office during the pleasure of the Government.

(2) An elected Director shall hold office for a term of three years and shall continue in office until his successor enters upon his office.

12. Filling of casual vacancy—A casual vacancy in the office of an elected Director shall be filled by election and the person elected to fill such vacancy shall hold office for the unexpired period of his predecessor.

Provided that it shall not be necessary to fill a vacancy for a period not exceeding three months.

13. Vacancy, etc., not to invalidate proceeding—No act or proceeding of the Board shall be invalid merely on the ground of the existence of any vacancy in, or any defect in the constitution of the Board.

14. Managing Director—(1) There shall be a Managing Director of the Bank who shall be appointed by the Government.

(2) The Managing Director shall be the Chief Executive of the Bank.

15. Functions of Directors—The Chairman, Managing Director and other Directors shall exercise such powers, perform such functions and discharge such duties as may be prescribed or assigned to them by the Board.

16. Resignation—The Chairman, Managing Director or any other Director may,

at any time, resign his office by notice in writing addressed to the Government.

Provided that no resignation shall take effect until it has been accepted by the Government.

17. Meeting—(1) The meetings of the Board shall be held at such times and at such places as may be determined by the Board.

Provided that a meeting may otherwise be convened by the Chairman when he so thinks fit.

18. Committee—The Board may appoint such committee or committees as the Board thinks to assist it in the efficient discharge of its functions.

19. Functions—The Bank shall provide credit with or without collateral security in cash or in kind, for such term and subject to such conditions as may be prescribed, to landless persons for all types of economic activities including housing, but excluding business in foreign exchange transaction, and may carry on and transact the several kinds of business hereinafter specified, that is to say—

   (a) the accepting of money on deposit;

   (b) the borrowing of money for the purpose of the Bank's business against the security of its assets or otherwise;

   (c) the issuing and selling of bonds and debentures;

   (d) for the purpose of securing loans and advances made by the Bank, accepting pledge, mortgage, hypothecation or assignment to the Bank of any kind of movable or immovable property;

   (e) Participation in the management, control and supervision of any rural organization, enterprise or scheme for the benefit and advancement of landless persons without financial investment;

   (f) with the approval of the Government, the buying, stocking and supplying of industrial and agricultural inputs and acting as agents for any organisation for the sale of inputs.

   (g) with the approval of the Government, the subscribing to the debentures, being debentures repayable within a period not exceeding ten years, of any body corporate concerned with economic activities in rural areas;

   (h) with the approval of the Government, the purchasing of shares of any body corporate, the object of which is to provide services to landless persons;

   (i) the custody of savings certificate, title deeds and other valuable articles and the collection of the proceeds, whether principal, interest or dividends of any such securities or saving certificates;

   (j) the paying, receiving, collecting and remitting of money and securities within the country;

   (k) the acquiring, maintaining and transferring of all movable and immovable property, including residential premises, for carrying on its business;

(l) carrying out survey and research, issuing publication and maintaining statistics relating to the improvement of economic condition of the landless persons;

(m) providing professional counsel to landless persons regarding investments in small business and such cottage industries as may be prescribed;

(n) encouraging investments in such cottage industries as may be prescribed and service projects by landless persons;

(o) providing services to the borrowers regarding all kinds of insurances;

(p) with the approval of Government, constituting, promoting, issuing, organising, managing and administering Mutual Funds or Unit Trusts of any type or character, and acquiring, holding, dealing, selling, paying or disposing of or dealing in shares, certificates or securities of such Funds or Trusts;

(q) rendering managerial, marketing, technical and administrative advice to borrowers and assisting them in obtaining services in those fields;

(r) the opening of accounts or the making of any agency arrangement with and the acting as agent or correspondent of any bank or financial organization;

(s) the investing of its funds in Government securities;

(t) the selling and realising of all properties, whether movable or immovable, which may in any way come into the possession of the Bank in satisfaction or part satisfaction of any of its claim and the acquisition and the holding of and generally the dealing with, any right, title or interest in any property, movable or immovable, which may be the Bank's security; and

(u) generally the doing of all such acts and things as may be necessary, incidental or conducive to the attainment of the object of the bank.

20. Prohibited business—The Bank shall not undertake or transact any kind of business other than those authorised by or under this Ordinance.

21. Bonds and debentures—(1) The Bank may, with the prior approval of the Government, issue and sell bonds and debentures carrying interest at such rates as may be approved by the Government.

(2) The bonds and debentures of the Bank shall be guaranteed by the Government as to their payment of principal and payment of interest at such rate as may be fixed by the Government at the time the bonds and debentures are issued.

22. Accounts—The Bank shall maintain proper accounts and prepare annual statement of accounts, including the profit and loss account and balance sheet, and shall comply in respect of such accounts with such general

directions as may be issued by the Government and the Bangladesh Bank from time to time.

23. Audit—(1) The accounts of the Bank shall be audited by not less than two auditors being chartered accountants within the meaning of the Bangladesh Chartered Accountants Order 1973 (P.O. No. 2 of 1973), who shall be appointed by the Government.

    (2) Every auditor appointed under sub-section (1) shall be given a copy of the annual balance sheet and other accounts of the Bank and shall examine it, together with the accounts and vouchers relating thereto, and shall have a list delivered to him of all books kept by the Bank, and shall at all reasonable times have access to the books of accounts and documents of the Bank, and may, in relation to such accounts, examine any Director or officer of the Bank.

    (3) The auditors shall report to the Government upon the annual balance sheet and accounts, and in their report they shall state whether, in their opinion, the balance sheet contains all necessary particulars and is properly drawn up so as to exhibit a true and correct view of the state of affairs of the Bank and, in case they have called for any explanation or information from the Board, whether it has been given and whether it is satisfactory.

    (4) The Government may, at any time, issue directions to the auditors requiring them to report to it upon the adequacy of measures taken by the Bank for the protection of the interest of the Government and of the creditors of the Bank or upon the sufficiency of the procedure in auditing the affairs of the Bank, and may, at any time, enlarge or extend the scope of the audit or direct that different procedure in audit shall be adopted or that any other examination shall be made by the auditors or any other person or persons, if in its opinion, the interest of the Government so requires.

24. Returns—(1) The Bank shall furnish to the Government such returns, reports and statements as the Government may from time to time require.

    (2) The Bank shall, within three months after the end of every financial year, furnish to the Government a statement of accounts audited by the auditors under Section 23 together with an annual report on the working of the Bank during the year.

    (3) The copies of the audited accounts and annual report received by the Government under sub-section (2) shall be published in the official Gazette and shall be laid before Parliament.

25. Reserve Fund—The Bank shall establish a reserve fund to which shall be credited such amount out of its net annual profit as the Board may determine.

26. Disposal of profit—After deducting the amount credited to reserve fund under Section 25 and making provisions for bad and doubtful debts, depreciation of assets and any other matters which are usually provided for by bankers, the net annual profit of the Bank remaining thereafter shall be utilized in such manner as the Board may determine.

27. Appointment of officers and other employees—The Bank may appoint such persons as it considers necessary for the efficient performance of its functions on such terms and conditions as may be prescribed.

Provided that in making such appointment, the persons who served under the Grameen Bank Project mentioned in Section 37 shall be given preference if they are otherwise eligible for such appointment.

28. Recovery of Bank dues—(1) All sums due to the Bank shall be recoverable as arrears of land revenue.

Provided that no sum shall be so recovered unless fifteen days notice has first been given by the Bank to the debtor or any other person liable to pay the sum.

Provided further that in so giving notice, the Bank shall inform the debtor or any other person liable to pay the sum that he may pay the dues in such instalments as may be fixed in the notice and that it will proceed as to the entire sum outstanding in case of any default in any instalment.

(2) In the application of the Public Demands Recovery Act, 1913 (Ben.Act III of 1913), for the purpose of recovery of the dues of the Bank, the provisions of Sections 7, 9, 10 and 13 of that Act shall not apply, and the certificates issued under Section 6 of the said Act shall be conclusive proof that the amount specified therein is due to the Bank.

(3) An officer of the Bank may exercise all powers exercisable by a Certificate Officer under the Public Demands Recovery Act, 1913 (Ben. Act III of 1913), within his jurisdiction for the purpose of recovery of the dues of the Bank only.

29. Delegation of powers—The Board may for the purpose of ensuring efficient functioning of the Bank and facilitating transaction of its daily business, delegate to the Chairman, Managing Director or any other Director or any officer of the Bank any of its functions subject to such conditions as it may think to impose.

30. Indemnity—Every Director shall be indemnified against all losses and expenses incurred by him in the discharge of his duties except such as are caused by his own wilful act or default.

31. Penalty, etc.—(1) Whoever wilfully makes a false statement or knowingly permits any false statement to be made or to retain in any document of title

or any other document given to the Bank by way of security or otherwise in respect of any loan or facility sought or granted under the Ordinance shall be punishable with imprisonment for a term which may extend to one year, or with fine which may extend to two thousand taka, or with both.

(2) Whoever without the consent in writing of the Bank uses its name in any prospectus or advertisement shall be punishable with imprisonment for a term which may extend to six months, or with fine which may extend to one thousand taka, or with both.

(3) Whoever wilfully withholds or fails to deliver to the Bank, which he is required to deliver under this Ordinance shall be punishable with imprisonment for a term which may extend to one year, or with fine, or with both.

32. Cognizance of offence—No court shall take cognizance of any offence punishable under this Ordinance except upon a complaint in writing by an officer of the Bank authorised in this behalf by the Board.

33. Exemption from taxes—Notwithstanding anything contained in the Income Tax Act 1922 (XI of 1922) or any law for the time being in force relating to income tax, super tax or business profits tax, the Bank shall not, for such period as the Government may, by notification in the official Gazette, specify, be liable to pay any such tax on its income, profits or gains.

34. Liquidation—No provision of law relating to the winding up of companies, including banking companies, shall apply to the Bank and the Bank shall not be wound up save by order of the Government and in such manner as it may direct.

35. Power to make rules—The Government may, by notification in official Gazette, make rules for the purpose of giving effect to the provisions of this Ordinance.

36. Power to make regulations—(1) The Board may, with previous approval of the Government, make regulations, not inconsistent with the provisions of this Ordinance and the rules, to provide for all matters for which provision is necessary or expedient for the purpose of giving effect to the provisions of this Ordinance and efficient conduct of the affairs of the Bank.

(2) All regulations made under this section shall be published in the official Gazette and shall come into force upon such publication.

37. Grameen Bank Project to cease to exist—(1) Notwithstanding anything contained in any other law for the time being in force or in any agreement or contract or other instrument, upon the Establishment of the Bank:

(a) the Grameen Bank Project, hereinafter referred to as the said project, shall cease to exist;

(b) all assets, rights, powers, authorities and privileges and all properties, movable and immovable, cash and bank balances, reserve funds, investments and all other rights and interests in, or arising out of, such property and all books of accounts, registers, records and all other documents of whatever nature relating thereto, of the said project shall stand transferred to and vest in the Bank;

(c) all debts, liabilities and obligations incurred, all contracts entered into and all matters and things engaged to be done by, with or for, the said project before establishment of the Bank shall be deemed to have been incurred, entered into or engaged to be done by, with or for, the Bank;

(d) the loans advanced by the said project before the establishment of the Bank shall be deemed to have been advanced by the Bank and shall be recoverable in accordance with the provisions of this Ordinance.

(2) The Government may, for the purpose of removing any difficulty in relation to the transfer and other matter specified in sub-section (1), make such orders as it may consider expedient and any such order shall be deemed to be, and given effect to as, part of the provisions of this Ordinance.

Explanation—In this section 'Grameen Bank Project' means the Grameen Bank Project sponsored by the Rural Economics Programme of the Department of Economics, University of Chittagong, in 1976 in village Jobra, police station Hathazari, in the district of Chittagong and subsequently adopted by the Bangladesh Bank and participated by new Banks and the Bangladesh Krishi Bank.

DHAKA
The 1st September 1983

H.M. ERSHAD, nde, psc
LIEUTENANT GENERAL
Chief Martial Law Administrator

SHAMSUR RAHMAN
Deputy Secretary

17

Self-help Groups and Bank Linkages

Unlike many countries which have implemented Self-help Groups (SHGs) after the mid-70s, as a part of the formal credit delivery system, India has been experimenting since 1960s with very flexible systems, giving a lot of freedom to the non-governmental organisations (NGOs) to set up SHGs based on various models. SHGs are mostly informal groups of people where members pool their savings and re-lend in the group on rotational basis, depending upon consumption, production or investment needs. SHGs have a common perception of need and improvise in collective decisions and actions. Many such groups are formed around specific production activities to promote savings among members and use the pooled common resources to meet emergent credit needs of members. Where funds generation is low in the initial phases due to low savings capacities, these are supplemented by external resources by NGOs.

Thus, SHGs have been able to provide rudimentary banking services to members on a cost-effective basis and meet urgent credit requirements in time which ensures almost cent per cent repayment of loans. Based on local requirements, SHGs have evolved their own characteristics of functioning. These are:

- The groups usually create a common fund by contributing their small savings on a regular basis.
- SHGs evolve flexible systems of operations, often with the help of NGOs and manage common pooled resources in a democratic manner.

- Loan requests are considered by groups in periodic meetings with competing claims on limited resources, being settled by consensus as regards greater need.
- Loaning is mainly on the basis of mutual need and trust with minimum documentation and without any tangible security.
- The loan amounts are small, frequent and for short durations, and are mainly for unconventional purposes.
- Rates of interest vary from group to group, depending upon the purpose of loan, and is often higher than that of banks but lower than that of money-lenders.
- At periodical meetings besides collecting money, emerging rural, social and economic issues are discussed.
- Defaults are rare due to group pressures and intimate knowledge of the end-use of credit as also the borrowers' economic resources.

SHGS in Orissa

India has about 1,50,000 credit outlets in the rural institutional sector, including cooperatives and the disbursements made by the banks for agricultural purposes during 1996–97 amounted to Rs 28,187 crore. In spite of this, rural people depend on money-lenders for all their consumption purposes. Even for production credit requirements, it is estimated that rural credit institutions supply only 12–13 per cent of the actual credit requirements with the remaining being met from own sources, friends and relatives, traders, money-lenders and landlords. With land reforms being a forgotten issue, gross capital formation in agriculture has also been falling. Banks are unable to meet rural credit requirements due to various organisational inadequacies. Very poor persons (estimated at around 240 crore) have little or no access to rural credit due to the:

- Attitude of bankers in view of rising NPAs and poor loan recovery rates.
- Attitude of borrowers in being wilful defaulters.
- Prevalence of illiteracy.
- High level of indebtedness due to natural calamities.
- Non-availability of consumption credit.
- Time taken to sanction rural loans (one month to 18 months)
- High loan transaction costs for both poor rural borrowers and rural banks.

With the help of some banks and a few committed NGOs, the number of SHGs in Orissa have been rising steadily (see Table 17.1).

Table 17.1
Number of SHGs—Orissa vs. All India

	1992–93	1993–94	1994–95	1995–96	1996–97
SHGs in India	255	620	2,122	4,600	8,000
SHGs in Orissa	—	180	203	461	753
Women SHGs in Orissa	—	180	201	459	703

Though there has been a tradition of thrift and mutual help in the villages, pooled cash savings in SHGs is an alien concept in Orissa. However, in some villages, the concept of grain 'goals' in tribal villages (at times of drought) and 'Kothas' or village funds, has been prevalent. The linkage process, emphasised by NABARD since 1992, has centred around the following broad concepts:

• Savings first, no credit without savings.
• Savings as partial collateral
• Bank loans to the SHGs for on-lending to members.
• Income-generation programmes to be popularised along with SHG concepts.
• Credit decisions for on-lending to be the prerogative of SHG members.
• Interest rates and other terms and conditions for loans to be decided by SHG members.
• Joint liability as a substitute for physical collateral.
• Ratio between savings and credit contingent upon credit worthiness and could increase over a period due to good repayment record.
• Small loans to begin with and then slowly based on repayment performance and needs, may graduate to higher credit amounts.

While SHG linkage has the capacity to develop into an alternative credit delivery system, the problem is of finding an adequate number of committed bankers and NGOs to carry forward this programme. In spite of the blessings of RBI and the initiative taken by NABARD on an all India basis, progress has not been encouraging. The status of banks/NGOs involved in the SHG programme since 1992–93 is given in Table 17.2.

Table 17.2
Status of Banks/NGOs Involved in SHG Programme

	Orissa	All India
No. of Banks	28	300
No. of Banks Linked with NGOs/SHG	7	15
No. of NGOs	5,817	23,780
No. of NGOs Involved in RD/Thrift	105	1,999
NGOs Linked with Banks in SHG Formation	9	87

Banks have been apathetic to SHG linkage partly because the concept has yet to percolate to the branch level with each bank having its own guidelines. Also, SHG lending is not perceived as normal lending activity but is treated as a concessional dispensation. Most bankers distrust lending to the poor and to NGOs due to the poor credibility of existing poverty alleviation programmes and poor interaction between NGOs and banks. On their part, NGOs also distrust banks and their bureaucratic procedures. Most NGOs are not interested in thrift-based programmes as they depend upon foreign funding on very generous terms and without much interference. Many NGOs feel that expert manpower is needed for maintaining thrift-based programmes especially keeping accounts. But, the major problem is that of linkage with banks due to the suspicious attitude of bankers as they are handling the money of other people.

Success Stories of a Few SHGs

Less Dependence on Money-lenders— Kalahandi/Bolangir

Usury in its most deplorable form exists where the lender tries to coerce the borrower into a dependency-relationship from which the borrower cannot escape. Rural money-lenders charge interest at the rate of 10 per cent per month in Sambalpur and 25 per cent per month in Bolangir and Kalahandi. NGOs have been able to organise SHGs comprising women in these areas and inculcate thrift and income-generation activities. Loans have been utilised for growing crops, blacksmithy work, making of hill-brooms, trading and business, collection of sal leaves, tailoring, etc. Repayment among these women SHGs is 100 per cent. These groups have also taken up community development like adult education, fair price shops, construction of village roads, mini-medicine banks and community grain centres. No lien on the deposits of groups have been taken in respect of loans advanced to SHGs by the Bolangir and Kalahandi Anchalik Grameen Banks.

Food Security—Koraput

The tribals of Koraput had set up grain banks in their villages in times of harvest and withdrew grain when absolutely needed. But the setting up of credit cooperatives forced the closure of these grain-banks. Under the active guidance of Ankuran, SHGs have re-established grain banks as a hedge against starvation deaths in most tribal villages of Narayampatna in Rayagada district.

Village Savings—Dhenkanal

Jahnitala in Dhenkanal district is a small village with nil-overdues. All 93 borrowers have repaid their loan instalments to Canara Bank. The village has a common fund with all households making deposits and needy persons take and repay loans within a year at the rate of 25 per cent per annum. As the interest amount adds to the fund, borrowers do not mind the additional interest. About 50 years ago, the village elders took up forest plantation on common village wastelands; today, the forests are guarded at village expense.

Another interesting innovation is that all houses in the village must be represented during all village meetings and a fine of 99 paise is imposed for non-attendance. The difficulties in gathering exactly 99 paise ensures that no household is unrepresented. Since 1947, no single police case has been registered in the village and no political meetings or smoking or drinking is permitted in the village. A model village, indeed! A community pond for development of fisheries has also been built.

Stopping Tribal Exploitation—Kalahandi

The poor tribals of Rampur and Kalahandi districts are exposed to cerebral malaria and hunger for four months in a year, apart from being exploited by money-lenders, middlemen and businessmen. Their main income is from shifting cultivation and collection of minor forest produce. Antodaya has been assisting these tribals and 800 tribal women have formed 35 SHGs with small savings. A loan of Rs 30,000 from the Kalahandi Anchalik Grameen Bank helped them to evade the clutches of money-lenders during the festive season and they avoided selling the forest agricultural produce to the money-lender traders, at nominal prices. The NGOs also helped the tribals to break the trader monopoly on hill-brooms and instead of Rs 3 per kg, the tribals now get Rs 15 per kg which has helped them pay their loans in time. Various production activities such as leaf-plate stitching, bee-keeping and *agarbathi*-making have also been taken up.

Production-oriented SHGs—Bolangir

Birmuda village in Bolangir district had 140 families with a population of 641. As the nearest bank branch was 25 km away, no credit facilities were available in the village. The milk production cooperative society could collect only 30 litres of milk daily. The Bolangir Anchalik Grameen Bank gave a credit support of Rs 3.55 lakh for 42 families and Rs 1.56 lakh deposits have been mobilised in 95 accounts. Thirty families have taken dairy loans and the milk collection by the cooperative has shot up to 320 litres per day. All loan instalments have been repaid in time and the government has extended infrastructural support like additional roads, water-harvesting structures, etc. A large number of trees have been planted and adult literacy programmes have been successful.

SHG for Mechanised Farming—Mayurbhanj

Twenty farmers in Badjore village of Mayurbhanj District formed a Farm Mechanisation Cooperative Society in 1993 and purchased a tractor with a loan from the Bank of India with IRDP subsidy. The farmers cultivate their land extensively with the tractor optimising productivity. During the off-season, the tractor is used for transportation of rural produce like construction materials, vegetables and other village handicrafts. The tractors has been a boon to the income-generation capacity. There is good unity among the members who meet on a monthly basis to review expenditure and accounts; district/bank officials also attend their meetings. A shed-cum-meeting place has been constructed.

Banning Social Ostracisms—Bhadrak/Cuttack

In Bhadrak, the first SHGs linked with banks were started by several poor Muslim women going against the conservative social customs with the help of the Balasore Gramya Bank and Fellowship, an NGO. Though the credit assistance was low, the impact on the economic conditions of the women members makes it worth emulating. A few members purchased indigenous varieties of cows with a very small investment and the assets created have added to their family income considerably. Kumari Usharani Das, an SHG organiser in Chaudwar, Cuttack district was ostracised and her house regularly stoned at night as she tried to organise women SHGs and mobilise their savings. Against all odds and with the support of the womenfolk, the SHG saved Rs 6,000 in four months and was linked to Indian Bank in 1994. Poor rural women are able to take up economic activities with common marketing facilities and increase their family incomes.

Operational Problems of SHGs

The emergence of SHGs as a supplementary credit channel and its evolution from a pilot project to a business opportunity for the banks is a departure from traditional banking practices. This has necessitated constant review of the functioning of SHGs and assessment of their strength and weaknesses.

The flexibility provided in operations and in the linkage process has encouraged and helped the groups/NGOs/banks to evolve procedures and patterns suitable to their needs. This needs to be continued. At the same time, standardisation may be attempted only in areas where flexibility has been misinterpreted or where imposition or rigidity is a necessity.

A study of all the SHGs, NGOs and banks where credit linkage had been established up to March 1995 was taken up by NABARD in mid-1996. All the existing models of linkage were covered. In all, eight NGOs, 11 banks and 14 SHGs were covered during the study covering almost the entire state. Structured questionnaires were used for collection of data besides field studies on the basis of interviews and non-participative observation at the SHG level.

The major findings of the study were:

- The repayment performance of SHG loans vis-à-vis those under the IRDP and the branch's overall recovery performance were compared. It was observed that the average recovery percentage in respect of IRDP, SHGs and branch as a whole were 36 per cent, 88 per cent, and 71 per cent respectively.
- An attempt was made to assess the initial costs incurred by NGOs in promotion and linkage of SHGs, and the source from which the same

is met. NGOs mentioned that when the number of groups were comparatively more, the initial costs incurred were less due to economies of scale.

- The study team attempted to evaluate the transaction costs incurred by banks for linking SHGs with bank credit. Similarly, the transaction costs for SHGs vis-à-vis other loans were also studied. Most of the bankers were of the view that the transaction costs for SHGs were low compared to those for small loans by banks, especially when the linkage was through an NGO.
- The record keeping and accounting procedures maintained at the SHG and NGO level varied depending upon the involvement of the NGO, level of awareness of members, etc. There is no need to impose a common system for the sake of uniformity.
- Documentation for sanction of loans and securities collected at the bank's level brought out certain interesting observations. The number of such documents varied from bank to bank (four to 11). While many banks kept the savings of the groups in fixed deposits as lien, a few preferred to keep the same in savings bank deposits and two banks did not keep any lien at all.
- The rules and regulations formulated and adopted by SHGs for smooth operations varied. There was a plethora of guidelines regarding group discipline, savings discipline and credit discipline among the groups.
- The choice of SHG members is limited to a few activities because the amount of loan is small in the initial years of the linkage programme. At a few places, group activities have been pursued with bank credit support and in most cases, there is provision for consumption loans. The repayment period was short in view of the low level of operations and to accommodate more members availing credit.
- The groups were found to take conscious decisions regarding utilisation of earned interest. While in most cases, the interest earned was ploughed back into the seed money, there were a few instances where the same was utilised for common welfare activity.
- The study team came across a few successful instances of conflict resolution and the role of peer pressure in ensuring that the SHG continued to operate. In some groups, SHGs debarred members who had availed of IRDP/DRI loans from banks but had not repaid them. In others, members paid off pending small bank loans before the SHG was constituted. In many instances, members forced repayment of SHG dues from recalcitrant members while in some cases, SHGs expelled persons who were of doubtful integrity and could not

be relied upon to repay loans. The amount of money lent and the interest rates charged by the SHG were subject to intense negotiation and justification of need by members. The desire to ensure that the SHG continues its operations, was reflected in the mature decision-making process.

- The study team also made a survey of the group decisions regarding amount of savings, frequency of savings and the source of savings and concluded that most SHGs had a mastery over financial intricacies and could manage lending decisions effectively.

- The income generated from small ventures undertaken by SHG members varied, depending upon the activity undertaken and the manufacture/marketing skills of the individual SHG member.

- The size of groups varied from group to group. However, it was observed that except in two groups, members never considered the size to be causing any problem in the functioning of the group.

- The rate of interest charged for consumption and production loans varied from group to group, ranging between 10 per cent to 36 per cent.

- The study team also explored the possibility of rotation in leadership to maintain the democratic character of the group. The majority opinion was that the SHG should decide the matter.

Issues

Thrift-based SHGs have proved that given flexible conditions, the poor can also save significant amounts. But thrift groups alone will not be able to help its members unless a loaning programme is also set up for enhancing their income-generating capacity. The example of United Artists Associates, Ganjam, reveals poor loan allocations capability if there is no bank linkage programme. Other SHGs, which had a slender resource base, utilised bank loans to augment their lending capacity. After about 3–5 years of building up the SHG's funds corpus, the NGO could withdraw and set up new SHGs.

Thus, concessional funds from NABARD in the initial years would be useful for SHGs to augment their funds and basically, would stabilise the funds resource base of SHGs. However, there is no easy access to funds for SHGs, given the hostile environment for SHG linkage, even after five years of having the SHG-bank linkage programme.

Banks are wary of giving excess credit, especially when they are very conscious about non-performing assets (NPAs) and preparing a 'healthy' balance sheet. The availability of concessional funds would enable SHGs to build up their financial resource base faster and help inculcate the principles of self-help as the corpus of SHG funds requires 3–5 years to build. The SHG would be able to generate more funds and rely on members rather than on cheap bank funds. The banks would also find this system of lending convenient as the recovery rates exceed 90 per cent in most cases and transaction costs are lower; at the same time, priority sector lending is carried out as per RBI targets.

The SHG linkage programme cannot be replicated without using NABARD refinance as the volume of funds is low. For Orissa, only an amount of Rs 22.57 lakh has been given as NABARD refinance for 404 SHGs as on 30 September 1995 (over three years). Each SHG comprising an average of about 20 members got only Rs 5,615. The availability of concessional refinance has been targeted at banks so as to popularise the SHG linkage programme and make it more attractive as banks otherwise generally treat NGOs with suspicion. The use of refinance is part of NABARD's strategy for healthy NGO–bank linkage to bring about integrated rural development with people's participation. No concessional funding is being contemplated under the NABARD bank linkage scheme. Refinance is available at the same rate as is available to banks for normal development purposes.

The issue of all NABARD refinance being concessional and the need for refinance when the process of economic liberalisation is being implemented, is beyond the scope of this paper. However, SHGs/NGOs should not be discriminated against by imposing higher refinance rates when other sections are being given concessional refinance for development purposes.

External funds do not dilute the self-help concept for NGOs; in fact, refinance helps in forging healthy linkages between banks and NGOs for more involvement in other rural development processes. Taking into account the various factors stated earlier, we conclude that if linkages between SHG members, banks and NGOs are usefully built, transaction costs will be lower for both banks and borrowers. Also there will be better loan recovery and mobilisation of deposits at low costs. The SHG linkage scheme, thus, will not merely add one more tier in the complex rural credit delivery system or dilute the principles of self-help as no subsidy is included. In the initial stages, as banks and NGOs are both wary of each other, RBI/NABARD intervention is necessary to enable SHGs to sustain/expand their operations. Over a period of 3–5 years, they will be able to stabilise their operations and build a healthy resource base. It is still too early to say if banks can provide funds from their internal resources (without recourse to NABARD refinance). However, it may be stated that many NGOs prefer not to have recourse to funds from banks given the problems in arranging linkages. Many NGOs have been suspicious about the performance of banks in spite of the need to augment SHG resources, and have firmly resisted the bank linkage programme of NABARD.

Thus, NABARD intervention to reduce mutual suspicions and encourage a healthy working relationship should continue. This will not dilute the principle of self-help as no concessions/subsidies have been envisaged in the linkage programme. But the sad truth is that due to the non-availability of a number of good NGOs which have a diversity of activities and for whom the bank linkage programme is one of many developmental activities, SHGs can only be an efficient supplement to the credit delivery system rather than form an alternative credit delivery system.

There are certain advantages in the NABARD–SHG linkage programme that must be noted. No subsidy is contemplated and the SHG is free to charge a higher rate of interest ranging from 18 per cent to 36 per cent per year. The bank charges a lower rate of interest (9.5 per cent) and a 3 per cent margin is available to the NGO to meet their transaction costs. No concessional lending to the SHG borrower is contemplated in the scheme as it would dilute the 'self-help' process and provide only temporary crutches to the poor to lean on. One of the findings of the ODA–PHEP Study, 'Credit for Fisherfolk' June 1995 states:

> There are a few NGOs who have started saving and credit programmes among marine fishing folk through SHGs. For lending they rely mainly on mobilisation of savings. But the amounts being very small, credit based solely on the savings of the community is not adequate to meet the requirements, particularly for assets.

Thus, the need for SHG–NGO–bank linkage under NABARD refinance support and guidance continues to be felt. It is surprising that the Micro-credit Summit held in Washington (February 1997) did not even discuss the need for bank linkages for SHGs. In the Indian context, where cheap, low-cost funds are not available, the need of bank linkages for SHGs is a necessity in view of the low initial savings capability of the really poor rural people.

18

Basic Policy Issues on Self-help Groups

The pilot project for linking SHGs with bank credit is an innovative programme that aims at banking with those who were considered unbankable so far. The essence of the programme as pointed out by bankers and NGOs alike is its flexibility in structure and operational guidelines, creation of awareness prior to provision of credit, conscious effort at group creation and economic empowerment through group effort as well as individual effort. At the same time, SHG financing has opened up a few issues that need to be discussd in detail and require appropriate policy interventions.

Group Size

SHGs are formed on the basis of the homogeneous character of group members—economic status, sex, profession and at times, place of residence or even caste. A large number of SHGs were found to have more than 20 members. Such SHGs attract the provisions of Sec.11(2) of the Companies Act 1956 which says,

> No company, association or partnership consisting of more than 20 persons shall be formed for carrying on business that has for its object the acquisition of gain by the company or by the individual members thereof, unless it is registered under the Act.

A few banks have issued instructions that informal groups consisting of more than 20 members cannot be financed unless they are registered. Some banks have advised their branches that such SHGs may be split into smaller groups and then financed. But any artificial splitting of the group may at times prove counter-productive, especially at the psychological level. Group composition becomes the first casualty. To encourage the participative and democratic character of the groups, NGOs are nowadays taking steps to restrict the membership size below 20. However, in some places where SHGs were formed on the basis of place of residence, say a village, there are more than 20 members. Similarly, there are instances—as in case of SHGs promoted by the Utkal Mahila Sanchaya Bikas (UMSB)—where the bigger SHGs were subsequently split into smaller SHGs. The 175 SHGs linked to bank credit were split into 308. Attempts at artificial splitting of groups were not favoured by group members in many cases.

The option to register the members has certain limitations. The pros and cons of various registration options open to SHGs are given in Table 18.1.

Table 18.1
Registration Options for SHGs

Options	Advantages	Disadvantages/Limitations
As Trust		Members of trust cannot become staff of the trust or in any way derive income from trust's activities.
As Partnership Firm		A firm with more than 20 members will attract the provisions of Sec. 11(2) of the Companies Act.
As Society	Membership to Society can be open to all those who subscribe to the business of the Society.	Society cannot declare any dividend or distribute profits to its members. As and when the Society is dissolved the common property cannot be distributed among its members. In such an eventuality, the SHG members stand to lose the savings money kept in the corpus fund.
As Cooperative Society	Registration as per Cooperative Societies Act of concerned State. Cooperatives provide for equal rights to members for participation in decision-making.	Control by Registrar of Coop. Societies and Govt. regulation over functional autonomy.
As Company		Registration procedures are lengthy and time consuming.

As registration under the present legal framework has limitations, steps need to be initiated to exempt SHGs, which are basically informal groups, from Sec.11(2) of the Companies Act.

Security Norms

The RBI has relaxed security norms for lending to SHGs and accordingly, group savings are the only security which can be offered by the SHG. It is thus, envisaged that the credit worthiness of an SHG need not be judged on the basis of the security it can offer. On the contrary, the cohesiveness, vibrancy, group discipline, level of awareness, collective decision-making, etc., should be assessed and given more importance than any tangible security. It was, however, observed during the study that a few bankers insisted on keeping the savings of the group as fixed/savings deposit. Such deposits affect the liquidity of the group and restricts lending among the members. When an SHG has received credit assistance that is three to four times of their savings, some banks insist on preventing the group from withdrawing their own savings until the full amount of the loan has been repaid. In Ganjam, where 308 groups have been linked to Canara Bank with credit to savings ratio of 4:1, the entire savings amount has been kept as fixed deposit with the Bank. Besides affecting the liquidity position of the group, the cost of credit to the group also goes up. For example, where the ratio of savings to credit is less, i.e., 1:1 or 1:2, and the savings is kept in fixed deposit, the rate of interest earned on fixed deposit (which is 12 per cent on a one year deposit) is same as the rate at which the credit is made available to the group. In other words, where the savings to credit ratio is 1:1, the group operates only with their savings. In case the savings is kept in a savings account instead of fixed deposit, the interest on deposit earned is only 4.5 per cent, whereas the interest paid by the group on the credit is 12 per cent. Unless the savings to credit ratio is increased to more than 1:1, it will be a loss-making proposition for the groups and also lead to less fund utilisation.

The study team found that the Dhenkanal Gramya Bank was in the habit of keeping the savings in a savings account as lien. They have been advised to take necessary corrective measures and keep SHG savings as a fixed deposit instead.

Credit Utilisation and Skill Training

SHGs are not formed just to corner more credit for the members unless the same can be repaid. It was observed that by and large, SHGs have been adept at mobilisation of savings. A loanee member must utilise the loan to make products which he or she can sell, otherwise he or she will be worse off as a result of having borrowed funds at high cost.

During the study, it was observed that group members at times did not have any specific skill to take up a productive activity. Also, most of the members being women were engaged in household work and did not have sufficient time to take up some activity independently. They may be encouraged to take up group activities during their spare time (as in case of Fellowship, Bhadrak) or take up small subsidiary activities (goat rearing, duck rearing, etc., as in Ganjam). The bank and the NGO should help members to choose the right activity besides providing skills training. In Orissa, NABARD through NFS promotional schemes, technical officers and extension agencies is providing skills training in a small way to SHG members whenever required.

At times, improper choice of activity without proper analysis of the cost and benefit may put the members further on the path of poverty. At Bhadrak, the members of the Gayatri Self-help Group were engaged in making bamboo baskets, a traditional profession. They were found to take seven to eight days for procuring, sizing, cutting, basket-making, curing and selling their products. An analysis of the cost (bamboo at the rate of Rs 70–80 per piece) and benefit (selling price of four to six baskets at Rs 90–100) by the study team found that the group members were able to earn only Rs 10–20 each for a week's labour. This was clearly inadequate and skills upgradation as also product diversification was needed.

Repayment Period

According to RBI/NABARD guidelines on SHGs, banks are required to sanction a term loan for lending to SHGs or NGOs repayable over a period of three to 10 years. Flexibility has been provided in collection of interest by the bank (at shorter intervals with quarterly or half-yearly rests) and in fixation of appropriate instalments of the capital depending on the rolling over of funds. However, the instructions are not clear as to whether NABARD will provide refinance support for three to 10 years even though the banks provide loans of short maturities (even less than 18 months at times) to the NGO/SHG. It needs to be decided whether NABARD should insist on a minimum repayment period (as applicable in the case of any term loan) for SHG finances with flexibility to banks in fixing the instalments. Accordingly, the repayment schedule can be fixed or the banks can provide term loans with shorter repayment period (one to three years). This has to be examined in the light of provisions in Sec. 29 of the NABARD Act, which mentions that all amounts received from borrowers as repayment of loans advanced by banks and refinanced by NABARD and realisation from any securities effected by the bank in respect of the said loan has to be repaid to NABARD. The Dhenkanal Gramya Bank, the Balasore Gramya Bank and the Koraput Panchabati Gramya Bank were found to have fixed repayment period at one year, as per field studies of a few SHGs.

Need for Cash Credit Limit to NGOs for On-lending to SHGs

With the amount of credit provided by banks to NGOs/SHGs being proportionate to savings and banks found to be shy of giving credit at a higher ratio in the initial phase, there is need for cash credit limits. However, it was observed that almost all banks have provided term loans for financing SHGs. This forces SHGs to operate with restricted/limited credit facility, which at times is insufficient till the first loan is repaid. Similarly, till the earlier loan is repaid in full the savings generated gets locked up for this period. This has forced some SHGs/NGOs to somehow repay the loans at a shorter period than stipulated and avail a higher credit limit against the accumulated savings. But each time the NGO/SHG approaches the bank for the loan, it has to go through the entire procedure for sanction which leads to unnecessary delay and documentation. Sanctioning short-term credit limits in proportion to the savings at the same rate of interest and similar conditions as NABARD refinance will go a long way in helping SHGs overcome this situation.

Rate of Interest: Exemption from Subsequent RBI Instruction

The rate of interest is governed by RBI directives. The rate of interest structure under SHGs is such that it provides some margin to the bank as well as to the NGO when the credit linkage is established through an NGO. However, any change in the rate of interest charged to the ultimate beneficiary or any change subsequent to the linkage disturbs the entire structure and margin available. For instance, the rate of interest being charged to the NGO by the bank, and by the NGO to the SHG were fixed at 9 per cent and 12 per cent respectively, when 175 SHGs were linked through Utkal Mahila Sanchaya Bikas with guarantee by PREM, an NGO in Ganjam and Gajapati districts. Subsequently, the rate of interest was revised to 10.5 per cent and 12 per cent respectively, adding the Deposit Insurance and Credit Guarantee Corporation premium—reducing the margin of the NGO by 1.5 per cent. As the UMSB had passed the credit amount at 9 per cent to SHGs without keeping any margin with them, it was in a difficult situation when the rates of interest were revised. A policy decision in consultation with RBI may be taken so that the rate of interest structure at the time of linkage should be immune from subsequent rate change.

Documentation

During the study, it was observed that banks have prescribed their own documentation procedure, which varies significantly from the flexibility they have been allowed. This was expected to be kept at the minimum and the banks were allowed to decide the same in consultation with their legal departments. It was, however observed that the documents collected by the banks varied from four to 11.

The loan being a group loan, some banks were found to have insisted on the signature of all the members of the group instead of their authorised representatives. At times, banks also asked for the photographs of all the SHG members. Where the credit had been given through an NGO to several SHGs, a few banks were found to have insisted that such SHGs submit loan applications along with their bye-laws through the NGO. This led to a considerable increase in the documentation expenditure and made the job of the NGO more difficult. This was found to be taking place mostly due to the over-cautious and overzealous attitude of the bankers, as they were dealing with such type of credit for the first time. Therefore while allowing flexibility to the banks, they should be guided by providing them with the model minimum documents needed for giving loans to SHGs directly or through an NGO.

It is felt that while providing credit to an SHG directly, banks should demand (i) interest agreement among members (ii) DP note and (iii) loan agreement. Similarly when credit linkages are established through an NGO, the bank should insist on, besides the memorandum and articles of associations, (i) DP note (ii) loan agreement (iii) loan application along with a statement furnishing detailed data regarding SHGs, linked to the bank. However, they need not insist on copies of the agreement between the NGO and the SHG.

Margin Available to NGOs

Initially, at the time of launching the pilot project, NGOs and banks shared a margin of 3 per cent and 2.5 per cent respectively. Subsequently, the DICGC premium of 1.5 per cent was added to the bank's margin and this reduced the margin of the NGOs to 1.5 per cent. As the loan amounts were not substantial, it was seen that this margin was not compatible to the efforts put by the NGOs. The cost of promotion, initial training, documentation, etc., being substantial, the margin to NGOs needed to be increased or else a mechanism would have to be evolved to ensure that the start-up costs for NGOs were compensated.

DICGC Premium

Financing banks have been paying premium to the DICGC at the rate of 1.5 per cent, which is recovered from the beneficiary by adding it to the rate of interest at which credit is made available. Initially, when the linkage was through an NGO, the margin available to banks was only 2.5 per cent which was insufficient as it itself paid a DICGC premium of 1.5 per cent. This was subsequently recovered from the margin available to NGOs, reducing the margin available to them from 3 per cent to a meagre 1.5 per cent.

Therefore, it needs to be considered whether the DICGC could be persuaded to charge only a nominal amount for SHG financing. Otherwise, banks should be requested not to seek a DICGC guarantee in view of the low level of risk involved when the linkage is through a reputed NGO.

Direct Financing by NABARD to NGOs for Linkage

For quite some time, the issue of direct financing by NABARD, especially in innovative areas, has been under consideration. But due to various factors, the issue has been shelved and direct financing by NABARD has remained a non-starter. Various other agencies, such as SIDBI, Rastriya Mahila Kosh and Rashtriya Gramin Vikas Nidhi (RGVN), have been providing direct assistance to NGOs for linking SHGs. The rate of interest charged by these agencies is 8.5 per cent. NABARD has decided to make available revolving fund assistance to a few reputed NGOs for on-lending to smaller NGOs. A few NGOs such as Fellowship, PREM and Ankuran expressed their dissatisfaction over the unhelpful, overcautious and bureaucratic attitude of the bankers and observed that NABARD should come forward to directly finance selected NGOs. If direct financing can be made available, it will leave sufficient margin with an NGO to undertake skills training for SHG members and facilitate marketing tie-ups.

Bulk Financing to NGOs Through Banks

In areas where formation of SHGs is difficult, bulk financing to NGOs through banks can be made available at an interest rate of 10.5 per cent per annum so that the groups may be formed and linked with bank credit. However, as bulk finance is made available through banks to NGOs, for which NABARD provides refinance support to banks, it has not yet gained popularity among NGOs in Orissa. This is because the rate of interest as well as the linkage through banks was the same as that under the original linkage programme. If NABARD directly provided bulk financing to selected NGOs at a lower rate of interest, NGOs would definitely opt for this method. Many bankers also feel that NABARD could directly finance SHGs through NGOs, without involving banks.

Threat Posed by Subsidy

It has been reported by SHGs that they are often being approached by DRDA officials and as also those implementing various government sponsored subsidy-linked schemes, to convert the SHGs into DWCRA groups or into IRDP groups (for group financing) so that the target set for financing beneficiaries could be fulfilled and subsidy provided to them. While a few SHGs, especially in areas linked in Rayagada district through Ankuran, have availed such assistance under DWCRA, a number of SHGs, as in case of Fellowship-promoted SHGs which have resisted such temptation. This subsidy and seed money assistance under DWCRA is a definite threat to the healthy growth and functioning of SHGs. It discourages the habit of saving among neighbouring SHGs. Besides, (even within the group) this is considered to be 'outside' money and adversely affects the functioning of the group as peer pressure will not be as strong as in the case of purely thrift money and bank loan. Thus, the availability of subsidies or cheap money from the government will definitely have an adverse impact on the repayment performance of SHGs.

Standardisation of Procedures

There is a feeling that too much flexibility is being accorded to NGOs/SHGs which could hamper the healthy growth and replication of SHGs elsewhere. In countries like Bangladesh, Indonesia and Malaysia where SHGs have been successful, a very rigid and inflexible system is followed and no freedom to change any parameter is given. Therefore, it is suggested that on certain matters like minimum documentation and systems of accounts maintenance at the SHG/NGO level, the system could be a rigid one, allowing flexiblity operations to individual members of the SHGs. This will help ensure that NGOs do not make mistakes or incur huge start up costs.

Subsequent Credit to SHG for Sustainable Development of Members

Contrary to target-based poverty alleviation programmes where one-time credit assistance is generally provided, it has been envisaged that an SHG should cater to the frequent credit needs of its members. During the initial linkages with bank credit, a cautious approach is followed by banks and the ratio of credit assistance to savings is low. This is often not sufficient to meet the credit needs of SHG members. However, as the savings amount of the group increases and performance improves, banks are expected to provide more credit. As most of the SHGs studied were linked only one year earlier, this aspect, which is very vital for sustainable development, could not be covered in detail. More emphasis for subsequent doses of credit to SHGs which have repaid their earlier loan amount has to be given. Guidelines should be issued to all banks, highlighting the need for subsequent doses of credit to SHG after proper monitoring by the controlling offices of the concerned banks.

Exemption from Share Capital Contribution in Case of Linkage through Cooperative Banks

As per the Cooperative Societies Act prevailing in many states, a borrower has to first become a member of a Primary Agricultural Cooperative Society (PACS) and contribute towards its share capital, which is a certain percentage of the loan he is seeking. This comes in the way of linkage of SHGs through cooperative banks, especially in areas where commercial Banks/RRBs do not have branches. A circular guideline, should therefore, be issued requesting state cooperative banks to initiate steps to amend the Cooperative Societies Act so that the SHGs may be exempted from contributing to the share capital or becoming a member of a PACS. As an alternative, the SHG as a group, should be permitted to become a nominal member of PACS, with a fixed nominal contribution to its share capital.

SHG Study—India/Kenya

At a seminar in ASCI, Hyderabad, the results of a SHG study in India (in Orissa, Karnataka, Maharashtra and Uttar Pradesh) and Kenya during 1996–97 were discussed. Prof. Malcolm Harper, who conducted the study along with a team of experts presented the findings of the study (20 October 1997). Some salient features of the study are:

Business Opportunities

SHG financing is a profitable new business for bankers and if the initiative is not taken, the market opportunity will be seized by others to their detriment. CDF, Hyderabad, has 12,000 SHGs in just two districts of Andhra Pradesh. There is no connection with banks, as initially bankers had not assisted the SHGs. With some of the SHGs having built up over a period of five years, funds amounting from Rs 10 lakh to Rs 15 lakh, banks have now evinced interest in them. However, SHGs have refused to have anything to do with banks. In Kenya too, commercial banks had initially not assisted SHGs and are now excluded from their business dealings. This could lead to a substantial loss of business, if banks do not take corrective steps now. SHGs are not part of a 'scheme' but involve real banking business and do not need charity or welfare.

Financial Intermediation

Unlike the Bangladesh Grameen Bank model, where loans are given to individuals and the group mechanism is adopted as a strategy for better recovery and where individual lending has been taken up since the 1990s, for term-loan borrowers, SHGs in India take bulk loans from banks and bring down transaction costs both for banks and borrowers, and ensure timely loans. Besides, SHGs reach a new and fast growing market, where a large number of SHGs already exist, and can work within the existing brand network, can borrow at market rates and also repay loans in time, besides doing the documentation, loan appraisal, disbursal, monitoring and recovery, without additional cost to the banks. However, SHG market-penetration which is 15 per cent in Sri Lanka, is only 1.15 per cent in Kenya and 0.04 per cent in India. A large number of SHGs already exist, but little effort has been made to link them up with institutional credit by banks.

Linking up SHGs

SHGs deal with 'hot' money (owned by its members) and also 'cold' money (if supplemented by bank funds). A SHG has to achieve some norms prior to bank linkage. These are:

- Should be in existence for a year.
- Have about 30 members.
- Regular meetings should be held and attended by all members.
- Homogeneous groups.
- A bank account should be opened.
- Loans for individual borrowers and not for group activities.

The spadework done for SHG linkage is slow and time-consuming and is estimated to cost about $200 per SHG for the bank/NGO.

Interest Rates and Collateral

Bankers insist on normal banking procedures and formalities. SHG should not be given special interest rates. NABARD gives refinance at the rate of 6.5 per cent to banks while SIDBI gives the same at 15 per cent directly to NGOs. There should be no concessional financing at all for SHGs, which can afford market rates as in Bangladesh. As far as collateral is concerned, SIDBI insists on 100 per cent security from an NGO. Many banks insist on keeping the SHGs, deposits as collateral, though this is not strictly necessary.

The study team concluded that SHG financing is restricted due to the bank(s) lack of initiative (or rural staff) and orientation to deal with SHGs as a prime business opportunity. As micro-enterprises organised by SHG members will become a major economic force in rural areas, banks need SHGs more than SHGs need banks!

PART IV

Strategies for Sustainable Rural Credit Delivery

19

Revival of the Rural Credit Delivery System in India

The rural credit delivery system now comprises banks which are performing poorly due to illiquidity, insolvency, mismanagement, violent fluctuations in interest/exchange rates and fraud. The macro-economic conditions have a major impact on bank performance and mismanagement leads to poor performance. Bank mismanagement can be characterised into four phases:

- Technical Mismanagement—non-maintenance of CRR/SLR, RBI norms of lending, etc.
- Cosmetic Mismanagement—window-dressing of deposits, laundering of illegal funds, etc.
- Desperate Management—deliberate non-transference of non-performing assets (NPAs), falsification of reports.
- Outright Fraud—bank scams, funds diversions, etc.

Even in the tightly regulated banking system, mismanagement can be caused by any or a combination of factors such as:

- Poor quality of top-level management.
- Poor supervision by the Reserve Bank.
- Poor internal accounting and records systems.
- Imprudent lending and asset acquisition.
- Violation of banking regulations.
- Inappropriate macro-economic conditions due to large-scale enterprise failures.

- Sudden financial market fluctuations due to devaluation, stock market collapse and disasters.
- Poor internal management controls, staff disputes or labour problems.
- Inexperienced staff operating in volatile, new fields.
- Errors in judgement or market strategy by top management.
- Fraudulent transactions.

The options available for overhauling the system, need to be evaluated.

Bank Restructuring

A review of the banking system and procedures, leading to a restructuring of the system, is long overdue, given the rising numbers of scam-related operations and poor viability of banks. However, this is not possible in the existing setup. A World Bank study by Andrew Sheng reveals that restructuring techniques vary according to the economic condition of the country and the resources available. Market-based solutions are the most cost-effective, with options like privatisation and liquidation being kept open.

In Malaysia and the Philippines, partial privatisation of government-owned banks could raise profitability and efficiency. The problem of bad assets haunts the banking system worldwide. Bad assets can be carved out of banks in exchange for government bonds or central bank loans or equity can be pumped in. The Government of India has apparently decided in favour of cleansing of bad assets by pumping in fresh equity for nationalised banks from budgetary resources and allowing them to access the share market, (Budgets for 1992–93 and 1993–94). The Narasimham Committee recommendation for the setting up of an Asset Reconstruction Fund (ARF) has not been well recieved. As a general rule, the central bank should not be involved in credit decision-making as this compromises supervisory authority. The Credit Authorisation Scheme (CAS) has been diluted considerably though the priority sector lending norms (40 per cent of total loans and advances) continue with the recent direct threat of RBI to impose penal action on banks for non-attainment of target; leaving the existing bank management to look after assets could lead to even greater losses. Retaining staff with suspect integrity at senior and supervisory levels can lead to continuing weaknesses in control over asset quality.

Some options available to the RBI for banking restructuring are:

- Directing that problems be remedied, with follow up inspections.
- Fine heavily the bank or persons responsible.

- Moral suasion by publicising the misdemeanor.
- Restrictions on branch expansion, loans growth or investments.
- Change in bank management.
- Increase capital base.
- Assume control of the bank in the public interest.
- Merge or consolidate institutions with stronger institutions.
- Liquidate the bank.

The two major aspects vital for achieving a turnaround in banks are solvency and management. The Indian banking system is in a state of crisis on both these fronts.

Solvency

In view of adequate back-up support from the RBI (lender of last resort), banks seldom face illiquidity problems. Though they can show signs of illiquidity problems due to ailing assets (non-performing loans being greater than the capital base), they can easily compensate for this from the market by borrowing in the inter-bank market or offering competitive terms and opening more branches. Also because of lack of transparency, they can easily hide their non-performing loans, losses or other failures by rolling over credits, lending more loans to float the balance sheet and undertaking high risk ventures. An extensive evaluation of the extent of losses, value of assets, internal controls and accounting records will show the extent of solvency. Bank managements commonly try to buy time and avoid showing losses. Also they assert that profits are just round the corner. By not making adequate provisions for bad debts, banks are only delaying recognition of losses. If not properly re-capitalised, banks will become sick. The Government of India and the Reserve Bank have attempted to tackle this problem by injecting new capital (in phases) and by imposing stringent provisioning norms, recognition of NPAs and imposing capital adequacy norms from 1992–93 onwards. However the slow bleeding of banks' assets can be stopped effectively only if errant bank managements are also revamped.

Management

The key to a purposeful bank turnaround is effective and responsive management. In view of vested interests and corruption in high places, it has become very difficult to assess the integrity and competency of bank managements, especially at the senior executive level. New brooms sweep cleaner because they can be more objective in assessing the extent of damage caused and, therefore, the need to:

• Recognise the extent of losses.
• Secure new lines of bank credit due to improved confidence.
• Stem old losses.
• Reduce overheads and staff, with retrenchment if necessary.
• Put in improved controls, accounting systems.
• Improve Management Information System (MIS).
• Introduce aggressive management and new profit opportunities.

Thus, strategic management in the Indian banking system is an imperative need, if it is to regain credibilty, operational efficiency, organisational effectiveness and profitability. The present disarray of the system should be perceived as a challenge to restructuring and strategic management.

Revamping the Indian Banking System

With the Government of India and the RBI having taken up the task of bank restructuring in phases, there is a need to inculcate strategic management techniques in banks so that the entire process becomes effective. Without these start-up measures, restructuring would be an ineffective and a futile exercise. There is an urgent need to start the strategic management process in banks. This will help consolidate the bank restructuring process, which is essentially a 'top-down' approach and an imposed system. The strategic management techniques can form a 'bottom-up' approach, which is participatory in nature, so as to improve the organisation culture and make banking institutions profit-oriented and cost-effective. Thus, a two-phase approach, outlined below, can hold the key to revamping the Indian banking system.

Elements of Strategic Management

The crucial elements of strategic management relevant to the Indian banking system in today's context are:

• General Management Perspective
• Personnel Management
• Financial Management

- Marketing Management
- Management Information System

Important elements from these five areas of management techniques have to be woven into an integrated management change system so that strategic management can become a way of life for the banking system. The techniques of strategic management, as defined by the top management, have to be swiftly inculcated at all levels and have to be made essential ingredients of daily work norms for all. These should not be confined only to the top levels.

1. GENERAL MANAGEMENT PERSPECTIVE

I) ORGANISATIONAL STRUCTURE

Banks are highly overstaffed, especially in urban and metropolitan centres and though the volume of business has been growing, little has been done to improve staff productivity or change operating systems. The easy way out that is to increase staff has been sought. This has further hampered productivity, increased industrial relations problems and eroded profitability. It has been estimated, on a conservative basis, that in urban and metropolitan centres, 25–30 per cent of the staff is more than the actual requirement while in semi-urban and rural branches, the figure comes to 10–15 per cent. This is because the pyramidical organisation structure is being followed, leading to the creation of useless layers of staff at the middle management level. These layers (seven of officers and two at subordinate levels, including supporting staff) hamper quick decision-making. This structure is an anachronism and has to be replaced by flatter organisations so as to minimise managerial costs.

RECOMMENDATIONS

Before 1858, under the East India Company, colonial India was a typical example of a 'flat' organisation and hundreds of district collectors reported to just nine provincial political secretaries, who in turn reported to the Governor-General. It was, indeed, effective. There have been several management theorists who have promoted the flat organisation structure. These include:

- **Frederick W. Taylor** (classical school)—believed in existence of the one best way to perform a task by the one best person in the organisation.

- **Mary Parker Follett** (behavioural school)—theories of authority sharing with subordinates (as well as groups and individuals).
- **Peter Drucker** (the management theorist)—predicted in the 1950s the demise of the pyramidical corporation structure, to be replaced by flat structural forms.
- **Michael Hammer** (re-engineering specialist)—organising work around outcomes other than tasks, requiring flat organisations eliminating narrowly defined jobs.
- **David Nadler**—advocated autonomous work teams to form corporate structures and spelt out objectives of all flattening exercises.
- **Edward Lawler**—theorised that empowerment is difficult when management does not surrender authority so roles could be changed to create small work groups and flatter organisations.

A 'flatter' organisation has both plus and minus points as under:

Plus Points	*Minus Points*
i. increased growth opportunities for performers	i. reduced promotion options for employees
ii. faster decision-making and market response	ii. increased workload as layers trimmed
iii. upgradation of skills within banks	iii. increased training and developmental needs
iv. better internal communication and interaction	iv. low staff morale during transition phase
v. decline in overall management costs	v. rigours of labour unrest
vi. better customer service	

The Indian banking system will benefit from a 'flatter' organisation as it will lead to staff participation, speed in responding to customers and competition, lower costs, quicker decision-making, productivity, result-oriented performance, removal of middle management tiers and more flexibility.

II) ORGANISATIONAL CULTURE

There are two distinct phases in the organisational culture of the Indian banking system (pre- and post-1969). Before nationalisation (1969 and 1980), banks were privately owned; some by large business houses like the Hindustan Commercial Bank (JK Singhania Group), United Commercial Bank (Birla Group), Dena Bank (Devkaran Nanjee Group), and Syndicate Bank (Pai Group).

These banks were run on commercial lines and followed prudential banking norms and were very conservative in their approach. Thus, they showed healthy profits. However, after nationalisation, the bureaucratisation of commercial banks began. Two resulting trends, in particular, caused tremendous harm to the banking system.

- Opening of large number of branches without considering viability aspects.
- Appointment of chief executives of banks by the Government of India.

The result was that a large number of untrained staff was let loose and quicker promotions followed, while the controls exercised from the top got diluted due to non-banking practices, non-exercising of powers, interference by vested interests, etc.

The high standards of rectitude followed by earlier bankers were diluted and a 'laissez-faire' culture imposed, leading to corrupt practices. The various target-oriented government programmes added yet another dimension to this. Much of the present ills of the banking system are due to rampant corruption and mismanagement. Poor recoveries are partly to be blamed on the 'sticky' fingers of the bank officials. Also, a plethora of forms, including those prescribed by the RBI and NABARD, especially in understaffed rural branches, are difficult to fill. There is a suspicion that figures relating to achievements under priority sector lending and government programmes are being 'overstated'. In some branches, house-keeping and internal controls are poor. With the introduction of the ARDR Scheme 1990, many field officials have stopped going out for recoveries in view of the adverse recovery climate. Of late, it has been observed that certain rural branches located in remote areas are not being opened for days. Also many bank officials prefer not to stay in the vicinity of rural branches where they are posted for two to three years, in view of inadequate facilities like houses, schools, colleges, hotels, etc., and prefer to commute from distant towns. Given their urban orientation and rural bias their involvement in the rural branches is minimal. As mostly junior-level staff are posted in rural branches, they have little personal commitment and, consequently, staff morale is poor. Also, for rural postings, there is no incentive for the staff instead, their allowances are reduced. Some officials have to maintain double establishments when they are unable to shift their families and their costs increase. The organisational culture is, therefore, very poor and the bank scam in 1992 has further demoralised the staff. With militant bank unions and poor quality of officials, customer service levels have deteriorated with declining productivity levels.

RECOMMENDATIONS

A sensitive and committed management can work wonders in toning up organisational culture. The management has to be perceived as legitimate, strong, responsive, caring and above all, fair. Further, rural branches should be opened in areas with good potential and on viability considerations alone, not on the basis of vested interests. State governments must also ensure reasonably good infrastructure. Opening branches, which will not be able to break even in the near future (i.e., after five years), does not make for sound banking. The recent RBI decision to relocate branches in rural areas and rationalising in branch licensing policies are welcome. There has to be a concrete move to rebuild the pre-1969 organisational culture in nationalised banks.

III) POOR CUSTOMER SERVICE

Customer services have been badly affected by the poor organisational culture, poor motivation and low staff morale coupled with increased volume of work in metropolitan and urban areas. Without an exit policy and strong trade unions, little disciplinary action can be taken against wrong-doers and non-performers. Also, promotions are largely 'seniority-based' and hence, outstanding performers cannot be rewarded. Customer services as also house-keeping operations have deteriorated and, as a result, frauds have increased. Customer-orientation has vanished and a branch-level banker generally carries out routine banking transactions, not perceiving himself to be a 'businessman' who has to develop good business for his branch especially as far as good loan proposals are concerned. At the most, their targets are deposit-oriented. The idea of a profit centre and proper use of scarce credit resources has yet to have a significant impact.

Further, applications are expected to be routed through the government agencies (DRDA, District Industries Centre [DIC], etc.,), especially in rural areas, and the realisation that a banker too has to move and secure good business proposals is yet to take root. Recoveries are also poor in such sponsored applications (IRDP—25 per cent to 30 per cent) and the vicious cycle of poor quality lending followed by poor monitoring and consequently, poor recoveries leading to further resistance in lending while maintaining targeted lending norms, has led to a steep fall in customer service standards.

RECOMMENDATIONS

The Reserve Bank had constituted a Committee for improving customer service and some of its recommendations have been accepted but implementation has been tardy. With the entire banking system in a state of flux as regards the shape of financial sector reforms (including the restructuring of the banking industry), the closure of bank branches, merger of weak banks with stronger banks etc. appears to be on the cards. Drastic restructuring is needed with computerisation/automation a must for good customer service, even at the cost of industrial relation problems arising from the retrenchment of surplus staff (also due to the the closure of unviable branches). If banks are to show profits, the management must be given a free hand in all aspects. The stranglehold of officials attached to the banking division in the Ministry of Finance needs to be broken, especially as they do not take any responsibility for the poor operational results of banks. Responsibility and authority needs to be given back to bank managements for better customer service and operational results.

IV) COMPUTERISATION/AUTOMATION OF BANKS

All over the world, banks have computerised their operations so as to provide efficient customer service. This also ensures good house-keeping for banks, as ledger postings, balancing, MIS are all taken care of. But, bank employees unions in the country have not allowed this to take place. In fact, despite the Rangarajan Committee recommendations, the Indian Banks Association (IBA) has been able to place automated ledger posting machines (ALPMs) only in some banks while only a few branches have been computerised and have back-up records for personnel, salaries, etc. Computerisation/automation for customer needs, understandably does not figure in the vocabulary of trade union leaders who have effectively set back the industry by almost 20 years. Indian banking is outdated and cannot be efficient unless large-scale computerisation as part of customer service orientation is carried out.

RECOMMENDATION

The restructuring exercise must include large-scale computerisation of routine operations and data handling. Simultaneously, decisions should be limited to bankers only. A sound, reliable communication system as also high-speed computers are essential in modern banking along with satellite hook-ups.

V) SYSTEMS AND PROCEDURES

Credit delivery systems need to be toned up if banks are to survive in the new deregulated environment.

New norms of asset classification, income recognition and provisioning for doubtful advances have forced banks to shift their emphasis from deposit mobilisation to profitability. Consequently, the emphasis is now on quality lending. Where previously there used to be a shortage of funds for lending, now it is the shortage of capital, owing to the new norms, which are inhibiting lending.

The main requirement of borrowers is speedy decisions which they feel are more important than lower interest rates. Foot-dragging in decision-making in banks affects borrowers to a greater extent than the interest rates, and this is one reason why hire-purchase, leasing and finance companies are doing so well even though they charge higher interest. Credit if not released in time serves little purpose and is thus often the cause of projects getting delayed, with related problems like cost overruns.

There is often heavy workload at the branch level, where the staff has to cope with a wide variety of work of which advances is only one segment. The branch manager, therefore, is a major factor in taking a decision if a proposal falls within his jurisdiction or in following it up with his higher authorities. This apart, he is tied down with equally important work such as deposit mobilisation, industrial relations, customer service and house-keeping.

One of the main reasons for delay in decision-making is lack of expertise. At the branch level, more often than not, generalists, and not specialists, are in charge and this leads to the delay. Acknowledging this shortcoming, more and more banks have started to open specialised business branches concentrating exclusively on industrial, finance and overseas business, respectively. However, such branches are currently located only in urban areas; more particularly, in metropolitan centres.

Besides, operatives at most decision-making levels are now wary of taking speedy decisions for fear of being put in the dock if it proves to be wrong at a later stage. This trend has become highly pronounced in the post-securities scam phase. The decision-makers, therefore, need to be convinced that investigations are conducted essentially to establish that systems have been strictly followed and not to victimise them. In other words, punishment will be meted out only if there is proof of malafide intention or gross negligence.

The other major reason for slow decision-making is a flawed system. In most banks, there is insufficient delegation of powers. Thus, most decisions have to be referred to higher levels resulting in delays. Further, at each successive level of decision-making different people look at the proposal and each one has his/her own queries which are sent back to the branch for further clarification.

RECOMMENDATIONS

One possible answer to this could be a group approach where all officers concerned with a proposal sit together and thrash out its pros and cons. A single questionnaire could then be prepared incorporating all possible requests for clarification. The State Bank of India is currently following this system. It also uses a chart, specifying the time frame within which all proposals have to be dealt with, incorporating a schedule for each stage of processing. The Reserve Bank of India has also acknowledged the importance of the time factor and it has set a time frame within which all proposals have to be cleared.

Ultimately, however, the solution depends on the attitude of the staff. It is largely due to the top management's lack of confidence in their subordinates that powers are not delegated. The introduction and implementation of the new systems will serve little purpose unless the staff is properly trained and equipped to discharge their duties properly.

VI) INTERNAL CONTROLS

Lax internal controls, such as managerial incompetency, militant staff, poor monitoring systems, non-submission of returns, falsification of returns etc., set the stage for possible frauds. Banking as a system rests on trust. Every bank has its internal controls systems, perfected over the years and which have been incorporated in routine, daily operations. Unfortunately, however, it is because of the routine nature of these controls that the top/ middle management levels appear to have forgotten the rationale for their imposition. As a result, existing control systems have been diluted. Also, with the changing complexities and new instruments, opportunities, and operational procedures, the majority of the staff is unable to cope up with the changes and indeed, change. This is especially true for the 'above 40' executives who resist change and who are in the middle managerial and executive cadres.

Modern banking requires swift and agile minds, capable of operating computerised equipment and taking on-the-spot decisions, especially in equity share market operations, currency deals and merchant banking. With a seniority-based promotion system and the need to have good industrial relations, promotions are often given to persons who are out of their depth and are either unwilling or unable to adapt to their new role. And, with no exit policy in sight, the possibility of a large number of lightweights floating to the top management levels, cannot be ruled out. With a large number of non-contributing executives, incapable of taking reasonable decisions, the banking system will not be able to withstand the process of change.

As a result, incompetence at various levels leads to weaker internal controls and leaves the gate open for clever manipulation (within the bank and within the banking system). Even minimum safety precautions are ignored and there are loopholes exploited by unscrupulous elements when they sense an opportunity. The number of frauds is increasing and many are perpetrated by bank staffers in connivance with cheats.

RECOMMENDATIONS

The internal control system of each bank has evolved out of various needs and has to be reviewed for efficacy. The bank scam—a result of system failures and the venality of a handful of corrupt bank officials—could have been prevented if the internal control system had been operating effectively. That over Rs 10,000 crores could be withdrawn from the banking system within one to two years, without the bank managements being aware, shows that a thorough revamp of internal controls is overdue. Also, bank staff should understand the implications of routine operational procedures, which are a part of the internal control system, so that they do not dilute these requirements.

VII) BANK FRAUDS

Defrauding nationalised banks has become a fine art in India with 27,317 cases involving Rs 707.14 crore being registered between 1976 and 1993 (see Table 19.1), as per PAC Report in Parliament quoted in newspapers—August 1997. Bankers are on the horns of a dilemma, coping with the growing ingenuity of fraudsters and the need to improve the quality of service dished out by public sector banks. The 34th report of the Estimates Committee submitted to the Lok Sabha in 1994 arrived at the conclusion that 'neglect of well-established procedures is the basic cause of most of the frauds'.

Table 19.1
Position of Frauds in Commercial Banks

Particulars	1991	1992	1993
i) No. of Frauds	996	1,063	340
ii) Amt. Involved (Rs. lakh)	4,960.14	13,425.38	1,129.00

The top brass of the banks can not remain aloof from charges of collusion. This was borne out by the fact that the RBI received 47 complaints up to 1990 against top executives, of which 38 were serious enough to warrant investigations while the rest were not substantiated.

Concerned over the increasing amounts lost, the Committee expressed its 'unhappiness over the complacent attitude of the managements of the banks and the government in the matter of frauds. . . The Committee has every reason to believe that in case of frauds which result in substantial financial loss to the government, top persons are allowed to go scot-free because of their clout rather than being subjected to exemplary punishment'.

Internal audits, an instrument of preventing frauds, has been seen in poor light by the Committee. It cited the case of the State Bank of Hyderabad where a fraud of Rs 1.48 crore was not detected even though the branch had been audited six times by the bank's internal auditors, once by a firm of chartered accountants and for the eighth time by officials of the State Bank of India.

The Committee questioned Central Bureau of Investigation representatives, who admitted that there were inevitable delays and that 70 and 80 months elapsed before a major fraud could be investigated. (A CBI probe is on into the massive Rs 2,000 crore a year racket involving the fraudulent encashment of crossed cheques and other instruments in Mumbai.)

According to RBI, frauds are generally committed in the areas of misappropriation of cash/remittances, fraudulent encashment of negotiable instruments, withdrawal through forgery, misutilisation of discretionary limits, non-observance of prescribed norms in granting credit facilities, opening/issue of letters of credit, bank guarantees and foreign exchange dealings.

The number of frauds registered a small decline in 1991 compared to 1990 but again rose in 1992. The recommendations of another committee appointed under the chairmanship of former RBI Deputy Governor A. Ghosh, were adopted in August 1992 and the banks were asked to implement most of its recommendations immediately. Some recommendations requiring government approval have also been accepted.

The RBI issued several circulars with guidelines on strengthening the control mechanism, conducted surprise inspections, impressed upon the banks the need for proper training of operational personnel, set up a special investigation cell and served caution notices to top bank executives regarding irregularities in borrowal accounts. It also reviewed the implementation of the guidelines.

Frauds are perpetrated by outsiders, banks' own staff and often by collusion between the two. Bankers, handicapped by an antiquated system of functioning, are called upon to wage a battle with increasingly innovative modus operandi and walk a tightrope balancing the demand for better services and the need to prevent embezzlement. Clearly, banks need to get their act together if they are to cut losses and survive the fierce competition when private banks begin expanding their operations.

RECOMMENDATIONS

A combination of factors like the lack of mechanisation and computerisation, bypassing of established procedures, inadequate staffing and low levels of morale is responsible for increasing bank frauds. Computerisation will definitely bring in swifter reconciliation of inter-branch accounts and make information available faster to cross-check facts before a decision is made. The banking system is in the process of computerising its operations and will have to build into the new working environment sufficient checks and balances. However, computerisation by itself is not a panacea for frauds. The tactics used to defraud the banks will also be upgraded by the unscrupulous. One of the ways to protect the new system would be to restrict access and check operations daily. An awareness of procedures laid down in the earlier days needs to be spread in order to ensure that the checks and balances are applied. After nationalisation, banks spread their network in leaps and bounds and the first casualty of this was measures to prevent frauds.

Bankers felt that the threat of a CBI inquiry hanging over the heads of the staff kills the enthusiasm of even the honest staff. To counter this, they prefer a mechanism, minus the CBI, to probe and hand out punishments, if necessary. Some of them hold the view that banks are in a business with high risks and the best they can do is to minimise the damage as these cannot be eliminated altogether.

2. PERSONNEL MANAGEMENT

I) RECRUITMENT AND STAFF SELECTION

Every organisation needs good quality staff, but the banking industry's requirements are more complex. Banking requires people with a minimum education (10+2 level), who then have to be suitably trained. Instead, the banking system currently has highly educated staff (due to the lack of employment opportunities elsewhere) who, however, have not been well trained. Banking is, by and large, a routine and boring profession at the lower levels and, therefore, for post graduates and others, it can be very frustrating. Thus, the job contents and the employees' expectations do not neatly match. The British banking system takes new recruits after school ('A' levels) and then exposes them to various aspects of banking (on the job training). Those who shape up well in this are exposed to further training and promoted to higher management levels. Thus, rigorous training is given for those who have an aptitude for the job.

The Indian banking system today, however, has a highly bureaucratised approach to selection. Banks do not have the powers to select their own staff, except at the messenger level (through employment exchanges where corruption is rampant). For officers and clerical staff, recruitment earlier had to be made through the Banking Service Recruitment Boards, which clubbed recruitment for various banks, and then made allocations as per choice/availability of vacancies. This system underscored that all banks had the same staff requirement. The needs of an individual bank were ignored. However, this system of common recruitment was scrapped in 1994. Depending upon their specific requirements, banks can now hire specific talents required for modern banking. With increasing globalisation, private sector banks as also foreign banks are being allowed in large numbers. There is an exodus of talented staff from nationalised banks to these banks, which offer better working environment, better challenges, less transfers, lucrative salaries, with computerised operational systems and less staff (without militant trade unions and incompetent staff). Also, there is no imposition of non-banking norms—interference with work due to other considerations (Rajbhasha, SC/ST quotas, etc). The consequent exodus from nationalised banks will have to be filled by trained staff from within, as recruitment to higher levels is a difficult proposition yet.

RECOMMENDATIONS

Banking has to be made more professional and de-bureaucratised, as it is a highly specialised field. Unlike the generalist, who can be fitted in anywhere, specialist requirements are different, as a good professional can mean a lot to profitability. Professionalisation of Indian banking personnel is long overdue, as is an immediate review of each bank's needs. Staff who are not trainable or who cannot adjust to new operational systems have to be eased out.

II) INCENTIVES AND PUNISHMENTS

A well-defined system of incentives and rewards is one of the most effective tools available to a management in motivating staff. There is no such system in most public sector undertakings and, in particular, in nationalised banks.

The most important asset in any organisation is its human resources. There has not been any serious attempt in the banking industry to nurture and develop this invaluable asset. Motivation is a key problem in the industry and some of the problems that the industry is suffering from can be traced to the low level of motivation of the staff.

The system does not give any rewards for outstanding performance nor does it provide incentives to enthuse staff to put in extra effort. Rewards or incentives can be of two types—cash or kind. Cash rewards can mean extra payment through vouchers or extra increments. The other type of reward could be through a promotion or some other recognition, such as an award or a prize.

In the banking industry, both these systems are limited in nature. Awarding of increments is generally not linked to performance and is a routine affair. There is also not much scope for extra payments. Given the government restrictions on payment of overtime, it is quite difficult for managements to offer monetary inducements to staff for extra work.

The promotion system is also a cause for much heartburn among bank employees. In theory, it is fairly broad-based and comprehensive, and takes into account a wide range of factors. Practically, however, seniority plays a major role in determining the success of the candidate and promotions tend to be time-bound. This weightage for seniority is there in the promotion of both clerks and officers. Promotion up to the executive cadre requires a period of minimum service at each level. It is only from the executive cadre level onwards that minimum service requirements are dispensed with and performance becomes the main criteria for promotion.

The situation in the banking industry is, thus, not a very congenial one for young, dynamic employees. The realisation that there is no reward or incentive for good performance can frustrate even highly capable individuals.

The flaws in the promotion system, with its emphasis on seniority, also mean that there is usually not much hope for entrants at the lower level to go beyond a certain level in the organisation. This can deter even the best of individuals from consistently giving their best.

The fallout of such a promotion system is two-fold. On the one hand, it deters juniors from exerting themselves beyond the needs of duty. On the other, it also means that those who have been lucky enough to get promoted are generally those who have had to endure their share of frustrations in the process. It is, therefore, understandable if their output is less than optimum. Seniority rears its head in many banks in other areas also; posts such as those of a computer operator or head cashier, where extra allowances are paid, have become the preserve of the seniors.

At the branch level, too, it often becomes very difficult for managers to motivate their staff. The problem is particularly acute in smaller branches and in those located in rural and semi-urban areas. Typically, such branches tend to be short of the requisite staff and also do not satisfy the criteria for mechanisation. As a result, staff there tend to be overworked. Without a proper system of incentives and rewards, motivating staff is a highly demanding task and much depends on the personal relations among staff members.

Not only is there no reward for performance, there is also no punishment for failure or non-performance. Again, in theory, there is a system to take care of this aspect. In practice, however, the realities of the system, at least in most cases, precludes punishment. Quite often, branch managers are unable to enforce discipline even in basic matters such as punctuality and courtesy to customers.

RECOMMENDATIONS

It is time for banks to think in terms of rewarding their employees in profitable branches. At a time when profitability has become the major concern of bank managements, staff or profit-making branches should receive lasting benefits—branches may be awarded extra points for the purpose of promotion or staff may be given extra increments as the performance of the branch is essentially the result of their efforts.

At a time when there is a lot of talk about financial sector reforms, it is to be noted that no serious attempt has yet been made to tackle human resources development. Reforms have so far concentrated on purely external factors. However, success of the reforms programme will ultimately depend on the attitude of the staff, their willingness and ability to adapt to the changing situation.

III) TRAINING AND EFFECTIVENESS

Every professional banker will swear by training, for it sharpens existing skills, imparts knowledge, changes attitudes and enables personal and organisational effectiveness. Banks have overhauled their training systems by holding one or two day workshops/seminars for senior executives and one to two week courses for middle/lower management levels. But, the rapidly changing economic environment has led to a host of banking opportunities and new avenues for bankers. Among the new possibilities are real estate, merchant banking, shares trading, financial restructuring, mergers and acquisitions, insurance, etc. But each of these are highly skilled tasks and hence, effectiveness of training will be sorely tested. There is bound to be resistance to change, especially from the above 40 age group, but this is where it has to rise to the challenge and deliver results in a very short time. Training has to be continuously augmented and upgraded.

RECOMMENDATIONS

Multiple skills development is very important in a service industry like banking and the successful induction of new technologies/systems is essential. Bankers have to change policies and procedures to keep abreast of changes in the economic scenario due to liberalisation. Training has to meet the challenges of foreign/private banks. Investing in HRD, and especially in training, is an investment in knowledge capital. And, capital resources are subject to both amortisation and obsolescence. Training needs to be continuously updated and expanded taking into account the following aspects:

- Qualitative Improvement in Training
- Multi-level Staff Training
- Training Needs Survey
- Management of Training Institutions

- Co-ordination among Training Institutions
- Post Training Evaluation
- Co-ordination with Placement

Investing in good human resources management and training will fetch good returns in the future.

IV) INDUSTRIAL RELATIONS

This is one of the weakest spots of the Indian banking system. The rise of multiple trade unions (affiliated to political parties) has coincided with management weaknesses. The long-term effects on the banking industry of short-sighted managements are being felt in ample measure.

Poor work culture, non-acceptance of responsibilities, rising incidence of frauds in collusion with bank staff, opposition to imposing discipline, non-accountability, poor work ethics, absence of disciplinary systems leading to delay/dilution in punishments and the non-availability of an exit policy—all have played havoc with industrial relations in banks. And, militant trade unions have played no mean part in forcing the banking system on its knees. There is very little discipline and even though bank employees are some of the highest paid in the country, their productivity is low due to over-staffing and is declining due to weak management. Their exorbitant wage demands and frequent strikes have been bleeding the industry dry for years as they are linked to productivity.

The takeover of banks by the government, in retrospect, has been an unmitigated disaster, especially in the field of industrial relations. The rise of bureaucratic functioning in banks has also been instrumental in creating an adverse industrial relations climate. Over-staffing with little automation/computerisation has resulted in inefficient functioning as ALPMs, note-counting machines, personal computers, mainframe computers, which could help in streamlining banking operations, have been resisted strongly by the trade unions.

RECOMMENDATIONS

The privatisation of banks (20 commercial banks and 196 RRBs), the debureaucratisation of cooperative banks and the functioning of the banking system purely on commercial terms needs to be implemented. The depoliticisation of trade unions is also desirable—this should promote healthier trade unionism. Financial sector reforms need to be pursued vigorously to its logical conclusion by:

- Closing down unviable branches.
- Restricting the banking system by systematic mergers and closing down of unviable banks.
- Retrenchment of undeployable staff.
- Massive re-training for efficient customer service and commercial re-orientation.
- Non-interference by the government in day-to-day operations.

V) CONSOLIDATION OF THE BANKING SYSTEM

As per conservative estimates, over 10,000 branches of commercial banks and over 1,200 branches of RRBs have been incurring losses for over five years. This is an unacceptable fact and the RBI branch licensing policy for the 1970s and 1980s, has been responsible for this. The Lead Bank scheme, Service Area Approach, priority sector lending norms, targeted lending, credit to the weaker/neglected sectors all have led to an increase in the number of bank branches. Population per branch has been brought down to about 12,000 (in 1991). But the cost to the banking sector of this largely unplanned growth has been phenomenal in terms of unviable branches set up in non-potential areas on non-commercial considerations. The uneven quality of staff in such branches, quick promotions and non-implementation of internal controls have contributed to the ills of the banking system.

RECOMMENDATIONS

Based only on commercial considerations and viability/profitability norms, banks should review the operations of their branches on a branch-by-branch basis. Branches which have been making losses for over five years should be closed. The RBI has already issued instructions to this effect (except for rural areas), but implementation has to be impartially carried out. This may lead to staff re-deployment and also retrenchment (with a voluntary retirement scheme) of those who are not needed. This requires hard decisions.

3. FINANCIAL MANAGEMENT

I) RISKS DUE TO FINANCIAL INTERMEDIATION

Financial intermediation helps in the process of savings and investment in the economy, as financial institutions reduce the risk of capital loss savers, their transaction costs and provide the investor/entrepreneur/consumer with funding in quantities and repayment schedules convenient to them. Financial institutions also help mobilise savings by issuing liabilities (financial instruments), tailored to the savings and transactions needs of the saver. They use these funds to provide loans or financial assets tailored to the needs of the borrowers (consumers or investors). By reducing the savings loss risk and timings of payment (liquidity) risk of the savers, the financial intermediaries are exposed to the following risks on both sides of their balance sheets:

Asset Management	*Liquidity Management*
Credit risk	Maturity mismatch
Country risk	Funding risks
Foreign exchange risk	Solvency/Capital adequacy
Counter-party failure risk	
Transfer risk	

Banks absorb all these risks and attempt to make a profit through a spread—the difference between their lending rate and their cost of funds and overheads. However, due to the administered interest rate structure, the spread is very very thin compared to the risks involved and it is often negative (even for RRBs). A bank is lucky if it makes 2 per cent per annum on gross assets over the long-term. This can be offset by poor recoveries (overdues exceed 56 per cent). Banks try to cushion losses from abnormal risks through their capital base. As banks are highly geared, even the margin of capital (2–3 per cent of total assets) may not be sufficient to withstand a large shock (e.g., ARDR Scheme, 1990).

RECOMMENDATIONS

The RBI exercises tight control over the banking system and a large number of returns are prescribed for monitoring the banks' performance and their compliance with statutory rules and regulations. The lack of transparency in accounts was done away with in 1992, with the revised balance sheets reporting system. Further, banks are now prohibited from entering certain types of business (non-banking business), where they may be in direct competition with their customers or where they would be having a distinct financial muscle. Controls over appointment of the board of directors (non-politicians and professionals encouraged), the branch licensing policy, limited foreign exchange restrictions, all these can check the excesses in the banking system, provided, however, the RBI does not dilute them (as in the bank scam). Risk control limits (credit risks, single customer, credit limits, prohibition of connected lending, selective credit controls, CAS, foreign exchange risk, interest rate/maturity risks) are exercised judiciously by the RBI. The problem arises when political pressures compel the RBI to dilute the norms. The RBI should be autonomous and not function under the control of the Ministry of Finance as per Narasimham Committee recommendations.

The liquidity requirements (CRR 12 per cent and SLR 34.75 per cent of total demand and time liabilities) are very stringent and need to be lowered as per the Narasimham Committee recommendations. However, banks have experienced problems of surplus liquidity with a slight lowering of the SLR and need to develop new lending instruments/business. The RBI has adopted the Cook proposals (Basle Committee on Bank Supervision), which allocate risk weights to different categories of assets and require that a bank should have a minimum standard of 8 per cent capital base by 1995. This approach also takes into consideration off balance sheet risks. The capital adequacy requirements will strengthen the Indian banking system and the government has provided Rs 5,700 crore in 1993–94 and Rs 5,600 crore in 1994–95 from the annual budgets, for shoring up bank capital resources. However, restructuring of the commercial and cooperative banking system has not been taken up yet. The most difficult part of assessing capital adequacy and solvency is the assessment of assets and loss provisions, particularly bad debts. The RBI has to be complimented on the very stringent capital provisioning norms for NPAs. The problem areas are accounting treatment of interest in suspense and loan provisioning procedures (including security evaluation) as these are based on subjective criteria. Banks also resort to ever-greening of bad loans to hide NPAs.

II) FINANCIAL DEEPENING AND INSTABILITY

An improved financial system fosters efficient mobilisation of domestic savings and allocates resources for optimum usage—due to the removal of barriers for compartmentalisation and segmentation of financial markets—and promotes financial deepening by creating more financial instruments, institutions and markets, as seen since 1991. However, financial deepening depends on positive real interest rates and carries the risks of greater instability. The theory of financial deepening is that while it pays to diversify into different types of assets, it is not true for liabilities. Diversification into assets, with little correlation to each other reduces risks.

However, diversification into a wide array of liabilities increases the risks. (Brignoli and Seigel, 1987). The spreading of assets reduces risks unless the liabilities are internally-generated funds or capital. Financial collapse is possible unless there is strict supervision by the RBI. The reasons for a strong RBI regulation are:

- Monetary Policy—the power to create money
- Credit allocation—channel of credit/investments
- Competition and innovation—to prevent cartels
- Prudential regulation—depository of private savings
                       —operators of payments mechanism
                       —vulnerability to collapse

RECOMMENDATIONS

The Reserve Bank has to be strong and effective. Today, over 50 per cent of its 33,500 staff is utilised just for currency management operations. Only 19.7 per cent of the staff is officers while messengers constitute 25.6 per cent and the remaining 54.7 per cent are clerical staff/typists/stenos/supporting staff. The RBI has to be an officer-oriented institution, with complete autonomy in its operations. To be effective, the RBI requires:

a) Autonomy: RBI must be protected from political/government interferences by an institutional arrangement.

b) Supervision: RBI must create an intelligence gathering wing to track the financial sector and co-ordinate with SEBI. Cost of supervision must be reduced by adopting on-line banking processing system by experienced officials.

c) Information: RBI must increasingly automate its systems so that decision-making is speeded up.

d) Monetary Control: RBI must use open market operations and interest rate policies to control government borrowings in view of the huge fiscal deficits and restrict debt for consumption.

e) Foreign Exchange Management: RBI's role in managing reserves and exchange rates will be important when full convertibility comes, if the Rupee is to remain stable.

f) Debt Management: RBI has a role in controlling government debt and keeping it easily marketable, by developing brokers and dealers in government paper on a professional basis.

Finally, adoption of the Nayak Committee Report on Currency Management, the Padmanabhan Committee Report on Bank Inspection Procedures, the Marathe Committee Report on Human Resources and the A.F. Ferguson & Co. Report on Restructuring of the RBI must be done without delay. The Reserve Bank must preserve continuity in the stock of money and in the flow of credit. The Reserve Bank has to exercise control as banks are particularly vulnerable to collapse due to:

- High gearing/leverage
- Mismatch of maturities between assets and liabilities
- Lack of transparency
- Settlement risk
- Contagion and systemic failure

III) OTHER FINANCIAL ISSUES

The profit centre concept has been accepted for commercial banks and RRBs but is yet to be followed for cooperative banks. The concept of strategic management as a key to profitable/viable operations has to be internalised. Cost reduction a* part of a strategy to ensure profits is not very easy in the context of 'no exit' policy or restructuring, but the need to expand into other profitable avenues of business like leasing/insurance exists. Banks have to diversify their business operations, spread risks and enhance profitability. However, with foreign banks and private banks moving in on profitable business, public sector banks have to be more creative and aggressive in their operations. The excessive liquidity of banks and the sharp drop in non-food credit (1993–94) is alarming. The emergence of new and innovative instruments like commercial paper afford credit at very favourable terms (12.5 per cent per annum). It is estimated that nearly Rs 4,500 crore has been raised through commercial paper. Current asset classification along with stringent credit rating norms would make it difficult for many companies to raise funds from banks. Companies prefer to raise funds by public deposits (14–15 per cent + 2 per cent service charges) at attractive rates and that too after offering attractive incentives. This has put pressure on deposit mobilisation efforts of banks.

The Government of India, Economic Survey (1993–94) stressed the need to revamp the rural credit delivery system. The system has suffered from the ARDR scheme (1990) and has led to a tendency to default wilfully and also deny credit to the genuine farmer. The rural credit delivery system suffers from poor recovery of loans, high cost of intermediation and the legacy of write-offs contributing to the culture of non-recovery. Added to this is the burden of subsidised interest rates inadequate to cover even transaction costs, let alone generating reasonable surpluses for declaring dividends and building up reserves to deal with the accumulated losses of banks threatened with the possibilities of becoming non-viable and functionally ineffective.

Banks have made provisions for bad debts totalling Rs 6,437 crore (March 1993) and the finance ministry has calculated that the NPAs of nationalised banks (for advances over Rs 25,000) range from 8–10 per cent of their total advances for the better banks and up to 34–45 per cent for the worst ones. The average NPAs for all public sector banks stands at a high of 21 per cent. In absolute terms, it totals Rs 43,000 crore. The repayment ethics that have to be inculcated among politicians and borrowers are:

a) a complete ban on generalised loan waivers
b) speedy and effective loan recovery process to prevent erosion of public deposits which should be recycled to new producers and borrowers who repay debts
c) careful targeting of concessional lending to the really needy.

The loan recovery tribunals (announced in the Budget for 1993–94) have yet to be set up.

RECOMMENDATIONS

The time has come for a complete revamp of the rural credit delivery system as promised in the Economic Survey (1993–94). There are many recommendations of the Khusro Committee (1989) and the Narasimham Committee (1991) which must be implemented. The cooperative credit system has to be strengthened on an urgent basis. Also, a decision has to be taken on CRR/SLR norms for the rural credit delivery system, which depends on funds from NABARD. Cooperatives need to be brought into the concurrent list as state governments have marginalised the cooperative credit system and thoroughly bureaucratised it. The time has come, but political will is yet to be mobilised in cleaning up the Augean stables of rural credit.

4. MARKETING MANAGEMENT

The days of easy money are over and the 1990s will see the market place as the final arbiter of the future of banks. 'Profit or perish' is the new watch word and those banks which do not shape up, have to get out. There is going to be stiff competition among banks and 1996–97 and 1997–98 were crucial for the future of the Indian banking system. The direction the system takes in the future will be based on the decisions taken them. Marketing holds the key to future performance and this has to be done aggressively. A 'level banking field' is being sought to be created and some nationalised banks are setting up computerised branches for large corporate clients. For the first time, nationalised banks have woken up to evolve a marketing strategy appropriate for their business.

RECOMMENDATIONS

The days of the 'generalist' bankers are over and now, specialists have to take over. 'Specialisation' is the need today and proper targeting of market segments a necessity. Do bankers have the skills to meet the challenges posed by the foreign/private banks? The market will decide on the survival of the fittest and banks which cannot make profits will have to be wound up. Banks will have to review their marketing strategies and decide on an appropriate mix, if they are to survive and only then can they concentrate on market share and business volumes. The banking business strategy has four crucial parameters as under:

- Product
- Price
- Place
- Package

Each bank has to successfully focus its distinctive strategies for the market segment it aims at. As most Indian banks are basically aiming at the same market segments, competition will be very stiff and they need to work out new marketing strategies, business mixes and aim at customer satisfaction to maintain and expand profitable business.

5. MANAGEMENT INFORMATION SYSTEM

A good database is a pre-requisite for good business and the banking system in India can never be accused of having inadequate information.

The elaborate returns and reports to various agencies, auditors, etc., are a nightmare for every branch manager. These reports and returns just seem to multiply and even though the IBA/RBI have attempted to have a rational report system, they have failed. The unfortunate truth is that the reports and returns are based on internal operations of the branch and little effort has been made to computerise this elaborate database. Worse still, these reports are systematically filed and rarely processed. An elaborate system of documentation is built up mainly for the protection of bank officials should things go wrong. Thus, the MIS as it exists today is largely redundant and of little use in a market-oriented economy. At the branch level, the MIS has little or no market-related information. A thorough revamping of the MIS needs to be taken up so as to make it market-oriented. Further, the elaborate system of returns being compiled manually has to be replaced by an on-line data processing system, with complete computerisation of operational data and competent back-up systems. Data retrieval and specific returns can easily be compiled and bankers can concentrate on basic banking rather than compiling records.

RECOMMENDATIONS

Computerised branches with work-stations and on-line data processing with computer/satellite hook-ups, as is done in many countries, should be set up in all metropolitan and urban centres so that quick transactions and loan decisions can be recorded. However, for low-volume branches in semi-urban and rural areas, partial computerisation with personal computers, etc., will be sufficient. Much of the drudgery involved in today's banking can be done away with, if computerisation is done. Trade unions should not dictate the pace of computerisation. Salaries, personnel records, loans monitoring, deposits and due date diaries could all be put on computers. The RBI has contributed a lot to computerisation, with the DICGC computerisation and the SAMIS reporting systems as also computerised clearing operations. Internal computerisation of operations is the next logical step, if the Indian banking system is to be competitive and operationally vibrant and in tune with economic liberalisation.

The Indian banking system, of which the rural credit delivery system is a significant part, is at the crossroads today and in the near future, momentous decisions will be taken as regards its rationalisation and for ensuring a healthy growth. The RBI needs to understand that to restore health to the banking system, it is competition and not compulsion that will succeed. A large proportion of professional bankers feel that privatisation and computerisation are the panacea for the present ills of the banking system. What is needed is an infusion of elements of strategic management and even re-engineering. Restructuring could be the next major step. Accountability has to be ensured and not only profit-making, but also the tasks of strengthening loan monitoring and loan recovery processes, have to be given importance. The setting up of loan tribunals is not going to be enough. The Service Area Approach and credit planning mechanisms have to be strengthened. The crisis of credibility due to the bank scam will fade from public memory, but bank systems need to be strengthened.

Banking is a highly sensitive and specialised industry and the faith of the layman in the banking system has to be restored. Privatisation and computerisation are not enough, if the example of the Japanese banking system is taken. The non-performing assets of the top 21 private sector Japanese banks stand at over yen 12,700 billion (as at end March 1993) and by February 1994, they increased by another 10 per cent. Eventually, the banks were allowed to set up a company to buy the bad debts. But the half-hearted banking reforms have met with no success and the banking industry in Japan, continues to have review problems!

The Narasimham Committee, 1991, also recommended the creation of an Assets Reconstruction Fund. What is required is not a mere shift to privatisation but a back to basics approach with strategic management focus at all levels. Restructuring the rural credit delivery system for better efficiency and effectiveness is the next giant step to be taken.

Another important aspect is the restructuring of RRBs and rural coop-erative credit institutions (SCBs/DCCBs and SCARDBs/PCARDBs) so that they are able to meet rural credit requirements. Recapitalisation is under way in a phased manner for 100 RRBs. The Government of India tentatively estimated that Rs 6,600 crore (in 1997) is required for writing off the losses of cooperative credit banks, and efforts are being made to tap the requisite financial resources. However, to ensure that financial re-structuring accompanies managerial restructuring of the cooperatives, the DAPs/MoUs being signed by the institutions with the respective state governments and NABARD need to be implemented in right earnest. Thereafter, the RRBs and cooperative credit institutions should manage their financial and human resources better so as to function effectively and efficiently, and contribute their efforts towards a healthy rural economy.

The linking of SHGs with credit institutions will not only reduce trans-action costs for banks and borrowers but also reduce risk costs through better recovery performance. However, half-hearted attempts at linking

SHGs to credit agencies will merely add another tier to the existing structure and the cost of lending may further increase. Notwithstanding the SHGs practice of charging high annual rates of interest (10 to 36 per cent), the prudent linking of SHGs with credit institutions will increase the demand for credit without commensurate increase in costs. The number of good NGOs and SHGs are limited and of them, many are wary of taking loans from banks; thus, only a few NGOs will be involved in setting up SHGs and linking them with rural credit agencies. Therefore, the supplementary credit delivery system will have a limited impact in the initial stages but the demand for such linkages will increase sharply when the efficacy of the SHG experiment is proved, in rural poverty alleviation.

20

Designing Appropriate Systems for Micro-enterprises

The credit requirements of micro-enterprises are not being adequately met by rural credit agencies. There is a need for supplementary credit delivery systems.

Informal Credit Markets

Informal credit markets form an important part of the financial system of developing countries in Asia. They play a significant role in channelling credit to the poorer sections of society and assist in generating employment, income and output. Moreover, informal credit markets contribute a major source of working capital for entrepreneurs and generally serve to reduce discrepancies in the allocation of credit from institutional sources. Also, banks do not provide consumption credit, which forms a significant portion of the credit requirements of the rural poor. The informal financial sector functions outside the purview of regulations imposed on institutional credit. Having no restrictions on capital subscription, liquidity, lending and deposit rates, informal lenders are able to avoid legal fees and reduce transaction costs relating to loan appraisal and documentation to levels sharply below those for institutional credit sources. At the same time, the interest rate flexibility for individual borrowers enables them to cover any risk of default as well as the opportunity cost of their funds. Besides, credit from informal sources is perceived as more reliable due to its timely availability as also its availability for consumption purposes.

As risks are higher and the market is small and fragmented, the cost of informal sector credit is generally higher than that of formal sector credit even when the informal lender is not making monopoly profits. Also, informal credit is more readily available to borrowers whose credit needs tend to be neglected by the formal sector due to (a) high risk factors, (b) lack of collateral, and, (c) high cost of administering small loans.

While informal lenders tend to rely on their own funds to a greater extent than lenders in the formal sector, some types of informal lenders also accept deposits (e.g., temple trusts in Rajasthan).

Informal lenders actually operate as individuals (e.g., relatives, rural money-lenders, agriculture traders and pawn brokers) or as groups of individuals organised for mutual interest, such as rotating savings and credit associations (ROSCAS) also called 'chit funds' in South Asian countries. However, in some countries, informal lenders are organised as 'indigenous bankers' and are partnership firms or even informal finance investment, leasing and hire-purchasing companies. Such lenders are usually exempt from central banking regulations and controls and take on the characteristics of the informal sector. The distinguishing feature of informal sources of finance is the informality and flexibility of lending operations, which help to lower transaction costs.

Only very tentative estimates of the size of informal credit markets are available. It is estimated that informal markets provide more than half of the rural credit in most Asian countries and a significant part of urban credit as well. Informal sources provide a relatively higher proportion of the credit requirements of small informal enterprises for trade, consumption and working capital. As their size depends partly on the sources available and partly on the degree to which the financial sector is controlled, informal credit markets will remain a significant feature in developing Asian countries and may even grow. A useful distinction has been made between that part of the informal sector which is to some extent autonomous and older than the institutional sector (e.g. indigenous bankers, chit funds, pawn brokers) and that part which developed in response to the tight controls (finance companies). It is this second component that grows and contracts in reaction to regulations and liberal policies in the institutional credit source.

In recent years, there has been a growing interest in informal credit markets for their role in the expansion of the rural credit system without incurring heavy administrative and overhead costs (as in banks) and by reducing transaction costs. The formal sector ought to provide more effective competition perhaps by adopting some of the informal sector's practices. Measures for enhancing competition within the informal sector could be part of this approach.

Another method would be to work through the informal sector in those areas and segments where competitive conditions do prevail but the cost of funds, rather than demand, tends to keep interest rates high. Lower transaction costs of the informal sector could be used to 'retail' credit. This would lower transaction costs of the informal sector and lower borrowing rates as intermediation costs would be lower. This strategy would strengthen and expand the existing linkages between the formal and informal sectors. Access to institutional credit would be strengthened for several groups, such as agricultural inputs dealers, traders and commission transport agents. They would take advantage of the inter-linkage between credit and commodity transactions to reduce intermediation costs and risk premia only if monopoly market conditions are absent. But the greater availability of formal sector refinancing might itself induce better competition.

Some developing countries like Sri Lanka have experimented with schemes to use agricultural dealers to 'on-lend' formally. There is a need for a pilot project and experimentation to test this hypothesis further. Apart from the operational interest in informal credit markets, other issues like informal market savings mobilisation, allocative efficiency, equity, monetary policy, etc., need to be looked into. In many developing countries, there is legislation in the informal sector, including usury laws, restriction on the amount of loan or the purposes for which money-lenders can lend, restrictions on deposit-taking, debt moratorium and registration requirements. Regulations may be framed keeping in mind the important trade-offs to be considered. There is conflict between restrictions on deposit-taking imposed in furtherance of selective credit controls and prudential concerns on the one hand, and the role of mobilisation of savings by informal credit markets, on the other. Decisions regarding trade-offs need to be taken, if an 'optimal' regulatory environment towards the informal sector is to be instituted in keeping with a country's broad policy objectives.

Informal talks with both registered and non-registered money-lenders reveal that they are aware of the problems affecting the growth of institutional rural credit, the high administrative and transaction costs, and poor recovery rates. They are very efficient operationally and meet existing demands but are restricted from wider coverage due to lack of funds made available through a bank. In fact, a few money-lenders, who charge interest between 3 and 5 per cent per month (depending upon opportunity costs, operating margins and risk costs), have offered to act as agents of various rural credit agencies, if they are permitted and granted credit on flexible terms, with an agency commission (1 per cent per month) to meet their operating (monitoring and recovery) costs.

Transaction costs (both for borrowers and lenders) for the non-institutional rural credit delivery system are very low mainly due to the lack of detailed documentation, immediate decisions about sanction and disbursement (as the limited procedures are well known), and the absence of information costs for the lenders. Involving them as agents for disbursal of crop loans or working capital needs of small borrowers (village artisans, rural service industries and tiny rural industries) would reduce the transaction costs and introduce better efficiency in the loan recovery mechanism. The Sri Lankan banking system has been experimenting with this system. The results are yet to be documented. A pilot experiment could be launched to test the applicability of the system in a few selected districts and the results documented for further replication, if found viable.

SHG—A Low Cost Concept

The Self-help Group (SHG) concept helps members to develop both economic and social strengths. The collateral substitute positively influences the resources of the SHG, whereby members meet their contingent obligations without going to money-lenders/private sources. The financing banks are convinced about the collective wisdom of the group while lending, and its persuasive capacity as also group pressure for recovery of loans. The repeated interaction among bank officials and the groups helps in developing trust and confidence. Such confidence-building process involves a marginal period of 6–8 months.

Using group pressure, strengths, assurance and persuasion as the collateral substitutes without any tangible security for availing of loans from banks and financing to/through the groups has proved to be an effective supplement o the institutional credit delivery system. From the bank's point of view, financing to/through groups has not only resulted in 44 per cent reduction in transaction costs, but there are also substantial improvements in proper utilisation of loans and recovery is more than 90 per cent without much direct involvement. Thus, the use of group pressure and moral/social security as collateral substitutes indirectly contributes to the viability of the bank through reduced transaction costs and prompt repayment, thereby increasing its resources for further lending.

Linkages with Financial Institutions

The credit needs of the poor arise due to growing family sizes, societal obligations (expenses on marriages and deaths, etc.). Credit is also required because they have no cushion to tide over adverse situations, which arise very often, and to survive in times of total disaster (natural or man-made), market uncertainties, etc. Financial institutions have not entered this particular credit market as:

- The existing framework of rules/guidelines do not permit meeting such requirements.
- The staff are not oriented to such marginal operations.
- Their functional style is not cost beneficial for generating viable operations.
- There is too much work involved (documentation, follow-up visits for monitoring operations).
- Lack of viable schemes for implementation unless a target is imposed.

While designing an appropriate programme, sound financial principles as also clear social objectives must be kept in mind. However, the problem is not meeting these objectives, which can often be debatable, but the participation of the poor, in the true sense, in programmes for poverty alleviation, especially those in the agricultural and rural development spheres. In addition to increasing agricultural productivity and promoting non-agricultural enterprises in rural areas, there have to be specific activities that enhance inputs of production like (i) natural resource management, (ii) human resource development, (iii) rural infrastructural development and (iv) savings and credit programmes. These can be secured only if the poor participate in the process of their poverty alleviation. The four kinds of participation sought are:

- Participation in decision-making, in identifying problems, formulation of alternatives, planning activities and allocating resources.
- Participation in implementation, in carrying out activities, managing and operating programmes and partaking of services.
- Participation in economic, social, cultural or other benefits, individually or collectively.
- Participation in evaluation of the activity, its outcome, which should provide feedback into the first three kinds.

Individually, a poor person tends to be erratic, uncertain in his behaviour. Group membership smoothens such rough edges making him more reliable. An individual poor person feels exposed to all kinds of hazards and requires guidance and advice from people he knows and can trust. Membership in a group gives him a feeling of protection and the benefit of collective perceptions, decision-making and implementation of programmes of common benefits. Thus, formation of a group can ensure the maximum participation of the poor in a credit programme. The approach towards poverty alleviation should be one of self-help. One should raise oneself by one's own exertions. Others should help them to help themselves.

The BAAC System in Thailand

The rural credit system in Thailand comprises commercial banks, the Bank for Agriculture and Agricultural Cooperatives (BAAC), cooperative institutions, both at the apex and intermediate levels and the farmers' cooperative societies. Thrust is now being placed on formation and development of autonomous, informal SHGs. The BAAC plays an important role in dispensing rural credit and undertaking various operations which are incidental and connected with such credit extension.

The BAAC provides financial services to about half of all farmer households in Thailand and is a state-owned enterprise. The chairman of its board of directors is the Finance Minister of Thailand. This envisages that there is no interference in the bank from the bureaucracy or the Central Bank.

The BAAC's method of administering credit through the group lending method has ensured a high rate of loan repayment. While cooperatives also embody the idea of group responsibility and group monitoring, the BAAC's success lies in small-sized groups of 8–15 people. Also, the BAAC has earned the rural people's goodwill for meeting the farmers' needs; it has become a reputed institution. The BAAC charges an additional 3 per cent interest per annum as personal charges and does not permit new loans to delinquent borrowers until all loans are cleared. The BAAC has achieved a high repayment rate at a small cost. The administrative costs are reported to be around 5 per cent of the loans outstanding while about 3 per cent of the loan outstanding are eventually written off. When the cost of funds was 12–13 per cent, the BAAC would lend without any collateral to the rural sector at 20 per cent. However, BAAC credit has a number of disadvantages, including a higher transaction cost of about 9 per cent. Thus, the collective interest cost should be 29 per cent which is below the rates in the informal markets. The BAAC has been useful in making available short-term working capital loans to a large number of people but is not able to expand its scope to poor farmers or in riskier areas or even to expand the scope of its activities.

The concept of lending through groups being implemented by BAAC, particularly under joint liability groups, is worth considering. Although, like in India, the BAAC also experienced certain difficulties in channelling more credit through cooperatives, particularly in view of poor recoveries, its emphasis on encouraging lending through autonomous SHGs is a point to be considered.

The BAAC's mandate in Thailand and the privileges it enjoys in formulating agricultural credit policies, extending credit facilities and undertaking non-credit activities in agriculture and other allied fields, places it in an important position in the country's rural credit delivery system. There is a genuine need for developing NABARD into an apex rural developmental credit institution on the lines of the BAAC in Thailand. The provisions of the present NABARD Act, 1981, allow it, only refinance functions. In spite of the mandate given in the preamble to the NABARD Act, 1981 to bring about integrated rural development, these provisions have prevented it from playing a powerful role in the field of agricultural credit, given its limited powers over commercial banks, cooperative institutions and RRBs. Even after 16 years, NABARD has rarely been able to assert itself in various spheres in relation to refinance functioning and credit planning.

There are certain good aspects of the BAAC's operation and its policies which can be taken note of and considered for implementation wherever feasible.

The lower rate of interest applied by it to the paddy pledge scheme is attractive. Farmers in Thailand get paddy pledge loans at 3 per cent interest per annum and are able to market the produce after a small waiting period. Similarly, a lower rate of interest could, perhaps, encourage Indian farmers to opt for produce pledge loans which will (i) increase recoveries in the short term as farmers can get better prices for their produce, (ii) result in the optimal and economic use of godowns of primary societies/ other organisations like state/central warehouses, and (iii) help stabilise the produce market. The rate of interest could be arrived at taking into consideration the fluctuations in market prices.

Similarly, the concept of group lending being implemented by the BAAC, particularly under joint liability groups, is worth considering. The Thai model could provide us a reference with regard to the need for model formation and development, and linking of such SHGs with the formal credit structure. While in Thailand, the members of a group mostly belong to a single religion and are engaged in a single activity, our SHGs could be multi-religious but single-purpose groups. Even in Thailand, single-purpose groups have a higher rate of success than multi activity groups. A useful point in this regard is the role played by the Community Development Department (CDD), an extension agency of the Government of Thailand. The CDD official acts as a motivator and he plays a prominent role in the formation and development of SHGs, particularly because SHGs are informal credit agencies outside the organised sector.

The Grameen Bank in Bangladesh

The Bangladesh Grameen Bank has an unique approach in providing credit to the rural poor. It imposes a strict discipline on borrowers as well as bank staff. The management also services the poorest of the poor in the rural areas, who would otherwise have not been eligible for credit from other institutions. The theory that the lack of capital is the major constraint faced by the poor and they know how best to improve their economic condition has been amply proved by the bank's success. By virtue of peer pressure among its borrowers and loan supervision, the Grameen Bank has achieved a repayment record in an area in which most other credit schemes fail. An elaborate system of discipline and supervision is incorporated into loan procedures and this characterises its credit operations as well as related social development activities. Individually, the procedures may not be significant, but together, they make a formidable system. The Grameen Bank recognises that the poorest in the rural areas are not the farmers but the landless, who are also excluded from traditional credit projects designed for farmers. The landless form a major productive asset in Bangladesh, though their labour is an underutilised asset. However, the landless lack the basic skills to take up non-traditional activities. The Grameen Bank tries to improve upon skills and productivity by testing appropriate strategies and providing suitable training on improved technologies.

In an Islamic country, women have less rights than men. But, the Grameen Bank has recognised their worth as individuals and as reliable instruments in the fight against rural poverty. When women become income earners, the incremental income is systematically oriented towards increasing family well being, which is not true for male earners. This feature of intra-household distribution of incremental income and well being is the basis of the bank's preference for women borrowers.

However, there are a few female staff members as the social constraints on employing women, especially as branch managers, have yet to be overcome. In some zones (i.e., Tangail), the recovery rate has come down, even though it is still very high when compared to those of other rural credit agencies.

It has been the Grameen Bank's experience that the first-time loanees' repayment record is much better than that of subsequent loanees. Fourth-time loanees had about 10 per cent of overdue loan instalments compared to 0.4 per cent for first-time loanees and 1.2 per cent for second-time loanees. Thus, repeat loanees fail to maintain regularity in repayment compared to fresh loanees. Further, even amongst repeat loanees, the repayment performance of female loanees is much better than that of males. Also, the Grameen Bank has to take a decision about granting fresh loans to members, who have benefited from earlier loans and are not as poor as new loanees, or expand horizontally with newer members. For those leaving the groups, only their deposits from the group fund can be returned. Thus, the Grameen Bank has to decide upon strategies for those who no longer qualify for inclusion in the group.

The repayment performance of collective loans is not particularly good. Members with excellent individual record of repayment do not do well, when they go in for collective enterprises due to lack of management skills and wrong investment decisions. Few documents are also available regarding loan proposals, which may not be necessary for individual loans, essential for collective enterprises to ensure the commitment of all involved. The emphasis on working out per week repayment and whether a borrower can afford it and ensure repayment for the bank does not ensure project viability or profitability. Loanees are aware of the need for weekly repayment but are unaware of break even through required daily production, cost of machinery and installation, etc. In a few cases, repayment is not possible from internally-generated funds and the loanees were forced to borrow from other sources. Long-term projects may not generate enough funds for repayment within the stipulated one-year repayment period. The weekly instalment, which works well in the case of individual non-farm activity does not work as well in case of collective enterprises, such as land lease, deep tubewells, shallow tubewells, pisciculture etc. The Grameen Bank is trying to improve the management structure of these collective groups and to change rules. In many cases, the bank has taken over collective enterprises and is teaching loanees to run them efficiently.

The Grameen Bank depends upon the honesty and dedication of its staff and borrowers and puts a tremendous workload on the field-level staff; the incentive payments are linked to government employees' scales, who do not work as hard. A better incentive structure may be needed in the future or productivity may fall. The expansion of the Grameen Bank has been too fast and consolidation efforts may suffer. The Grameen Bank should not expand too fast due to pressure from the government donor agencies or the rural elite and, instead, should proceed at a manageable pace. Dependence on foreign funds (72 per cent) needs to be minimised, as self-sufficiency in funds management is necessary. Though the bank has taken steps to mobilise borrowings from members and has also accepted deposits from non-members, more effort is required on this front. Also, the bank's tendency to impose social objectives may not always be welcome.

The crucial factor in the Grameen Bank's operation is the high cost of supervision. The risk in this direction has not manifested so far in view of the bank's ability to attract large doses of financial assistance at incredibly low interest rates from foreign funding agencies. Its average borrowing rate is about 2.5 per cent and it lends at 18 per cent. But, it carried a heavy load of overhead expenses and its blocked assets in the form of buildings, etc., amounted to tk 12.66 crore, forming 32 per cent of its own resources of tk 38.14 crore in December 1988. Most activities financed by the bank were low profile and devoid of any extension facilities to either improve productivity or eliminate drudgery or physical stress through modern technologies and gadgets. Extension facilities came from the bank only when sought for by the participants. The average loan size is also small and though the bank claims that the economic conditions of the participants have improved greatly, it is aware that the nature of low profile activities is such that a single loan will not take the participants beyond a certain economic status. The most important drawback is the absence of any effort on the part of the bank to find markets for the products of its borrowers.

Although, the bank's theme of self-reliance through savings mobilisation is laudable, different types of compulsory contributions have proved to be a sore point in this regard. The contributions to the group fund at 5 per cent of the loan amount disbursed each time; the one taka per week to the Children's Welfare Fund; and 25 per cent of the interest amount to the Emergency Fund, all of which can not be reclaimed by a member leaving the group, increased the costs for the borrowers and were, perhaps, silently accepted by them as part of the several disciplines imposed by the bank. The vertical expansion by the bank could sooner or later be constrained by the low level of productivity of many of the activities financed by it.

A study conducted by IFAD revealed that with increase in the size of the loan, the rate of return decreased and that the present average loan size appeared to provide the optimum returns. The joint enterprises encouraged by the bank for larger investment have not produced better results due to management deficiencies and the bank's policy of non-intervention in activities pursued by the group members. The bank has been in existence since 1976 and naturally, therefore, its manpower is full of vigour and is in its youth, with the average age of employees being 22. Their ascendancy to higher ladders at definite intervals is also one of the motivating factors. One should not, however, miss the limitations in this regard that may arise in due course of time, when the bank reaches its optimum growth. Although sufficient training has been imparted at all levels, in order to equip the staff to climb up in the ladder of hierarchy, decentralisation and a distinct management style and system should be evolved to continue the progress.

The rapid expansion of the Grameen Bank project since 1976 has already demonstrated its replication potential. However, one should not fail to notice that even in Bangladesh, it has not been replicated in other rural credit agencies. This is due to the fact that the Grameen Bank started as a unique institution, different from traditional approaches in many respects and has been allowed to continue to do so. It would, therefore, be difficult to implant its operations in other institutions. In other conditions, many of the policies followed by the Grameen Bank and even its organisational structure, appear to be revolutionary.

The Grameen Bank, in the first instance, does not fit into any existing banking system. It was created by a special legislation, having shades of both a cooperative venture and commercial banking. It is exempt from the rigours of banking statutes in matters such as liquidity ratio, credit control measures, etc. Its operations even deviate from necessary minimal requirements such as legal documentation. The central bank exercises little supervision over it in the form of statutory returns (except annual balance sheet) or inspections. The bank has dispensed with even minimum documentation and collateral for its lending.

In Indian conditions, all these are considered as sacrilege and to think of such an institution is itself impractical. It is often stated that the package of practices prevalent in the Grameen Bank has alone contributed to its success and not one among them could be discarded. It is, therefore, suggested that the scheme should either be adopted in its totality or abandoned altogether. The various practices are interlocked and replicating some of them alone cannot be feasible.

An important factor is that the Bank was created under an Ordinance in 1983 under Martial Law and has never been formally regularised by an Act. The structure has been deliberately kept loose so .1at the permanent control of Dr. Mohammed Yunus, its founder, can be perpetuated. Out of 12 members of its board of directors, nine are members of SHGs (of which eight are women) and the other three are government officials. The majority, thus, act as a rubber stamp as they are not very educated or assertive or have little practical experience of running a bank. Basically, therefore, it is a one-man show, with the control being retained by Dr.Yunus. There is no democratic control or signs of a succession plan. From a banker's point of view, there are several inconsistencies. These include:

- A major source of funding is cheap foreign credit at very low rate of interest and on favourable repayment terms.
- No charge on assets is created but only social collateral or group pressure and hence, technically, there is no chance of recovery in case of deafult.
- Only tk 5,000 (maximum) can be given per borrower. Thus, a large number of otherwise viable activities are not being financed as per the bank's norms.
- Assets creation is poor as borrowers are encouraged to be dependent on the bank for consumption/production finance. Also, with repeated doses of loans of small amounts, families rising above the poverty line will be very few.
- The income pattern of the bank reveals that 61 per cent of it is from interest repayments while 39 per cent is from grants/foreign aid invested in commercial banks (8–10 per cent interest spread is available).
- Staff dropout rate is too high: over 40 per cent of the newly-recruited staff drop out in the first six months.

Application of Grameen Bank Experiment

The Grameen Bank project in its totality is not feasible in all countries, as it not only required a special ordinance, but also dedicated leadership, as found in Dr. Mohammed Yunus, who was given unfettered freedom on directional matters. Further, the concepts are revolutionary and cannot be introduced in India, unless a ground is prepared, even amongst the policy makers, for their acceptability. It would only be worthwhile to apply select practices of the bank, in specified areas as a pilot scheme in order to test its results under Indian conditions. Backward and tribal areas, having concentration of poverty would be ideal for testing the project. It is also necessary to identify the target group, which as in the case of Grameen Bank, could be those below the poverty line. Also, as in the case of the Grameen Bank again, women should get greater attention within the target group (in view of the identical culture of women in the two countries and the quick results it is capable of producing. Also, some development projects implemented in India with women as the target group have already shown good results).

Group Formation and Intermediation

The group concept of the Grameen Bank project should be adopted, given the advantages embodied in it. Group formation on the pattern of SHGs should be encouraged in identified areas. Already, SHGs are operating in India on the pattern of the Grameen Bank but very few have linkages with banks. Most of these SHGs operate with very limited resources on the pattern of chit funds run by individuals. These SHGs could first be linked with various rural credit agencies. Also, to begin with, voluntary agencies and educated persons (school teachers, postmasters, etc.) could be involved in group formation, but it should be gradually left to the borrowers themselves to motivate others to join the group. Homogeneity in groups is essential to avoid domination by better placed persons from amongst the rural poor. The IRDP scheme could be initially introduced in such identified groups. Government departments and banks should not be involved in the process of identification of the beneficiaries and it should be left to the group members, under the overall supervision of the voluntary agencies. This would, to a great extent, eliminate the grievance of corrupt practices alleged against bank/government officials.

The groups may consist of not more than 15 members and five groups should form a centre. No legal formalities such as registration, etc., should be insisted upon. Regular meetings of the groups and centres should be insisted upon. Initially the voluntary agencies should assist the groups and centres in holding such meetings but as and when they stabilise, the agencies should withdraw. The voluntary agencies should also undertake supervision of group meetings, recoveries and utilisation. But, here again, they should impart these disciplines to the groups in a phased manner and endeavour to withdraw themselves and make the groups independent as quickly as possible. Bank officials should, however, visit the group meetings at least once a month, as it is essential to build a strong relationship between the bank and the groups. Such visits should not be in the nature of supervision but for guidance on operational matters. The voluntary agencies may be assisted with token grants to meet initial expenditure. The selection of NGOs should be restricted to those agencies which have a good track record and which are interested in the SHG experiment. Many NGOs are used to grants-in-aid from foreign agencies without much supervision and may not be interested in SHG promotion with the help of bank credit.

SHG Linkages with Banks

Formation of SHGs enable banks to save on expenditure for:

- Appraisal costs of non-viable cases which are rejected by the NGOs.
- Appraisal costs as application forms are scrutinised and recommended by the NGO.
- Loan monitoring and repayment costs as NGOs assist loan recovery.

The NGOs gain is limited as their capital is not locked up and they can form more SHGs with bank linkages.

A substantial number of rural poor do not have access to funds from banks as they are perceived to be risks and not creditworthy for the banks. The limitations of the banks due to the legal framework and their inability to deal effectively and economically with a large number of small borrowers, makes operational linkages with SHGs a necessity.

Banks in India have been based upon old Scottish principles: adopting a culture of functioning on the principle of 'Suspect and Respect' and not the reverse. The more poor the clientele are, the more they are suspected because of their vulnerability to socio-political and economic pressures. Loans in the South-East Asian countries, the low cost external funds available for SHGs through IFAD, Ford Foundation, etc., have certainly assisted in boosting SHG efforts. An important element in the success of the SHG experiment has been the borrower discipline in rural areas.

Another phenomenon, which requires more detailed study, is the tendency of SHGs to break up as the poor graduate to relative economic prosperity levels. The borrower discipline imparted in the SHGs is then used for sanctioning loans to individual borrowers on a selective basis, depending upon their ability to manage the economic activity/asset. The results of the SHGs set up by the central government in selected districts for the Development of Women and Children in Rural Areas (DWCRA) have to be compared with those of successful SHGs set up by voluntary agencies so that replicable, low-cost models can be set up. The differences in the efforts of voluntary agencies and government agencies can certainly provide clues to the success and sustainability of the SHGs in the long run.

If the SHG linkages are successful, a large number of small borrowers could effectively be financed through the SHGs, while the bank can concentrate on monitoring a small number of large borrowers. This would enable extended coverage while keeping supervisory/monitoring staff levels within manageable limits. Small savings would be tapped at low cost, recoveries and profitability would improve and business development could definitely improve. Two problems, however, persist: the problem of lending to such groups due to absence of any legal status, and the high demand for consumption loans. Rural financial institutions, therefore, have to come to terms with certain harsh realities.

Initiatives

Based on the efforts being made to form SHGs, there is a need to encourage various types of initiatives being taken. Basically, there are three types of SHGs that are being considered for formal linkage with banks:

* SHGs set up by banks.
* SHGs set up by voluntary organisations.
* SHGs set up by the state governments and the cooperative system.

A multi-agency approach for setting up SHGs needs incentives, if the movement is to thrive and build a cheaper and more viable rural credit delivery system. Such a system would not only meet the credit needs of the people over time but also reduce transaction costs both for rural credit agencies and poor borrowers.

The supplementary rural credit delivery system seeks to develop strong linkages with rural credit agencies and extension of government agencies, so that SHGs are able to mobilise internal resources and savings, meet the needs for new technologies and inputs of members through extension agencies, and also meet demands for consumption credit, production credit and term credit needs.

The rural credit system being proposed will cater to all types of rural credit such as:

* Consumption Credit—Currently given only by money-lenders and relatives.

- Production Credit—Given by credit agencies, money-lenders, etc.
- Term Credit—Given by rural credit agencies only.

The supplementary rural credit system will not replace the existing system but will supplement its efforts. Further expansion of banking systems have to be cost-effective and should not enhance the cost of credit for needy rural borrowers and the loan servicing costs for banks. Instead, a low-cost viable rural credit system needs to be implemented which will help banks. The goals should be to:

- Maintain the volume/flow of rural credit especially for priority sector borrowers.
- Reduce transaction costs for borrowers and loan transaction costs for banks.
- Make credit available in time to rural borrowers.
- Motivate NGOs/banks/cooperatives in building up SHGs.
- Build up a healthy and viable rural credit system.
- Enable effective preparation and monitoring of service area plans for rural credit agencies without opening new branches and enhancing manpower costs.
- Enable better recovery as patterned on the Bangladesh Grameen Bank Model, where recovery exceeds 96 per cent of loans outstanding and this in a country where the average recovery by other banks is only 10 per cent.
- Enable rural borrowers (especially the weaker sections of society) to have a single-window credit facility for all types of rural credit.
- Involve NGOs/other organisations in developing concepts of self-help for the rural poor and disadvantaged sections and to make a dent in poverty alleviation.
- Enable the rural poor to have ready access to credit norms and to help them in micro-entrepreneurial enterprises, which will enable them to meet their consumption/working capital needs.

The Viable Rural Credit Delivery System

The supplementary system envisages two sources of credit for an SHG, the savings of its members and the seed fund at the bank (rural credit agency). For the banks, the transaction costs would be sharply reduced as NGOs would be providing intermediation services both for deposits and loan disbursements/recovery. There is, thus, (a) effective intermediation, (b) low transaction costs for loans, (c) low cost deposit mobilisation,

(d) effective monitoring and recovery of loans, and (e) involvement in group activities.

Thus, the supplementary rural credit delivery system needs to be given a fair trial for the poorer sections of society.

Credit operations. The bank will initially operate through a voluntary agency (NGO) and the initial period of linkage creation will involve a series of confidence-building measures on the part of the NGO, the SHGs and the bank. Certain linkages are proposed in respect of credit operations in the first phase of operations. Only after the linkages and the SHG functions are established, will the need to establish direct linkages between the SHG and the bank be felt. However, the SHG will function only for small loans for consumption, production and investment purposes up to Rs 10,000 per person. For large loans to any individual, the SHG may directly recommend cases to the bank and the loan may be given on an individual basis.

Banking requirements/ norms. The formation of SHGs by the voluntary agencies and availability of bank finance from commercial banks has to be facilitated by the issue of relevant central banking instructions. The maintenance of accounts by the SHGs/NGOs should fulfil the normal requirements of banks. However, more important are the linkages between the banks and SHGs which are dynamic in nature. The role of the NGO 'is basically that of a facilitator' or 'catalyst' and the NGO should build up the bank–SHG relationship and gradually merge into the background after the linkages have been established as also create more SHGs for helping the poorer sections of society.

Perspectives

As stated above, SHGs need to have a linkage with banks so as to be able to expand their lending for productive purposes. However, banks are hesitant to extend credit support to groups, except on a limited basis to a few individual members, and on terms required by them because of the absence of any legal status and inadequate information and knowledge about the role and functions of SHGs. There is also a related problem of differentiating good SHGs from the poor ones. Notwithstanding these problems, the case for exploring possibilities of developing a linkage between banks and SHGs appear to gain strength from the fact that in a general environment characterised by widespread repayment delinquency, the experience of SHGs is strikingly different. This advantage could perhaps be exploited through a linkage programme.

With SHGs being non-legal entities and banks having difficulties in dealing with them within the framework of the existing regulations, it would be desirable to try out a few pilot projects between banks, on the one hand, and SHGs and NGOs on the other, to try out various models of linkages and different savings and credit instruments. Subsequently, these can be evaluated to learn lessons for future replication. The pilot projects could perhaps throw light on the nature of the risks involved, and the compensation and guarantee mechanisms necessary thereafter. There must be flexible options for SHGs/NGOs/banks and the minimum of operational guidelines.

SHGs are functioning in remote and scattered areas and banks are not able to assess whether the concerned groups are suitable for promoting any linkages with regard to credit and savings operations. It would, perhaps, be desirable to develop an information base on the activities of these groups and also evolve suitable criteria for identifying eligible SHGs for bank linkage. SHGs could be associated with other government programmes like health care, extension, etc., so as to provide an informal recognition to their existence and working before the banks are involved in the linkages.

As SHGs are found to operate with considerable flexibility, with regard to terms of lending and saving operations, interest rates, security norms, margin, etc., free from guidelines, and also as these are considered critical for their performance, it may not be necessary to ensure any rigid norms in the operations of SHGs. The micro-enterprise concept should be coordinated with the SHG lending system so that rural women, tribal people and the rural non-farm sector, who have been deprived of credit, could have their fair share of credit.

Micro-finance Institutions

The role of new micro-finance institutions, which do not follow the group concept of micro-lending, has gained importance with the World Microfinance Conference held in Washington in February 1998. The strength of these institutions lie in their profitability, poverty reduction potentials, the very high loan recovery rates, the existence of insurance-linked savings facilities, mobile cash collection systems, cost-covering interest rates and incentives, both for the clients and staff. Some of the very innovative and successful micro-finance institutions are ASA in Bangladesh, BRI/BKD in Indonesia, Bancofol in Bolivia and SEWA in India. These lend directly to individuals without any collateral. Many micro-finance institutions have been set up with innovative designs and practices, and their profitability leads to sustainability and rapid growth in lending, creation of employment opportunities by borrowers, leading to poverty reduction.

The informal organisational structures and the effective loan recovery methods, along with innovative savings instruments, have led to considerable growth of such institutions in many developing countries, including India.

However, a 1998 report of the United Nations, Department for Economic and Social Affairs, states that programmes providing small loans are not effective in reducing poverty due to limitations when tried as a substitute for development efforts due to the limited availability of micro-finance funds. The author of the report, James Kans, has also warned against siphoning of development assistance funds away from agriculture, health, education and infrastructure sections of the rural economy.

Within a limited area of operations, the micro-finance could be developed into an useful additional strategy in the fight against rural poverty. However, micro-finance institutions have yet to develop a strategic alliance with the banking system so as to access large funds for on-lending. This alliance, if nurtured, could develop into a symbiotic relationship, useful for the rural poor, micro-finance institutions and also for the banks. But, certain teething problems have to be taken care of before micro-finance institutions in India develop into an additional strategy in the fight against rural poverty and as a useful supplement to the rural credit delivery system.

References and Select Bibliography

Adams, Dale W. 1986. 'Rural Financial Markets—Cases', *The FAO Review*, Jan–Feb: 15–18.

Adams, Dale W., Graham, Douglas H. and Von Pischke, J.D. 1984. *Undermining Rural Development with Cheap Credit*, 318 p. Boulder: Colorado Westview Press.

Anand, Virmani. 1982. 'The Nature of Credit Markets in Developing Countries', Staff Working Paper No. 524, World Bank.

Anand, V.K. 1984. 'Alternative Approaches for Rural Economic Development: A Note', *Indian Journal of Economics*, 64(254): 233–42.

Asia Pacific Regional Agricultural Credit Association. 1989. 'Linking Self-help Groups and Banks in Developing Countries', Bangkok.

Bardhan, Pranab and Rudra, Ashok. 1978. 'Interlinkage of Land, Labour and Credit Relation: An Analysis of Village Survey Data in East India', *Economic and Political Weekly*, 13 (6 & 7).

Bedhak, Hrushikesh. 1985. 'Cost of Institutional Finance in Priority Sectors—Reduction of Credit Acquisition Cost is Vital, An Empirical Study', *Indian Cooperative Review*, 22(3): 263–81.

Bell, Clive and Srinivasan, T.N. 'Agricultural Credit Markets in Punjab Segmentation, Rationing and Spillover', 54p, Working Paper No. 7, World Bank, Washington D.C.

Bhaduri, Amit. 1982. 'The Role of Rural Credit in Agrarian Reforms with Special Reference to India', *Economic Bulletin for Asia and the Pacific*, 33: 104–11.

Bhaduri, Amit. 1977. 'On the Formation of Usurious Rates in Backward Agriculture', *Cambridge Journal of Economics*, 341–52.

Bhatt, V.V. 1962. *Structure of Financial Institutions*, Mumbai: Vora and Co.

Bhende, M.J. 1986. 'Credit Markets in Rural South India', *Economic and Political Weekly*, 21 (38–39): A119–24.

Bottomley, Anthony. 1975. 'Interest Rate Determination in Under-developed Rural Areas', *American Journal of Agricultural Economics*, 57(2): 274–91.

Bouman, F.J.A. and Horstman, R. 1988. 'Pawnbroking as an Instrument of Rural Banking in the Third World', *Economic Development and Cultural Change*, 37, ADB, Manila.

Brignoli, R. and Seigel, L. 1987. 'The Role of NGOs in LDC Growth', Mimeo, World Bank.

Chandavarkar, A.G. 1965. 'The Premium for Risk as a Determination of Interest Rates in Underdeveloped Areas', *Quarterly Journal of Economics*, 79(May): 322–25.

Committee on Banking Regulation and Supervisory Practices. 1988. Report on International Developments in Banking Supervision.

Cueras, Carlos E. 1987. 'Transaction Cost of Agricultural Lending in Developing Countries', Occasional Paper No. 1418, Ohio State University, Columbus.

Cueras, Carlos E. and Graham, Douglas H. 1985. 'Transaction Costs of Borrowing and Credit Rationing in Agriculture: Simultaneous Equations Approach', 12p, Unpublished Paper, Department of Agricultural Economics and Rural Sociology, Ohio State University.

Datey, C.D. 1978. 'The Financial Cost of Agricultural Credit. A Case Study of Indian Experience', Staff Working Paper No. 296, World Bank.

Desai, B.M. 1984. 'Performance of Group Based Savings and Credit Programmes in Rural India', 28p, I.I.M., Ahmedabad.

Desai, D.K. 1988. 'Institutional Credit Requirements for Agricultural Production —2000 AD', *Indian Journal of Agricultural Economy*, 43(3): 326–55.

FAO/APRACA. 1985. 'Mobilisation of Rural Savings in Selected Countries in Asia and Pacific', Bangkok.

Gadgil, M.V. 1987. 'Agricultural Credit in India—A Review of Performance and Policies, I & II', *National Bank News Review*, Feb/March.

George, P.T. et al. 1985. 'Rural Credit and Farmers' Borrowing Costs, A Case Study', *Prajnan*, 14(3): 255–272.

Ghatak, Subrata. 1983. 'On Inter-regional Variations in Rural Interest Rates in India', *Journal of Developing Areas*, 18(Oct.): 21–34.

Ghate, P. 1985. 'Some Issues for Regional Study on Informal Credit Markets', 41p, Asian Development Bank, Manila.

Giddy, I.H. 1984. 'The Principles and Practice of Bank Supervision— Main Features and Evaluation and Possible Alternatives, Mimeo, IMF Central Banking Seminar.

Hartman, Jack D. 1985. 'Agricultural Credit: A Global Enigma', 156 p, Danville, Illinois: The Interstate Printers and Publishers.

Iqbal, Farukh. 1988. 'The Determinants of Moneylender Interest Rates, Evidence from Rural India', *Journal of Development Studies*, 24(3): 364–78.

Morris, Felipe. 1985. 'India's Financial System', 76 p, Working Paper No. 739, World Bank, Washington D.C.

Panda, R.K. 1985. *Agricultural Indebtedness and Institutional Finance*. New Delhi: Ashish Publishing House.

Prasad, J.V.S. and Naidu, M.K. 1986. 'The Role of Cooperative Production Credit to the Indian Farmer—Analysis', *Indian Cooperative Review*, 23(4): 400–09.

Quinones, Benjamin R. 1988. 'An Overview of Agricultural Credit Systems in Selected Asian Countries', 20 p, Asia Pacific Regional Agricultural Credit Association, Bangkok.

Rajput, S.S. 1986. 'Rural Credit and Its Cost—A Case Study', *Indian Cooperative Review*, 23(3): 301–10.

Ranade, Sudhanshu. 1984. 'Rural Banking Adrift', 126 p, Delhi: Jaico Publishing House.

Rao, Ananth S. and Dandekar, M.N. 1989. 'Non-Monetary Transaction Costs of Formal Credit Institutions—An Empirical Study,' *State Bank of India Monthly Review*, 28(4): 187–209.

Rao, S.R.K. 1989. *The Indian Money Market*. Allahabad: Chaitanya Publishers' House.

RBI. 1981. Report of the Committee to Review Arrangements for Institutional Credit for Agricultural Rural Development, Mumbai.

RBI. 1990. Report of the Agricultural Credit Review Committee, Mumbai.

Sheng, A. 1990. 'Bank Supervision: Principles and Practice', EDI Working Paper, World Bank.

Srinivasan, Aruna and Mayer, Richard L. 1987. 'Transaction Cost of Reserve Bank Branches in Bangladesh' Occasional Paper No. 1352, Ohio State University, Columbus.

Srivastava, D.R. and Kumar, Vinod. 1985. 'Cost of Credit', *Financing Agriculture*, 17(1): 14–17.

Tinberg, T. and Aiyar, C.V. 1984. 'Informal Credit Markets in India', *Economic Development and Cultural Change*, 33: 43–45.

Tinberg, T. and Aiyar, C.V. 1984. 'Informal Credit Markets in India', *Economic and Political Weekly*, Annual Number.

Index

About the Author

K.G. Karmakar is Chief General Manager in an apex rural financial institution in Mumbai. A Ph.D. in Management from the Jamnalal Bajaj Institute of Management Studies, Mumbai, he worked as an officer in the State Bank of India and the Reserve Bank of India before joining the rural financial institution in 1983. He has participated in many training programmes in India and abroad including the Rural Finance Course of the EDI, Washington, and the Development Banking Programme at the University of Strathclyde, Glasgow. Dr. Karmakar has previously co-authored *Agricultural Project Management for Banks,* besides having published a number of articles concerning rural financing and self-help groups in various journals and newspapers.